BREASTFEEDING RIGHTS IN THE UNITED STATES

**Recent Titles in
Reproductive Rights and Policy**

Who Decides? The Abortion Rights of Teens
J. Shoshanna Ehrlich

BREASTFEEDING RIGHTS IN THE UNITED STATES

Karen M. Kedrowski and
Michael E. Lipscomb

Reproductive Rights and Policy
Judith Baer, Series Editor

Westport, Connecticut
London

To my husband Tim, and my children Jonathan and Suzanne.

KMK

To Mom and Jen, who continue to remind me that we don't travel alone.

ML

Library of Congress Cataloging-in-Publication Data

Kedrowski, Karen M.
Breastfeeding rights in the United States / Karen M. Kedrowski and
    Michael E. Lipscomb.
        p. cm. — (Reproductive rights and policy, ISSN 1558–8734)
    Includes bibliographical references and index.
    ISBN 978–0–275–99136–4 (alk. paper)
    1. Breastfeeding—Social aspects—United States. 2. Breastfeeding—Political
aspects—United States. 3. Breastfeeding—Law and legislation—United
States. I. Lipscomb, Michael E. II. Title.
    RJ216.K397 2008
    613.2'69—dc22   2007032621

British Library Cataloguing in Publication Data is available.

Library of Congress Catalog Card Number: 2007032621
ISBN-13: 978–0–275–99136–4
ISSN: 1558–8734

First published in 2008

Praeger Publishers, 88 Post Road West, Westport, CT 06881
An imprint of Greenwood Publishing Group, Inc.
www.praeger.com

Printed in the United States of America

10 9 8 7 6 5 4 3 2 1

Contents

Series Foreword

*B*reastfeeding Rights in the United States is an important addition to Praeger Publishers' Reproductive Rights and Policy series. Karen Kedrowski and Michael Lipscomb's magisterial study combines quantitative and qualitative research methods to show that any right to breastfeed that exists in this country exists only as a weak negative right: You can do it unless someone takes you to court to stop you. The authors' exploration of the context in which a significant parenting choice takes place reveals that mothers of infants are confronted with a classic example of that familiar phenomenon known as the double bind. Mothers of infants are encouraged, indeed urged, to breastfeed their babies. But the nursing mother encounters barriers and frustrations. Social norms approve breastfeeding, but social practices make it difficult.

To become a mother, as many women have discovered, is to become the target of advice and admonition. This process starts as soon as a woman is known to be pregnant and continues indefinitely. Much, though by no means all, of this exhortation has come from accredited experts; some of it comes from strangers encountered in public places. "Breast is best" has become professional and cultural orthodoxy. The medical establishment endorses breastfeeding; practitioners urge their clients to nurse; and publications targeted to women of childbearing age praise breastfeeding. The pendulum has swung so far that a mother who chooses not to nurse her baby often meets with professional and social disapproval and may be labeled a bad mother. Government has also joined the chorus. From 2004 to 2006, the federal Department of Health and Human Services co-sponsored the National Breastfeeding Awareness Campaign, which strongly emphasized what it called the "health risks of not breastfeeding" in rhetoric that verged on scaremongering. New York City's current campaign to support exclusive breastfeeding for six months includes not only incentives such as providing breastfeeding counselors but also coercive disincentives to bottle feeding such as ending formula giveaways.

These endorsements of breastfeeding have gone much further in making claims for its benefits than the available evidence warrants. It is true that many studies have shown a reduced incidence of a host of diseases and conditions in breastfed babies. But these studies are inadequate science. They are not controlled trials: For ethical reasons, no investigator has randomly assigned babies to breastfeeding and bottle-feeding groups. Therefore, no study has controlled for the effects of intervening variables. No sound evidence that bottle-feeding is risky exists. Relying on studies like these to tell people what to do partakes more of propaganda than of science.

Nevertheless, mothers are getting the message. Well over half of American mothers initiate breastfeeding, although few continue for the full year recommended by the American Academy of Pediatrics. The best predictor of how long mothers continue breastfeeding is how soon after childbirth they return to work. This finding calls attention to one formidable set of barriers to breastfeeding.

Kedrowski and Lipscomb point out that breastfeeding is not easy. Nursing may be "natural," as its advocates claim, but it is not instinctive for human beings as it is for other mammals. It is a learned skill, and acquiring and practicing this skill requires considerable time and energy. Breastfeeding is demand-driven; establishing the milk supply requires putting baby to breast every few hours, and sometimes more often. Especially at the beginning, the demands made on the nursing mother may approach those of a full-time job. Because the majority of mothers of infants are in the paid labor force, work and mothering may add up to an arduous, exhausting double shift. The nursing mother meshes badly with the concept of the "ideal worker" on which the workplace is premised: the worker who has no distractions during the working day. Kedrowski and Lipscomb document that many women have been fired for breastfeeding or have been discouraged by workplace policies that deny them the opportunity to nurse or to express milk. The ideal mother is incompatible with the ideal worker. This conflict is worsened by the fact that the majority of working women hold clerical or service "pink-collar ghetto" jobs that do not easily accommodate a nursing schedule.

Not all barriers to breastfeeding are work-related. A second powerful incompatibility exists: between the valorization of breastfeeding and the prominence of the breast in American culture as a sexual object. Social discomfort with exposure has led to many instances of women being expelled from public places or being required to cover up—which is not always convenient or, with an active baby, even possible. These social attitudes, like workplace barriers, may lead women to stop nursing against their own wishes or to curtail their activities by avoiding places where they might encounter interference. The double bind creates coercively structured choices and is incompatible with the meaningful exercise of rights.

Kedrowski and Lipscomb conclude that the solution to this problem requires new theory and new strategy. The authors' democratic, feminist breastfeeding right makes several valuable contributions to theory. First, it is not a right to breastfeed, but a right to choose to breastfeed. Second, it is a woman's right to choose, not a baby's right to be breastfed. Third, it is a right, not a duty. The authors predict that framing the right in this way would encourage breastfeeding advocates and liberal feminists, who have historically been wary of one another's rhetoric, to unite to demand policy changes. The degree of success such a coalition could achieve would depend on its political strength and its ability to convince the powerful that implementing these rights would serve their own interests. *Breastfeeding Rights in the United States* provides an important step in the right direction.

Judith Baer
Series Editor

Preface

M any research projects are borne of personal experiences. Yet, this one is perhaps more personal than most. One of us is a mother, which hardly makes her unique. Like many other mothers in contemporary society, she faced those who judged her parenting decisions negatively. Yet, her case is unique in that those judgments often focused around her decision to, or not to, breastfeed.

Her first child was born in 1996 and was a large baby: just under 10 pounds at birth. And despite her good intentions, her efforts to breastfeed lasted eight long, horrible days: days marked by childbed fever (the postpartum infection that used to kill many women), mastitis, split and bleeding nipples, an inadequate milk supply, and a hungry, crying baby whose spit-up was colored pink with blood. Once the child was switched to formula, he was satisfied, and mom was able to recover. However, the following months were guilt-ridden, as her child developed eczema, a serious case of pneumonia and other, less serious infections. Moreover, she was sure her baby would be obese and mentally retarded because he was raised on formula. The language of breastfeeding advocates, including phrases such as "all women can breastfeed if they try hard enough," which was intended to be supportive, did nothing to assuage these feelings of guilt, and in fact compounded them.

When her second child was born in 1998, she was determined to breastfeed, but refused to set any goals for duration: a day, a month, or a year would all be considered a success. As it happened, her daughter was adept at nursing, and breastfed with wild enthusiasm. Mom watched her growth and development with awe. "I did this," she would think. The first year came and went, and she decided not to wean her daughter, so that she would receive greater benefits during her second winter of life. The child was not fully weaned until age three.

When her daughter was 18 months old, her mother was chastised for breast-feeding in a public place, her child care center, no less. At this point, the author discovered the constitutional protection stemming from the *Dike v. the School Board of Orange County, Florida* (1981), and the center publicized to staff and parents alike that it fully supported mothers' efforts to breastfeed. Yet, this experi-ence led the author to think, "I am a perfectly bad mother. I'm damned because I didn't breastfeed my son and I'm damned because I am breastfeeding my daugh-ter." The Political Scientist in her wanted to understand this paradox, and the seed was planted for this project.

This seed was fertilized when Judith Baer sent out a call for manuscripts for a new series on reproductive rights sponsored by Praeger. The author/mother pro-posed a book chapter; Judith proposed a book length manuscript. At this point, Dr. Lipscomb was invited onto the project, and we were on our way. This book is the final product.

Along the way, we have accumulated many debts. First, we wish to thank Judith Baer, series editor, and Hilary Claggett and Robert Hutchinson, our editors at Praeger/Greenwood, for their many insightful comments on our proposal and their unflinching support of this project. Second, several other scholars provided insightful comments on portions of this manuscript presented at professional con-ferences, and we are grateful. Third, we are indebted to the Winthrop Univer-sity Research Council, which provided financial support of various components of this project, and the Winthrop University Social and Behavioral Research Laboratory and its director, Dr. Scott Huffmon, for including questions about breastfeeding in one of its regular surveys of public opinion. Fourth, Renee Cap-straw, Erin English, Ashlie Evans, Emily Heckl, Patrick Jebaily, and Jamie Rose worked as undergraduate research assistants on various phases of this project. Their contributions are invaluable. Fifth, April Lovegrove, the Political Science department's Administrative Specialist, provided much assistance in the prepara-tion of this manuscript, and sixth, we thank Rachel Miller for vetting a key passage.

The babies who were the inspiration for this project are now in elementary school. They both are happy, healthy, well-adjusted children. The formula fed child is neither obese nor mentally retarded; in fact he is both athletic and academically gifted. His breastfed sister is a kind, loving, empathetic child who loves animals and people. Is this trait a product of being breastfed herself? Perhaps, but more likely it is a product of her generous, kind-hearted nature. We are grateful to them, too. This book, and whatever contributions it makes to understanding civil rights and breastfeeding policy in the United States, would not exist without both of them.

1

Introduction

"What interest do you, as a political scientist, have in breastfeeding?" This question, asked of both authors in social and professional contexts, is at the crux of this book. After all, many Americans do not think of breastfeeding as a political matter at all. To the degree that Americans think of breastfeeding, we conceive of it as a private act: a nurturing, intimate connection between mother and infant. We envision it in an idyllic setting: the privacy of one's own bedroom or the baby's nursery in a dark, sleeping house, with only the participants as witnesses.

The way that political scientists look at the world almost immediately complicates this warm and fuzzy ideal. Political scientists, after all, study the exercise of power. We study the transfer of power from one group to another, whether the power is transferred through elections, revolutions, or wars. This world of dusty battlefields, marbled hallways, ornate courtrooms, and unadorned bureaucratic offices—a world populated primarily by men—seems to be as far removed as one can imagine from a mother and baby locked in a quiet embrace in a peaceful, dimly lit room.

In fact, the moment the breastfeeding mother bundles up her baby into a car seat and leaves the house, breastfeeding ceases to be private, personal, and intimate. From the baby's first hungry murmur in a shopping mall, during a religious service, at a public swimming pool, or while her mother is at work, breastfeeding becomes a public act, one in which multiple actors, some of which are in formal positions of authority, become involved. They include police officers, charged with enforcing public obscenity laws; store clerks or private security officials worried about other customers' sensitivities; employers who are asked to accommodate an employee's need to express milk or nurse an infant during the work day; and passersby who may be unaccustomed to witnessing public breastfeeding.

Indeed, the question of breastfeeding *in public* has become a matter of *public policy* debate. In the United States, the word *public* has two meanings. The first is "not private" or "in the open," such as a public place like a grocery store. The other is predicated upon the notion that the citizens, otherwise known as *the public*, choose elected officials—sometimes called *public servants*—who then form the government and make and enforce laws. Consequently, government laws and regulations are often referred to collectively as *public policy*. As breastfeeding mothers are more likely to move into public places—whether it is as a consumer in a shopping mall or as an employee in the workplace—they are seeking protection of their breastfeeding rights by petitioning public officials to change public policy. Parenting decisions, including breastfeeding, are often considered private actions. Consequently, seeking support for these private practices through public means, such as legislation, is ironic.

It is at this intersection, where the intensely private moves into the public eye—in both senses of the term—that we as political scientists find ourselves studying breastfeeding. This book is a systematic exploration of breastfeeding rights, to the degree that they exist, in the United States.

What is breastfeeding? At first blush, this question appears absurdly obvious. However, definitions and the ramifications of those definitions vary. Because many advocates argue that one of the benefits of breastfeeding is the nurturing, human touch it provides, breastfeeding for them means that the child nurses at the mother's breast, period. Thus, breastfeeding does not include expressing breast milk by hand or with a mechanical pump to be fed to the child by bottle later. Others will combine these two activities—suckling and expression—under the term *breastfeeding*. Pediatricians also refer to *exclusive breastfeeding*, which means that the child receives only breast milk—whether from the breast or bottle—but no supplemental formula, cow's milk, semi-solid foods, teas, or water.

Another point of contention is the definition of a breastfed baby. Formula manufacturers, who, ironically, were the best sources of data on breastfeeding practices in the United States until very recently, define a child as breastfed if the child received any breast milk at all, even if only for one day or one feeding. Others differentiate between exclusively breastfed children and those who receive supplemental formula or other foods. The most sophisticated medical studies now differentiate by how long babies receive breast milk, whether supplemented or not. Extended breastfeeding refers to breastfeeding a child for more than one year.

For the purposes of this discussion, we define breastfeeding to include both nursing at the breast, or the expression of milk, unless otherwise specified. Similarly, we typically do not attach a specific duration to the term *breastfeeding*, though there are contexts where we are clearly thinking about something longer than one feeding or one day of feeding. When necessary, we define a specific duration in our discussion.

The remainder of this chapter is divided into four major sections. The first section provides important context for subsequent chapters by providing a discussion of the women's health movement, especially its focus on reproductive rights. The second section discusses the myriad ways in which breastfeeding is both a feminist and a public policy issue. The third section discusses breastfeeding as a civil rights issue, and the final section outlines the remainder of the book.

BREASTFEEDING AND REPRODUCTIVE RIGHTS

A Brief History of Reproductive Rights Debates in the United States

Debate over reproductive rights in the United States has often focused on a woman's right to terminate a pregnancy—or in other words, her right to choose *not* to become a parent. Also wrapped into this discussion is individuals' right to prevent pregnancy. For feminists especially, women's ability to control their own fertility permits women to pursue a wide range of new careers and reduces the health risks associated with multiple pregnancies. Moreover, birth control seems to make rational economic sense for first-world parents. By limiting fertility, families can maintain a higher standard of living, and parents can devote more time and attention to their children.

However, the flip side of the debate—that reproductive rights also imply that women and men have a right to choose to *become* parents—is equally important. Not only do many people desire to have children, children are important to society. All of us who hope to collect Social Security benefits, for example, depend on the next generation to pay its Social Security taxes. Any of us who may need nursing care in our final years will depend on well-trained, caring health care professionals who may not yet be born. Recognizing the importance of children, the government has instituted a variety of public policies for families and children, including lower tax burdens for families with dependent children, child care tax credits, and universal, free public education.

The second wave of American feminism roughly marks its beginning in the 1960s with the publication of Betty Friedan's *The Feminine Mystique*.[1] The women's rights movement of the mid-twentieth century was complex, encompassing a wide variety of approaches, assumptions, and goals. Moving from early efforts aimed at improving women's educational access and their political and economic equality, feminists also began to critique American medicine, particularly in the areas of health care delivery. Because pregnancy, delivery, and routine gynecological care are unique to women, and because health care services were delivered almost exclusively by male providers, the feminist critiques of health care in the 1970s focused on reproductive health almost exclusively. Their critiques were multifaceted. Feminist health care activists criticized male doctors for their paternalistic and disrespectful attitudes toward their female patients and the doctors' tendency to dismiss women's complaints.[2] They documented how traditional women healers and midwives were condemned as witches in the Middle Ages, and women were banned from many healing professions. Consequently, women's knowledge about childbirth, nursing, and child care was lost. The loss of women's accumulated knowledge and perspectives has been compounded by women's exclusion from the new, scientific, medical profession that began to dominate the delivery of health care in the early twentieth century. Even as recently as the 1950s, formal protocols permitted few women to enroll in medical school, ensuring the male dominance of the profession.[3]

In the 1960s and 1970s, feminists in the women's health movement critiqued the medicalization of pregnancy and childbirth and various hospital practices, including the extensive use of anesthesia and shaving the pubic area before delivery. They advocated home births and worked to revitalize midwifery as a profession. They taught each other how to conduct gynecological exams and began to spread the word about home remedies, such as using yogurt to treat yeast infections. Feminists also taught women how to demand respect from their health care providers and to educate themselves about their own bodies. Crucial to this effort was *Our Bodies, Ourselves*, first published in 1973 by the Boston Women's Health Collective.[4]

By the 1980s and 1990s, the definition of women's health had expanded beyond reproductive health to include various conditions associated with aging, such as breast cancer and osteoporosis. Health activists also recognized that certain conditions are not particular to women and girls, but affect them disproportionately, such as depression, eating disorders, and domestic violence. They also decried the lack of attention paid to women's health on the part of medical research professionals and pressured the National Institutes of Health to create an Office of Women's Health and to promote more medical research into women's health issues. One consequence of these efforts was an exponential increase in the federal funding for breast cancer research.[5]

One unrelenting theme from the 1960s to the present, however, remains the debates in the United States over abortion and the associated discussions over reproductive technology and embryonic stem cell research. Feminists saw the ability to control one's reproductive capacity as essential to achieving political, economic, and social equality. The development of the birth control pill, and its legalization in *Griswold v. Connecticut*, enabled women to experiment sexually without the fear of pregnancy. Similarly, the ability to terminate an unwanted pregnancy was key. In a world where work was and is structured by the economic demands of efficiency and production (rather than around the living needs of the human beings who do the work), working women risked being demoted, losing seniority, or being fired if they became pregnant, and the social stigma attached to unmarried, pregnant women was severe.

In addition, feminists were concerned with who had the right to exert control over women's bodies. Expressed concerns for the unborn child, or the presumed fragility of the pregnant woman, led to various social practices and attitudes that effectively kept women—whether they were pregnant or not—from participating fully in the workforce or other activities. By the same token, feminists also decried state policies that advocated involuntary sterilization of persons the state deemed unfit. Feminists saw in all of these outside forces, whether it came from the state, a male husband or sexual partner, or an employer, barriers to women's ability to fully exercise autonomous control over their own bodies. Men, of course, faced no such competitive constraints in the labor market or the public sphere. Feminists, seeking to shift public attitudes about women away from their duty to children and family toward the individual woman's right to choose her own life path, pointed out that women are citizens and subject to legal recognition and rights. Fetuses, while they are real and quite tangible—especially in the latter stages of pregnancy—hold no legal status until they are born.

Roe v. Wade, the 1973 Supreme Court decision that legalized abortion nationwide, did nothing to resolve the controversy surrounding abortion. Abortion rights activists continue to argue that women's legal status, agency, and personal autonomy trump any rights that a fetus might or should have. Abortion opponents point to what they see as the human carnage, the mass murder of millions of innocent children. Various state laws and federal cases have sought to restrict access to abortion through parental notification and waiting period requirements. However, these attempts at compromise have done little to achieve any consensus on this painfully divisive social issue.

Feminists' concerns with reproductive health practices and reproductive rights, however, have not extended far past the delivery room. Infant feeding decisions were ignored by women's rights activists for two primary reasons. First, the 1960s and the 1970s came at the end of a trend that breastfeeding advocates have come to term *scientific motherhood*.[6] Similar to the "medicalization of pregnancy," medical professionals also provided a variety of infant and child care advice that emphasized not "spoiling" a child by becoming too responsive to the child's crying and advocated strict sleeping and eating schedules and formula feeding by bottle. Not only was infant formula *scientifically* designed to provide infants with necessary nutrients, it was *scientifically* manufactured in sterile conditions, and infants' consumption could be *scientifically* measured, monitored, and compared to national norms. Breast milk, by contrast, was seen as inferior, possibly unsanitary, and difficult to measure. By the 1960s, breastfeeding rates in the United States were low, and few women—feminists and nonfeminists alike— even considered breastfeeding as an option when they had children.

The second reason is the ideological perspective of *liberal feminists* who dominated the second wave of American feminism. Liberal feminism espouses the belief that men and women are equal and should be treated identically under the law as much as possible. Consequently, liberal feminists reason, women can drive forklifts and pour concrete; men can be kindergarten teachers and beauticians; and parenting and child care responsibilities can and should be shared equally between parents. Formula feeding allowed parents to share responsibilities of infant care and nurturing. Liberal feminism saw in formula feeding another technological possibility for minimizing the kinds of child care responsibilities that had long been thrown up as a barrier to women's full participation in the public sphere. The rise of scientific feeding schedules actually dovetailed with this feminist impulse; schedules were seen as a way of shaping children's feeding habits and of habituating them to the demands of other people's, such as the mother's, schedule.

Moreover, given their desire to downplay the differences between men and women, liberal feminists of the second wave of feminism were very uncomfortable with special treatment legislation for working women. Such legislation, such as mandatory break time for working women but not working men, weight-lifting restrictions, or other such requirements, resulted in some of the systematic discrimination in the workplace that these liberal feminists sought to avoid.

Consequently, the biological reality of reproduction stands out as an exception to the general logic of liberal feminism. As Judith Galtry argues, second wave feminists in the 1970s, as represented by the National Organization for Women (NOW), drew a "bright line" around pregnancy, delivery, and recovery. These are special circumstances when the biological differences between men and women cannot be ignored, and working women need special protections to secure their jobs, benefits, and seniority. Breastfeeding continued, however, to be problematic for NOW and other liberal feminists because breastfeeding appears to consign a mother to a role as the infant's primary caregiver and espouses traditional definitions of motherhood. These perceptions were enhanced by the ideology of La Leche League, the primary organization promoting breastfeeding in the United States and abroad, which advocates that breastfeeding mothers should stay at home to care for their children. Consequently, Galtry argues, NOW's support for any legislation protecting the rights of working mothers to breastfeed came late and was less than enthusiastic.[7]

Breastfeeding as a Reproductive Rights Issue

However, breastfeeding is and should be considered a reproductive rights issue, just as controlling whether one becomes pregnant or continues a pregnancy are also reproductive rights issues. The decision of whether or not to breastfeed an infant is also a logical consequence of the decision to become a parent. The decision to breastfeed also has biological consequences. During pregnancy, women's bodies prepare to provide nourishment for the baby. As such, breastfeeding, like other female reproductive functions, is a biological reality that distinguishes men from women. The breastfeeding question does differ from questions about abortion because it avoids the divisive, value-laden discussion about whether a fetus has—or should have—recognized rights under the law. Instead, the fetus is replaced with a baby that exists as a legal, rights-bearing entity, alongside its mother and father.

Moreover, breastfeeding, like pregnancy, carries with it biological realities that shape a mother's daily experiences and differentiate her from her nonbreastfeeding sister. For instance, we are all well acquainted with the physical changes that occur during pregnancy, and most are aware of the illnesses and complications, such as morning sickness, that may accompany pregnancy. Yet, from a biological perspective, lactation also shapes a woman's life. For instance, her milk supply is demand driven. Without frequent nursing, a mother's milk supply will diminish. Similarly, without frequent nursing, lactating women risk the pain of engorged breasts and the embarrassment of wet clothing that results from leaking breast milk. Expressing milk by hand or pump is less efficient than suckling and also may fail to maintain a mother's supply.

Furthermore, breastfeeding should be included in a discussion of reproductive rights because of its potentially long duration. Given current trends and public health recommendations, the breastfeeding relationship may continue for years or longer—making this particular reproductive function longer than pregnancy itself. Yet, like pregnancy itself, breastfeeding is temporary, even if it lasts a period of years.

In addition, what was once rare is now commonplace. Since the early 1970s, breastfeeding rates have steadily risen. Today about 70 percent of all mothers breastfeed for some period after birth. Breastfeeding rates increase with the mother's level of education and socioeconomic status. Second, feminism itself evolved with the emergence of *difference feminism,* which argues that women's traditional roles and contributions—including breastfeeding—need to be recognized and valued by men and women alike. Thus, breastfeeding not only became a healthy choice for children and families, it became a way to demonstrate women's power and importance.

At the same time, the efforts to expand women's employment opportunities continue to bear fruit. Growing numbers of women are in the workforce, including steady increases in the numbers of mothers with young children. As of 2002, over half of all mothers with children under age three were employed.[8] Consequently, these two trends are on a collision course. More and more women want to work outside the home *and* breastfeed their children. Thus, we see at the same time, a collision between the public and the private spheres and confluence of traditional and modern forms of mothering that neither the liberal feminists of the 1970s nor the La Leche League founders of the 1950s foresaw.

BREASTFEEDING AS A PUBLIC POLICY ISSUE

Breastfeeding is not just an issue with which feminists must come to terms. Rather, it is one that increasingly demands the attention of public policy makers themselves. Breastfeeding has moved onto the policy agenda because of its public health effects, its place in the civil rights debate, and its implications for family law and women's employment. This section will document the health benefits of breastfeeding, which then leads to a discussion of public policy in terms of promoting public health, and ensuring women's right to breastfeed in a variety of circumstances.

Public Health: Benefits for Babies

Human breast milk offers infants a variety of health benefits, which are well-documented in the medical literature. Mothers impart some of their own antibodies to their infants through breast milk. Thus, the breastfed infant receives some protection against every infectious disease that the mother contracted during her life, any disease she contracts while breastfeeding, and any disease against which she has been immunized. The breastfeeding mother also manufactures antibodies to any illness her infant contracts while breastfeeding, even if she herself does not fall ill, and passes some of those antibodies to the child through breast milk. Consequently, even if the breastfed baby does become ill, the child stands a better chance of survival, may have a less serious form of the disease, and may recover more rapidly than infants who are not breastfed.

In other words, breast milk is, literally, lifesaving. The benefits for children born into the developing world are indisputable. For instance, breastfeeding can reduce the incidence and duration of diarrhea, one of the leading causes of infant death in the developing world. Not only do the children have more antibodies with which to combat infections, the exclusively breastfed baby does not ingest contaminated water or unpasteurized cow's milk, which may contain pathogens that cause diarrhea. The World Health Organization estimates that 1.5 million lives would be saved worldwide if all infants were exclusively breastfed from birth through the first six months of their lives.[9] However, the health benefits of breastfeeding children born into developed countries such as the United States, which has ample supplies of clean water and pasteurized cow's milk formula, as well as high immunization rates, was questioned by some.[10] In the last two decades, however, the medical evidence that breastfeeding is associated with various health benefits for infants in industrialized countries has mounted. The American Academy of Pediatrics (AAP) estimates that postneonatal infant mortality rates in the United States are 21 percent lower in breastfed infants than in their formula-fed counterparts.[11] The health benefits of breastfeeding are myriad. For instance, breastfeeding may protect against a variety of gastrointestinal track diseases. These conditions include:

- *Necrotizing enterocolitis (NEC):* a serious condition in which parts of the intestines die. It affects primarily premature and low birth-weight babies and has a mortality rate of 9–28 percent.[12] Approximately one percent of exclusively breastfed infants develop NEC, compared to seven percent of formula-fed infants. Exclusive breastfeeding would prevent an estimated 250 deaths from NEC each year in the United States.[13]

- *Alpha-1 Antitrypsin Deficiency:* a hereditary disease where the liver does not manufacture enough of the alpha-1 antitriypsin protein, which is necessary for digestion. It affects approximately 1 in 2,000 live births, or approximately 2,000 babies in 2004. Approximately 10–20 percent of infants born with this condition develop liver disease, or approximately 200–400 infants in 2004.[14] One study of a small number (*n* = 32) of these infants found that all babies who died from this condition were formula fed. None of the breastfed babies with this disease died.[15]

- *Crohn's Disease:* a disease that results in intestinal inflammation and affects about 7 of every 100,000 children under age 18, or less than one percent of the population. Approximately 20 percent of all cases of Crohn's disease are diagnosed in children under age 15.[16] Children who were formula-fed, however, are nearly four times as likely to develop Crohn's disease than are children who were fed breast milk.[17]

- *Celiac Disease:* occurs when the body cannot process the glutin in wheat products. This condition affects about 1 in 250 Americans.[18] Breast milk appears to protect against developing this disease; bottle-fed children were four times more likely to develop this disorder than were breastfed children.[19]

- *Urinary Tract Infection (UTI):* while most commonly associated with adults, UTI affects one to two percent of children each year.[20] One study of infants aged zero to six months found that bottle-fed infants were more than twice as likely to develop UTI than breastfed infants.[21]

- *Infectious diseases:* that lead to vomiting and/or diarrhea. While not a leading cause of infant death in industrialized nations, infants in industrialized countries still may acquire infections that lead to vomiting and diarrhea. Breastfed infants are about half as likely to develop such gastrointestinal infections, and when they do, they experience illnesses of shorter duration.[22]

Similarly, breastfeeding is associated with lower risk of numerous respiratory ailments, including:

- *Lower respiratory tract ailments,* such as wheezing and croup. These common childhood diseases afflict millions of children each year. Breastfeeding is a particularly important preventative when children have other risk factors, such as exposure to second-hand smoke, sharing a bedroom, or day care attendance. Moreover, rates of recurrent wheezing are much lower for breastfed children, even at age six.[23]

- *Infectious respiratory diseases,* such as influenza, respiratory syncytial virus (RSV), rhinovirus—and before a vaccine was developed, Haemophilis influenzae Serotype B, commonly known as Hib—and other respiratory infections. Several of these infections can lead to lower respiratory infections such as bronchitis or pneumonia. Hib can lead to meningitis and bacterial pneumonia.[24] However, breastfed babies are less likely to develop all of these diseases—34 percent less for all respiratory infections, excluding Hib—and they often experience less severe illnesses. Prior to the development of a vaccine in the 1990s, Hib infected up to 10 percent of children under the age of five.[25]

- *Inner Ear Infections (Otitis Media),* which may result from an upper respiratory infection. This condition is very common. Approximately 75 percent of children will experience an ear infection during childhood. If left untreated, repeated ear infections may result in hearing loss, and rarely, sepsis. Breastfed infants are less likely to develop ear infections. One study found that incidence of otitis media was 19 percent lower in breastfed infants as compared to formula-fed infants. Breastfed infants develop fewer ear infections over time, and infants breastfed exclusively for four months develop only half the number of ear infections as their counterparts who are not exclusively breastfed. Because ear infections are more common among babies who are fed in a supine position, like bottle fed babies, some speculated that breastfed babies had fewer ear infections because they are not fed lying down, but on their sides. The evidence seems to indicate that the breast milk, rather than feeding position, is key. One study of infants with cleft palate compared babies who were bottle fed expressed breast milk to babies fed formula. The babies receiving breast milk developed fewer ear infections. [26]

In addition, children benefit by having reduced risk of other diseases or conditions of genetic or unknown origin. They include:

- *Sudden Infant Death Syndrome (SIDS) or "crib death"*: SIDS is the unexplained sudden death of an apparently healthy baby. While rates of SIDS have declined by half in the last decade, primarily due to encouraging parents to lay sleeping babies on their backs, SIDS remains the third leading cause of infant death and the primary cause of death for infants over one month old. The National Center for Health Statistics reports that 2,162 infants died of SIDS in 2003.[27] While the cause of SIDS is unknown, breastfeeding appears to lower babies' risk of SIDS. Babies who are breastfed have about a 40 percent lower risk of dying of SIDS than do babies who were not breastfed. Babies who were exclusively breastfed have even lower risk.[28]

- *Diabetes*: Type I diabetes occurs when the pancreas ceases to make insulin as a result of an autoimmune reaction. Approximately 176,000 people under the age of 20 have Type I diabetes in the United States.[29] Complications of this condition can include coma, poor circulation, blindness, and premature death. Breastfed children are less likely to develop Type I diabetes in childhood, and several studies have found a dose–response relationship. In other words, the longer a child is breastfed, or exclusively breastfed, the less likely the child is to develop this disease. The reason for the protective effect of breastfeeding is unclear; however, early exposure to cow's milk, such as through cow's milk-based formula, may trigger the autoimmune response that leads to this condition. In addition, breastfed babies are less likely to be obese, and thus are at lower risk of developing Type II (adult onset) diabetes later in life.[30]

- *Childhood Cancer:* specifically lymphoma and leukemia. Childhood cancers are rare. In 2006, an estimated 9,500 new cases of cancer were expected to be diagnosed in children under the age of 14, and approximately 1,560 children were expected to die. The most common form of childhood cancer is leukemia, about 30 percent of all cases. Hodgkin's and non-Hodgkin's lymphoma comprise another 8 percent of all childhood cancers. Several studies, while not definitive, found that breastfed infants were less likely to develop leukemia or lymphoma in childhood.[31]

- *Atopy:* a group of disorders that include food and respiratory allergies, eczema, and asthma. Allergies are an inherited, genetic condition that affect about 40–50 million Americans. Atopic dermatitis—commonly known as eczema—affects some 15 million Americans.[32] However, the onset of symptoms of atopy may be delayed or prevented in children who are breastfed, and the protective effects increase with the duration of breastfeeding. One study found that children who were breastfed for one to five months were about one-third less likely to develop atopy between infancy and age 17.[33]

Are breastfed babies smarter? Finally, breastfeeding is associated with faster rates of cognitive development. Several studies have found that breastfed babies score higher on various tests of cognitive development at one year[34] and at two years.[35] The latter study also found a dose–response relationship, whereby the longer the duration of breastfeeding, the higher the average scores. A 2002 study found that the duration of breastfeeding also led to higher intelligence in adulthood, with an average of a five-point difference on an IQ test between those who were not breastfed as infants and those who were breastfed more than nine months.[36]

These associations are important ones, and clearly, they indicate that breastfeeding leads to healthier infants, fewer infant deaths, and possibly more intelligent children. However, we must add an important caveat that is standard fare in statistical interpretation: correlation is not causation. This means that while breastfeeding is *associated with*—or correlated with—these various outcomes, one cannot state definitively that breastfeeding *causes* these benefits. Arguably, breast milk does prevent or mitigate the severity of infectious diseases because of the presence of the mother's antibodies in the breast milk. However, causation in other situations is less clear-cut. For example, breastfed children are also less likely to die from injuries. Yet, there is no reason to expect that breast milk would protect from the severity of injuries. Rather, mothers who breastfeed may also be more attentive; thus, their children are less likely to become seriously injured.[37] Similarly, the scientific evidence does not tell us *why* breastfed babies score higher on IQ tests than their formula-fed classmates. The difference may be due to some unidentified factor in breast milk that leads to faster rates of cognitive development. Alternatively, the relationships may be due to intervening variables that are associated with both breastfeeding and human intelligence. For instance, given that highly educated women in the United States are more likely to breastfeed, the difference may be due to the fact that breastfeeding mothers have high IQs themselves and are more likely to engage in play, reading, and other activities that stimulate brain development.

Public Health: Benefits for Mothers

Women who breastfeed receive some health benefits as well. First, breastfeeding helps women recover from pregnancy and childbirth more rapidly. For instance, breastfeeding induces uterine contractions, which reduces the risk of postpartum hemorrhage and infection.[38] Breastfeeding women also return to pre-pregnancy weight more rapidly. One study found that women who breastfed for at least a year lost about twice as much weight as their counterparts who breastfed less than three months. Moreover, the longer women breastfed during the first year of their infants' lives, the more weight they lost.[39]

Second, breastfeeding is a form of birth control and helps to space pregnancies. Breastfeeding suppresses ovulation as a result of higher levels of the hormone prolactin and lower levels of the luteinizing hormone. Though the use of artificial birth control measures may interfere with milk supply or lead to other complications, the vast majority of women who breastfeed exclusively during the first six months after birth will not ovulate, making breastfeeding about as efficacious as other forms of birth control during this period. Ovulation, however, is likely to occur when supplemental foods are introduced, or after six months of exclusive breastfeeding.[40]

Third, breastfeeding provides some long-term health benefits to women. For instance, women who breastfeed have a lower risk of osteoporosis. Osteoporosis occurs when bone mass lowers and bones become porous and fracture. This condition affects some 8 million women, or approximately six percent of the adult women in the United States.[41] Women who breastfeed for at least eight months have higher bone densities, placing them at lower risk of osteoporosis.[42] Similarly, another study found that women who breastfed were at decreased risk of hip fracture, and the longer a woman breastfed, the lower her risk of a broken hip.[43]

In addition, women who breastfeed have a slightly lower risk of developing premenopausal breast cancer. The median age for developing breast cancer is 61 years, which indicates that premenopausal women comprise fewer than half of the 200,000 cases of breast cancer diagnosed in the United States each year. However, premenopausal breast cancer is more serious and has a higher death rate.[44] Women who breastfeed experience about a 20 percent reduction in their risk of developing premenopausal breast cancer.[45] Similarly, women who breastfeed have lower rates of ovarian cancer. Ovarian cancer is fairly rare in the United States, comprising only three percent of cancer diagnoses in women each year.[46] However, even breastfeeding as little as two months per pregnancy can reduce a woman's risk of developing this disease by 20–25 percent.[47]

Breastfeeding Barriers

Breastfeeding is not right for everyone and under all circumstances, however. In its 2005 policy statement on breastfeeding, the AAP advises that infants who suffer from galactosemia—a rare, inherited disorder in which the body is not able to process lactose properly—should not be breastfed. In addition, the AAP advises that women who have active tuberculosis, or who test positive for human t-cell lymphotropic virus (HTLV) type I or II, active Hepatitis A, or who have herpes lesions on the breast should not breastfeed. The AAP also advises women in the United States who are HIV-positive or who have AIDS to forgo breastfeeding. In addition, the AAP advises women undergoing chemotherapy or radiation treatments, or who are exposed to radiation for some other reason, to refrain from breastfeeding. Other prescription drugs may be transferred through breast milk and could be potentially harmful to infants, and women who use illegal drugs also should not breastfeed.[48] In addition, diseases such as West Nile virus can be transmitted through breast milk, and an infant can contract chicken pox if exposed to active lesions during breastfeeding.[49] Both the U.S. and Canadian governments have found dangerously high concentrations of the pollutant dioxin in human breast milk.[50]

Moreover, some women develop painful complications from breastfeeding, which include mastitis (breast infection), plugged milk ducts, engorged breasts, sore nipples, and split nipples. Other women report that they are unable to produce an adequate milk supply to feed their babies. The latter may be a result of a baby who is unable to latch-on effectively, infrequent feedings, or postpartum complications. While most of these conditions do not preclude successful breastfeeding, they can make breastfeeding difficult and, combined with the stress of new motherhood, sleep deprivation, inexperience, and a hostile environment, may undermine a mother's efforts to breastfeed and result in early weaning.

Finally, a lack of familiarity with how to breastfeed and the overt hostility of family members and others may undermine a woman's breastfeeding efforts. For instance, breastfeeding is not instinctive. For generations, new mothers depended upon the advice of mothers, aunts, older sisters, and midwives to navigate the early weeks when breastfeeding is being established. Yet, many mothers and aunts of today's new mothers never breastfed, leaving these new mothers without an important source of support and advice. Other mothers face outright hostility from their male partners or extended family members who discourage or disparage breastfeeding, or are uncomfortable with breastfeeding in public or in the home around other individuals. These subtle pressures are often inextricably tied with the Western idea that the breast is a sexual object, an idea that they cannot escape even when the context clearly involves the breast's biological—not a sexual—function.

Public Health Emphasis

Given the many health benefits that result from breastfeeding, the U.S. Department of Health and Human Services (DHHS) made increasing breastfeeding rates one of its public health objectives in its report *Healthy People 2010*.[51] DHHS estimates, based on a 1998 Ross laboratories survey, that 64 percent of mothers breastfed in the early postpartum period, less than one-third (29%) breastfed at six months, and few (16%) breastfed a year or longer. DHHS wants to increase these percentages to 75 percent in the early postpartum period, 50 percent at six months, and 25 percent at one year by 2010.

At mid-decade 2005, some progress had been made nationally to reach these goals. According to the 2005 National Immunization Survey, conducted by the Centers for Disease Control and Prevention, approximately 73 percent of mothers reported that they "ever breastfed," nearly the three-fourths benchmark in *Healthy People 2010*. Other measures also showed some improvement as well; over one-third (39%) of mothers reported they were breastfeeding at six months, and one-fifth (20%) were breastfeeding at one year.[52]

These improvements are not consistent across all groups of women, however. The chances that a mother will breastfeed depends, in part, on education and income, where she lives, her racial and ethnic background, and her marital status. For example, African American women are less likely to breastfeed than mothers of other races or ethnic backgrounds. Just 60 percent of African American mothers initiate breastfeeding, compared to over 70 percent of white, Latina, Asian, and Native American mothers. Similarly, college-educated mothers (85%), those with incomes three or more times the poverty level (82%), mothers over age 30 (78%), and married women (78%) are more likely to initiate breastfeeding than their counterparts who did not graduate from high school (64%), are unmarried (60%), live in poverty (64%), or are teenagers (64%). The same patterns hold for duration of breastfeeding.[53]

In addition, there is a strong regional component to breastfeeding practices. States with the highest rates of breastfeeding initiation are in the West, parts of the upper Midwest, and New England. States in the southern and Appalachian regions have some of the lowest breastfeeding initiation rates. For example, the state of Washington has the highest reported rate of breastfeeding initiation: 90 percent. One-third of mothers in Washington report they are breastfeeding at one year. On the other extreme, fewer than half (48%) of new mothers in Mississippi report that they "ever breastfed," and fewer than six percent (5.8%) are still breastfeeding at one year. Other states with high breastfeeding initiation rates are California (86%), Alaska (84%), Wyoming (84%), and Vermont (83%); other states with the lowest breastfeeding rates are Louisiana (50%), Kentucky (51%), West Virginia (52%), and Arkansas (54%).[54]

BREASTFEEDING AS A CIVIL RIGHTS ISSUE

The decision whether or not to breastfeed occurs at the intersection of colliding social trends. At the same time that breastfeeding rates have increased, so has the percentage of mothers of infants who are employed. As of 2002, 55 percent of all mothers of infants were in the labor force, compared to 31 percent in 1976.[55] This represents a dramatic increase over the same decades that breastfeeding rates have increased. However, breastfeeding and employment are difficult to manage together. Breastfeeding mothers must either nurse or express milk at frequent intervals to maintain their milk supply. To nurse, the mother must bring the baby to work, have a child care provider bring the baby to work, or leave work to go to the baby. Alternatively, a mother who pumps breast milk needs a private place to express milk and a safe place to store it. At best, working mothers must interrupt their work to express or nurse. At worst, they must forgo breaks and mealtimes to accomplish the task.

Consequently, how do these colliding social trends manifest themselves? First, we see that labor force participation also is associated with the educational attainment of the infant's mother. Mothers who hold college degrees are more likely to return to work during the first year of their infants' lives (63.5%), compared to the mothers with a high school diploma (55%) or less (39%).[56] Consequently, many of the mothers who are most likely to breastfeed—those with college educations—are also more likely to be in the workforce. These women also may be in professional positions that allow them to balance the countervailing demands of work and breastfeeding.

At the same time, we find some hints in these social trends that might help explain disparities in breastfeeding rates. African American mothers of infants have higher rates of labor force participation (66%) than their non-Hispanic White (57%), Latina (45%), and Asian/Pacific Islander (56%) sisters, which may explain their lower rates of breastfeeding, especially if they are not in professional positions with considerable autonomy. Married mothers whose husbands are present are less likely to be in the labor force (55%) than their counterparts who are widowed, separated, or divorced (63%).[57] Consequently, these mothers in stable relationships may be able to leave the labor force, which would facilitate breastfeeding.

As breastfeeding rates have increased, so has the conflict between mothers who breastfeed and others who are uncomfortable with the practice. Breastfeeding mothers and advocates abound with anecdotes about unsupportive family members, harassment in restaurants or public places, and concerns in cases of divorce and child custody. Breastfeeding advocates have increasingly turned to the courts and to state legislatures to ensure that the rights of breastfeeding women are protected. The first federal court case, and one of paramount importance, is *Dike v. the School Board of Orange County, Florida* (5th Circuit, 1981). In this case, the Fifth Circuit found that breastfeeding a child is a constitutional right, protected under an individual's right to privacy. More than a decade later, this court case is followed by a major legislative initiative, passed by the state of Florida, to guarantee the rights of breastfeeding mothers. This effort sparked a national movement to guarantee mothers' rights to breastfeed in a variety of situations.

Yet, the right to breastfeed is anything but absolute. Any discussion of a mother's right to breastfeed, or a child's potential right to be breastfed, comes against the competing rights of fathers, employers, the state, and the child. A father's parental rights in child custody or visitation disputes may interfere with a woman's right to breastfeed. At the same time, the federal government wishes to promote breastfeeding as a public health goal.

Thus, to return to the question that opened this chapter: What interest do you as political scientists have in breastfeeding? Our interest is untangling the thickets of competing and contradictory policies and rights that surround this intimate act, putting us in a position to prescribe our vision of optimal breastfeeding policies.

SUMMARY OF THE BOOK

This monograph will analyze several facets of breastfeeding policy and practice. Specifically, Chapter 2 provides a short history of infant feeding practices in the United States and the development of breastfeeding advocacy as a social movement. The contemporary breastfeeding movement in the United States began with the founding of La Leche League in the 1950s, but has since grown to include the current attachment parenting and natural mothering movements. This chapter also explores contemporary issues in the breastfeeding movement, including concerns about environmental pollutants in breast milk.

Chapter 3 measures public attitudes about breast milk and breastfeeding. Breastfeeding advocates believe that American society is generally hostile to breastfeeding. In this chapter, we turn their assumption into a question: Is American society hostile to breastfeeding? To answer this question, we present findings from various public opinion surveys and a study of media coverage of breastfeeding, which includes a comparison of mainstream news coverage with coverage in women's and parenting magazines.

The fourth chapter examines public policy toward breastfeeding at the federal level. In this chapter, we provide lengthy descriptions of the *Dike* case, subsequent cases at the federal levels, and the federal policies designed to encourage breastfeeding. We use social construction theory[58] to better understand the legally defined "right" to breastfeed and the limits of this right. Social construction theory is a way to organize and understand public policies that lends itself nicely to this analysis. In Chapter 5, we provide the same kind of summary and analysis of state laws and court cases.

In chapters 2 through 5, breastfeeding is the lens through which we analyze other aspects of women's lives, such as work, family, and recreation. In Chapter 6, we place breastfeeding in the broader context of women's lives, to include how women are situated in different social, economic, and biological contexts. This woman-centered, rather than breastfeeding-centered, analysis allows us to recognize how women's decisions to breastfeed and how long to breastfeed reflect these various contexts.

In Chapter 6 we also articulate what we see as an optimal response to the question of breastfeeding rights. Drawing upon feminist and democratic philosophy, we hesitate to impose a specific definition of "good mothering" that includes breastfeeding, because "good mothers" may reach vastly different conclusions about whether to breastfeed. We want to live in a society that encourages women to breastfeed and recognizes and values the benefits of breastfeeding to infants, women, and society. At the same time, we want to ensure that women who choose to breastfeed can fully participate in the public sphere as citizens and workers; and ensure that those mothers who make reasoned, informed decisions not to breastfeed are not stigmatized. This goes beyond merely encouraging women to breastfeed, but entails reforming the legal, policy, and social environments in which we live.

2

A Brief History of Breastfeeding in the United States

The purpose of this chapter is twofold. First, it offers a brief history of infant feeding practices in the United States. Second, it briefly traces the development of breastfeeding advocacy as a movement, moving from the founding of La Leche League in the 1950s to the contemporary attachment parenting and "natural mothering" movements. By tracing the histories of feeding patterns and the breastfeeding advocacy movements, we can start to see some of the cultural, social, and economic frameworks that have governed attitudes about breastfeeding and breastfeeding practice itself. Establishing this social and historical context puts us in a position to examine the new terrains that breastfeeding rights advocates are now encountering, such as the ways in which the struggle for breastfeeding rights connects with other struggles for rights and justice, including environmental justice and the fight against HIV/AIDS.

EARLY HISTORY

Of course, no compact, contextualizing history begins at its beginning, and the history of breastfeeding practices in the United States cannot be completely separated from its prehistories. In fact, any history of the cultural development of breastfeeding in the United States is impossible to disentangle from its natural history, or the European traditions from which it emerged, and remembering that history provides an important basis for claiming a right to breastfeed.

The prehistory of breastfeeding, from an evolutionary perspective, helps us understand the unique physiological benefits that accrue from nursing, for both the mother and the child. Breastfeeding, as Patricia Stuart-Macadam has pointed out, is a quintessentially biocultural behavior that reflects the evolutionary history out of which it emerges. Stuart-Macadam points out that for more than 99 percent of our history as a species, infants were primarily breastfed. During that long evolutionary history, a reciprocal physiological relationship has developed between mothers and infants, with each depending on the other for optimal health. In that context, the cultural alteration of ancient evolutionary patterns of breastfeeding "can have profound implications for the physiology, growth and development, and health of human infants and children as well as for the physiology and health of women."[1]

Despite differences in practical arrangements, human breast milk remained the primary way that civilizing humans fed babies. That holds true for the cultural traditions of Western Europe that most directly inform the historical continuity of breastfeeding practices in the United States; breastfeeding remained the dominant method of infant feeding throughout the course of the Medieval era in preindustrial Europe.[2] As Valerie Fildes puts it, the question remained much the same as it had throughout human history, not "'Was an infant breastfed?' but, 'Was an infant breastfed by its own mother or a relative, friend, or wet nurse?'"[3] Wet nursing had become a norm for upper-class European women throughout the Medieval era, "while in poorer families the mother nursed her own child."[4] Later on, breastfeeding continued to be the dominant form of infant feeding, though certain regions are notable for not breastfeeding their infants. In those areas, such as "parts of Germany, Bohemia, Northern Italy, the Austrian Tyrol, Finland, Sweden, Iceland, and Russia," children were fed with differing combinations of animal milk and cereal paps.[5] Though the colder climates in these areas were more hospitable to storing milk products, the infant mortality rates in these areas appear to have been substantially higher than in the remainder of Europe where breastfeeding was the norm.[6]

BREASTFEEDING IN COLONIAL AMERICA

As one would expect, breastfeeding practices in the American colonies largely mirrored dominant European practices, particularly those inherited from England. Breastfeeding one's own children continued to be the norm in the colonies throughout the seventeenth and eighteenth centuries.[7] Certainly, some members of the upper classes followed the European fashion of using wet nurses, but most

American mothers, given relatively low rural population densities and the lack of financial wherewithal, did not have this option.

Tracking breastfeeding practices in the colonies from the sixteenth to the early parts of the eighteenth century, one can see the way breastfeeding practices are entwined with larger notions of women's roles as mother and wife. Far from being matters of social indifference, these roles, in turn, are often subsumed under broader notions of the common good and the unique role that women played in operative notions of what constituted that good. Women's roles, then as now, are often dictated by authorities and experts, typically male, who are determined to govern women's sexual and reproductive activities.

The Puritans, for example, emerged as one of the primary advocates for maternal breastfeeding. Puritan theologians and ministers saw breastfeeding one's child as part of a mother's Christian duty to populate the flock for future generations. Those women who avoided breastfeeding were counted, according to Cotton Mather, among those "Careless Women, Living at Ease" who "are Dead while they Live."[8]

These programmatic assertions by social and religious experts remind us that decisions about breastfeeding never occur in a social vacuum. Rather, they tend to emerge within broader narratives about what is proper for women, children, and society as a whole. Presaging the increasing role that medical and scientific expertise have come to play in determining breastfeeding norms, seventeenth-century colonial mothers were warned not to breastfeed their children for several days after birth. At the time, many physicians believed that colostrum (the light yellow fluid secreted by mothers before and after birth as a precursor to the production of breast milk) was harmful, perhaps even fatal, for infants. Today, we know that colostrum provides nutrients and antiallergens that protect newborns from disease and infection.[9] It is difficult to know with any precision the degree to which this repeated public advice was heeded by nursing mothers, but, at the very least, this advice suggests that expert, scientific advice, despite its importance, and despite its elevated position in modern societies, is necessarily partial and runs the risk of peremptorily denying the importance of practices developed by women and children themselves in their actual feeding practices.

This observation is not meant, in any way, to discredit a scientific approach to breastfeeding. In fact, contemporary breastfeeding advocacy is largely based on the now undeniable avalanche of scientific evidence about the health benefits of breastfeeding for both mother and child, but it does remind us that modern society's faith in science can be marshaled in ways that deny women their autonomy and which prevent them from making the best feeding choices for their child and themselves. Even during a time where mothers can have greater confidence about an advanced scientific consensus about breastfeeding, that perspective can preclude other dimensions that rational mothers might consider in deciding not to breastfeed.

The expectation that colonial wives should be available for their husbands' sexual gratification often conflicted with their duties to care for their children. On the one hand, this tension can help explain the practice of wet nursing among the economic classes who could afford it. It also gives us some insight into how breastfeeding operated as a form of birth control, delaying the onset of ovulation between 8 to 12 months, thus allowing women a modicum of control over the size of their families.

Furthermore, it was the belief of many during this time period that sex during the breastfeeding period was detrimental to the health of the child. From the early colonial period throughout the nineteenth century, the experience of mothering always occurred under the threatening shadow of infant and childhood mortality.[10] Nancy Schrom Dye and Daniel Blake Smith, however, note a change in the way women responded to this ever present threat in the nineteenth century. Early Americans, they claim, expressed "a more passive attitude of Christian resignation," but, by "the early decades of the nineteenth century, except among evangelical families, Divine Providence was giving way to exalted motherhood in the care and protection of children."[11] As the modern sensibility that humans could use their reason to successfully respond to the problems of their experience began to take hold in modern cultures, and as the advances of modern medicine began to be felt across society, mothers would increasingly see infant mortality as a problem to which they could successfully respond in this world.

THE BREAST AS A SEXUAL OBJECT

The historical record also reminds us that women's decisions to breastfeed are further complicated by their relationships to men. It is worth pausing here to consider the ways in which the breast occupies a fascinating, charged place within our culture. Utilized by Karl Linnaeus in the nineteenth century to demarcate mammals from the rest of the animal kingdom within his taxonomic system, the breast marks that familiar yet unsettling intersection of the human and the animal, the maternal and the sexual. As Londa Schiebinger summarizes its broad range of cultural meanings:

> Long before Linnaeus, the female breast has been a powerful icon within Western cultures, representing both the sublime and bestial in human nature. The grotesque, withered breasts on witches and devils represented temptations of wanton lust, sins of the flesh, and humanity fallen from paradise. The firm spherical breasts of Aphrodite, the Greek ideal, represented an otherworldly

beauty and virginity. In the French Revolution, the bared female breast—embodied in the strident Marianne—became a resilient symbol of freedom. From the multibreasted Diana of Ephesus to the fecund bosomed Nature, the breast symbolized generation, regeneration, and renewal.[12]

It is not entirely clear that the erotic role that the breast plays in Western cultures necessarily reflects an intrinsic biological norm. Katherine A. Dettwyler points to studies by C. S. Ford and F. A. Beach that found "only 13 out of 190 cultures report that men view women's breasts as being related to sexual attractiveness, and only 13 out of 190 cultures report male manipulation of female breasts as a precursor or accompaniment of sexual intercourse."[13] In her own studies in Mali, Dettwyler reports that

> When I told my friends and informants in Mali about American attitudes toward women's breasts, especially sexual foreplay involving "mouth to breast contact" by adult men, they were either bemused or horrified, or both. In any case, they regarded it as unnatural, perverted behavior, and found it difficult to believe that men would become sexually aroused by women's breasts, or that women would find such activities pleasurable.[14]

This evidence clearly seems to suggest that the contemporary fascination with the breast as a sexual object reflects a culturally determined, rather than a biologically inherent, obsession. Within Western societies, Marilyn Yalom has traced what she sees as a shift from the sacred breast, celebrated in both prehistoric and Christian medieval cultures, to increasingly prevalent representations of an erotic breast beginning in the Renaissance, frankly depicted as the desired object of the male sexual gaze.[15] The idea that the breast can mean different things, or, at the least, that different dimensions of its meaning can be accentuated, during different historical eras seems to reinforce this emphasis on the culturally determined, rather than the biologically based, meaning of the breast.

Nonetheless, the tension in which the breast is situated, oscillating in the Western imagination between the maternal and erotic, may not be entirely a matter of shifting cultural attitudes about women and their roles as mothers and sexual objects. Freudian psychoanalysis points to the breast as the original infant fixation, the erogenous focus of the first stage of the child's sexual development, which eventually progresses toward a fascination with the genitals.[16] Melanie Klein would depart from this Freudian orthodoxy, developing an "object relations theory" that makes the breast the central fixture of the developing psyche.[17] Regardless of the ultimate accuracy of these theories, their general assertion that a child's original desire for the nourishing breast remains an unconscious fulcrum for their experience of sexuality and intimate relationships throughout the rest of their life may have some merit. At the very least, it is important to note that up to 41 percent of women "regularly experience sexual responses during breastfeeding."[18]

That internal response, whether its cause is physiological or socially constructed (or some mixture of the two), is worth noting because it gives us some insight into the difficult sociosexual space that women are asked to negotiate when making decisions about whether or not to breastfeed. On the one hand, the unease that many people feel when confronted with a woman breastfeeding her child in public reflects pervasive assumptions about the breast's function as a primary object of sexual fascination. In the context of public breastfeeding, that connection between the breast and sexuality manifests itself as a taboo against displaying one's breast in public, a taboo that has often been reinforced by charges being brought against mothers for breastfeeding their children. It is reasonable to assume that this connection underwrites the discomfort that many report with breastfeeding of toddlers (see Chapter 3).

On the other hand, breastfeeding advocacy is often couched in barely concealed sexual imagery, via "the sanitized and normatively acceptable language and imagery of adult heterosexual romance and traditional feminine sexual submissivenenss."[19] Rebecca Kukla offers examples, such as this excerpt from *Mothering* magazine: "I'm in love with the little guy, head over heels, what can I do. He can get my bra off faster than anyone I ever met, no hands at all, just a hungry look."[20] To be explicit about the physiologically felt feelings of sexual arousal reinforced by these socially images, however, particularly when it is not mediated by the indirect language that typifies official breastfeeding advocacy, runs the risk of being marked as deviant. One sees this policing at work in the story of Denise Perrigo, whose child (a female toddler) was taken from her after she sought help from the La Leche League in understanding her sexual response while feeding.[21]

These conflicting currents, that see the erotic understanding of the breast being used to both promote and police breastfeeding, remains an important, often confusing tension that continues to shape the overall field in which breastfeeding practices are determined. As we will emphasize in our conclusions about the prospects and consequences of breastfeeding rights in the United States, different women are differently positioned to respond to these cues, and it is important to consider those different circumstances when evaluating the efficacy and justice of actually practiced breastfeeding rights.

BREASTFEEDING IN THE NINETEENTH CENTURY AND BEYOND

The early nineteenth century saw the rise of "the cult of domesticity," a pervasive social sentiment that "entrusted women with the nurturance and the maintenance of the family."[22] This valorization of the mother in the United States may shine some light on the different social structure in which nineteenth-century women faced decisions about how to feed their infant children. Even as urbanization began to bring women closer together, the lack of a firmly established aristocratic class made wet nursing a less common practice than in Europe.[23] Furthermore, as Linda Blum suggests, maternal breastfeeding "became almost an emblem of new democratic ideal, as images of 'nature' were linked with equality, the rejection of decadent, aristocratic 'culture,' and the rising health and wealth of the middle class of the young nation."[24]

At the same time, this emerging norm of the good mother who sought to breastfeed her baby was part of a broader effort to police distinctions between the middle class and the lower class of European immigrants who were seen as dirty and whose milk was, therefore, less pure.[25] In the South, despite concern about the fitness of black slave women's milk, up to 20 percent of plantation families used slaves to wet nurse their children.[26] The irony, of course, is that black slave women were often denied the ability to nurse and care for their own children.[27]

That evolving sensibility of the cult of domesticity created a space in which women could realize their agency within the limits of the domestic sphere, but it also entailed a responsibility for the children entrusted in their care.[28] In fact, even as the increasing valorization of women reinforced extant norms of mothers breastfeeding their own children, the rise of a scientific world view and the belief that mothers should use the best means possible to optimize the health of their children began to create the antecedents for the precipitous decline of breast-feeding rates in the twentieth century.

Spurred by concerns about the ability of mothers to deliver wholesome milk to their infants, by suspicions about the purity of milk from immigrant and slave women available for wet nursing, and by the higher rates of infant mortality associated with cow's milk and other human milk substitutes, physicians and scientists began experimenting with finding formula substitutes for human breast milk.[29] The effects of the industrial and scientific revolutions had an increasing impact on all aspects of mothering during this period, and those changing material realities began to profoundly affect breastfeeding practices in a variety of ways. The organization of economic production around time schedules in the 1800s, for example, introduced a logic of efficiency and mobility that eventually began to colonize child rearing practices.[30] The idea that infants should be fed on a more regular, more efficient schedule worked against practices of feeding on demand, which is requisite for successful breastfeeding. Because breastfeeding is demand driven, feeding according to a schedule "is a particularly efficient way to diminish milk supply,"[31] and it is not surprising that the change to scheduled feedings led to increasing reports that women were having difficulty producing sufficient quantities of milk for the nursing infants.[32]

Riding the wave of momentum created by the women's suffrage and the settlement house movements during the progressive era,[33] the last decades of the nineteenth century and the early decades of the twentieth century witnessed the emergence of women's voices as a public, political force capable of casting attention on the problem of infant mortality, and middle- and upper-class women began to mother their children in a more openly caring way.[34] This new public presence put pressure on the State and the medical community to effectively respond to the infant mortality problem.[35] That response, in the early part of the new century, entailed a public health campaign that urged women to breastfeed, but that same campaign also hints about how the increasing medicalization of infant feeding points to alternative feeding methods.

We see a fusion here of a norm of good mothering attached to class status coming into contact with the logic of medicalization. As these factors coalesced over the course of the twentieth century, and as they eventually hooked up with women's entrance into the work force in the latter part of the century and with the increasing commercialization of the erotic breast during the same time period, they had the overall effect of driving down breastfeeding rates in the United States.

In fact, breastfeeding rates in the United States have been relatively low over most of the last century,[36] fluctuating because of a variety of cultural and economic reasons manifested in the changing nature of expert discourses about mothering and infant feeding. At the beginning of the century, from about 1900 to 1930, it appears that between 85 and 90 percent of mothers breastfed their babies at birth.[37] However, feeding cow's milk or other supplements to infants was considered a major cause of infant mortality and a public health crisis by 1900.[38]

With the medicalization of pregnancy and childbirth, infant feeding practices also came under medical supervision. As understanding of human nutrition increased and supplies of clean water and pasteurized cow's milk became abundant, formula feeding increasingly replaced breastfeeding. Consequently, American breastfeeding rates fell, and reached their nadir approximately in the 1970s.[39] The late part of the nineteenth and early part of the twentieth centuries witnessed an increasing medicalization of childbirth and child rearing practices that have directly impacted norms of infant feeding. For many, this process of medicalization, which saw the male dominated medical profession assume power over decisions about childbirth and child rearing practices, is a fundamental cause of the steady decline of breastfeeding rates throughout most of the twentieth century. As Penny Van Esterik defines this term:

> Medicalization of infant feeding refers to the expropriation by health professionals of the power of mothers and other caretakers to determine the

best feeding patterns of infants for maintaining maximum health. There follows from this definition no judgment as to how medicalization of infant feeding relates to infant morbidity—only an argument that what was in the past largely the concern of mothers and women is increasingly part of the medical domain.[40]

Van Esterik's definition captures the reaction against the disempowering, denaturalizing effects on breastfeeding mothers, but, as she points out, it may oversimplify the case on at least two fronts. First, during the early part of the twentieth century, the scientific and medical communities actually advocated breastfeeding in reaction to the number of infant deaths associated with diarrhea caused by unpasteurized and unsanitized cow's milk.[41] As a poster used in this campaign clearly states, "To lessen baby deaths let us have more mother fed babies. You can't improve on God's plan. For your baby's sake—nurse it!"[42]

Second, the medicalization of childbirth and child rearing began to gain predominance within the ideology and practices of childbirth and child rearing because of its increasingly apparent effectiveness. The fear of infant mortality ceased to be the primary shaping force of mother's self-understanding by 1920.[43] The passage of the Federal Food and Drugs Act in 1906, which gave the Bureau of Chemistry (which later became the Food and Drug Administration) the responsibility of regulating consumable substances,[44] and the invention of antibiotics in 1928 were among the achievements and practices that began to change women's self-understanding of their burden as mothers. These accomplishments in health care were a crucial "post-material" fact that contributed in important ways to the acceptance in the rise of artificial feeding methods through the 1950s and 1960s. The scientific revolution that had led to miraculous achievements in many areas of health care and medicine made a convincing case that women should heed health care professionals' infant feeding advice. To assert that women's increasing acceptance of bottle feeding meant that they were being duped would overstate the case. It may be that this consensus was reinforced by the development of vaccination, and medical and sanitation advances, which improved infant mortality rates and, thus, masked the benefits of breastfeeding (including the further reduction of infant mortality at the margins).

The increasing medicalization of infant feeding and care was reinforced by the United States' capitalist economy. On the one hand, women's increasing participation in the work force (only 19% of women were in the labor force in 1900, while over half of mothers with children under age three were in the labor force by 2002)[45] has, over the course of the twentieth century, created a new incentive for women to seek greater flexibility in their feeding options. The greater prosperity enjoyed by many families and women during the twentieth century also gave women the option of being able to afford formula and, thus, made breastfeeding less of an economic necessity. In this context, the discourse of liberal feminism, which seeks to downplay the differences between men and women and to maximize women's ability to choose public and professional careers, reinforced the attractiveness of bottle feeding.

On the other hand, infant feeding research and its application was increasingly funded by formula companies, and by the 1950s, those companies were aggressively promoting their product with aggressive marketing campaigns that courted physicians with junkets and other perks.[46] The interrelationship of medicalization and capitalism has tended to normalize our understandings and expectations of what constitutes natural feeding practices, leading to a severe decline in breastfeeding rates, and continues to shape feeding practices even as an increasing understanding of the health benefits of breastfeeding has piled up over the last 30 years.[47]

LA LECHE LEAGUE AND ITS HEIRS: THE REVOLT AGAINST SCIENTIFIC MOTHERING AND THE RISE OF THE NATURAL MOTHER

Against this backdrop of an increasing medicalization of infant feeding practices and its emphasis on formula feeding, some women began to resist the kind of disembodied mothering that these approaches entailed.[48] Though this resistance had been simmering throughout the rise of medicalization, it began to gain momentum in 1957. That year, seven Catholic women came together to offer an alternative to the increasingly dominant paradigm of "scientific motherhood."[49] Searching for a name that reflected their philosophical commitment to breastfeeding, the group called itself La Leche League after a shrine in St. Augustine, Florida, Nuestra Senora de la Leche y Buen Parto, or "Our Lady of Milk and Good Delivery."[50] From its modest beginnings, La Leche League, now known as La Leche League International (LLLI), has grown into a major international organization that, by the beginning of 2001, was serving 200,000 people every month in 66 countries and responding to breastfeeding questions from an estimated 750,000 American mothers every year.[51] LLLI's publication *The Womanly Art of Breastfeeding* now boasts a circulation of more than 2.5 million copies and has been published in eight languages and in Braille.[52]

On its Web page, La Leche League summarizes its core philosophy with the following statements:

- Mothering through breastfeeding is the most natural and effective way of understanding and satisfying the needs of the baby.

- Mother and baby need to be together early and often to establish a satisfying relationship and an adequate milk supply.

- In the early years the baby has an intense need to be with his mother which is as basic as his need for food.

- Breast milk is the superior infant food.

- For the healthy, full-term baby, breast milk is the only food necessary until the baby shows signs of needing solids, about the middle of the first year after birth.

- Ideally the breastfeeding relationship will continue until the baby outgrows the need.

- Alert and active participation by the mother in childbirth is a help in getting breastfeeding off to a good start.

- Breastfeeding is enhanced and the nursing couple sustained by the loving support, help, and companionship of the baby's father. A father's unique relationship with his baby is an important element in the child's development from early infancy.

- Good nutrition means eating a well-balanced and varied diet of foods in as close to their natural state as possible.

- From infancy on, children need loving guidance which reflects acceptance of their capabilities and sensitivity to their feelings.[53]

As these statements make clear, the position and activity of pro-breastfeeding groups, such as La Leche League, go beyond the health benefits of breast milk to include a valorization of the bonding contact between the mother and infant, which itself is warmly nested in the nurturing love of the attentive husband and father. By focusing on the bonding effects of the mother–child dyad, this discourse has been able to extol the psychological and emotional benefits that accrue to both the child and the mother. For mothers, this bonding effect can take the form of a renewed appreciation of their own bodies. In fact, many women reported that La Leche League's celebration of the embodied act of breastfeeding helped them recognize alternatives to the predominant cultural scripts that had previously contoured their understandings of their bodies. One small-breasted La Leche League leader, for example, talked about how this emphasis helped her overcome the denigrating view of her body imposed by male expectations: "I did not feel so good about my body before nursing. I feel my breasts have a use now and I have much more confidence in my body. My breasts are not just there for men!"[54] Another mother, Nicole Strickler, enthused, "Overall, I think the nursing relationship has enhanced my sexuality in the sense of making me feel more comfortable and that my body is more valuable and beautiful in a way that I had not realized before."[55]

An important dimension of the La Leche League ideology rests on how it connects the practice of breastfeeding to an ethos, to a total way of life, which addresses important questions of meaning and purpose for many of its adherents.[56] As Julie DeJager Ward points out, this ideology was crafted, both consciously and unconsciously, by drawing on ideas made current by modern science, the Second Wave of feminism, and the traditions of the Roman Catholic Church.[57] As Ward notes, La Leche League, in resisting the medicalization of infant feeding practices, did not reject science. On the contrary, they recognized that "many women who wished to breast-feed did not achieve that wish because they had received poor information from the medical community."[58] One might say that the organization sought to use science and sound medical advice from professionals to save infant feeding patterns from the misguided consensus of the mainstream medical community of the time. Though feminists often criticize La Leche League for its complicity with traditional and, from many feminists' perspectives, stifling notions about women's proper role as the good mother, League adherents shared the feminist belief that women need to share information with one another in order to liberate themselves from the misinformation disseminated by a male-dominated culture.[59] And though it may be true that La Leche League's religiously inherited picture of a good mother suggests a traditionalist strain of its ideology, it is also the case that its immense success can be attributed to the way in which it integrates the practice of breastfeeding into a larger philosophy of life emerging across different sites in American culture during the late 1950s and early 1960s.

In fact, the amazing success of La Leche League cannot be understood apart from feminist, women-centered celebrations of natural ways of being that began to emerge in the 1960s, and the commitments of La Leche League are undoubtedly part of the broader foci of the natural mothering movements and attachment parenting movements.[60] It is not uncommon, in fact, for La Leche League followers to count themselves as adherents of these philosophies, and there is clearly some overlap between "natural mothering" and "attached parenting." Chris Bobel, in fact, describes "natural mothering" as a way of mothering that emerges at the intersection of the lifestyle choices of the voluntary simplicity, attachment parenting, and cultural, or difference, feminist movements.[61]

Natural mothers, according to this description, eschew the fast-paced consumerism typifying modern life, seeking instead the voluntary simplicity of living "frugally, rejecting material preoccupations and opting for recycling, bartering, and trading in place of traditional market exchange."[62] In doing so, adherents seek to actively recognize that "individual well-being is entangled with the well-being of society at large." The respect for the natural world that this mode of living entails spills over into a belief, drawn from the ethos and insights of difference feminism, that women occupy an important, biologically distinct role, that positions them "as nurturing, intuitive, and relationship oriented, regardless of class or race."[63] Often, those traits are assumed to be natural, or essential, though it is not impossible to accentuate those womanly virtues without such an essentializing move. Even if those qualities are culturally and historically conditioned, it could be reasonably argued that they are worth preserving.

The attachment parenting movement reinforces this emphasis on women's nurturing, relational virtues, emphasizing the careful cultivation of the close bond between mother and child. As advanced by William and Martha Sears, whom Bobel credits with coining the term, attachment parenting entails much that sounds common sensical, such as connecting closely to one's baby in a way that allows the parent to recognize the child's needs, but it challenges many norms of mainstream twentieth-century parenting by asking parents to keep their baby wedded to their body in a baby sling and to sleep with their baby. Of course, it also mandates that mothers should breastfeed their babies.[64]

Moreover, the ultimate success of La Leche League and these corollary movements is grounded in the increasing scientific consensus about the importance of breastfeeding. As Ward points out, for La Leche League founders, "it was the solidity of their scientific knowledge base that grounded the other elements of their philosophy."[65] By the first decade of the twenty-first century, the proclamations of the scientific mainstream have given increasing ballast to advocates' long-held assertion that "breast is best." The American Academy of Pediatrics, for example, now states flatly,

> Human milk is uniquely superior for infant feeding and is species-specific; all substitute feeding options differ markedly from it. The breastfed infant is the reference or normative model against which all alternative feeding methods must be measured with regard to growth, health, development, and all other short- and long-term outcomes.[66]

The American Dietetic Association takes the position "that exclusive breastfeeding provides optimal nutrition and health protection for the first 6 months of life, and breastfeeding with complementary foods for at least 12 months is the ideal feeding for infants."[67] The strategic plan of the United States Breastfeeding Committee of the Department of Human Health and Services, referencing *Healthy People 2010*, has set goals for 2010 of 75 percent rate of initiation, 50 percent at 6 months, and 25 percent at 1 year. This enthusiasm for breastfeeding as the optimal form of infant feeding is echoed by the position of the American Medical

Association. As these and similar position statements from groups ranging from the Centers for Disease Control and Prevention, to National Organization for Women, to the March of Dimes suggest, La Leche League's general mission to promote breastfeeding finds ample support from the scientific, medical, and advocacy communities.[68]

CONTEMPORARY BREASTFEEDING ISSUES

The total commitment to an ethos of mothering championed by La Leche League, particularly its connections to the natural mothering movement, points to the ways in which the struggle for breastfeeding rights is connected to broader struggles by women for environmental and social justice.[69] Environmental pollutants contaminate mothers' breast milk, which can be passed along to their children, and to the degree that poorer women and, by extension, women of color are more likely to suffer the effects of environmental degradation, this degradation accentuates the race and class dimensions of breastfeeding politics. The connection between breastfeeding and environmental protection seems obvious—breastfeeding women should want an environment that does not pollute the breast milk that they are feeding their children—but it is important to note that many breastfeeding advocates have been wary of endorsing or emphasizing this coalitional partnership.[70] Faced with what they perceive as a medical and cultural atmosphere that remains hostile to breastfeeding, these advocates fear that talk about toxins in breast milk could discourage women from breastfeeding. These advocates argue that in almost all cases of toxins in breast milk, the health benefits of breast milk still outweigh the negative impacts of the toxins.

In a similar fashion, breastfeeding advocates struggle with how to relate their support for breastfeeding with the national and global HIV/AIDS crisis. Research accepted by most of the medical community indicates that HIV-infected women who breastfeed double the risk of infecting their children with the virus. This has lead to a dilemma for breastfeeding advocates, particularly in developing countries where unsafe and unreliable water supplies make breastfeeding more important for children's development: Replacing breastfeeding in order to curb the spread of this devastating virus seems to put those children at risk for nutritional maldevelopment or, even more pressingly, death from diarrhea.[71] Some breastfeeding advocates argue that children of HIV-infected women should breastfeed, because their children may live longer before developing AIDS than they would if they develop diarrhea. Others have gone so far as to question whether the HIV virus can be transmitted through breastfeeding.[72]

But just as the idealized picture of motherhood championed by La Leche League, and by the natural mothering and attachment parenting movements, served as an important corrective to the ideology and practices of scientific motherhood, that ideal also carries with it certain blind spots. As Bernice Hausmann puts it, "Moral ideals of maternal duty continue in contemporary advocates' common assumption of a traditional heterosexual family structure, replete with economic support from the male spouse and idealized financial dependence on the part of the mother."[73] Certainly, these assumptions and the financial wherewithal that makes "natural" mothering possible allow some women to make the choice to follow these sets of practices. At the same time, not all women have the economic luxury of making this choice, and some women may have good competing reasons for not making this choice. On this point, Christina G. Bobel has suggested that La Leche League models of good mothering offer a form of "bounded liberation" that, on the one hand, empowers women to take back mothering practices from the impersonal, male-dominated purview of experts, but that, on the other, reinscribes mothering practices within the expectations of the male-led family.[74]

In fact, it is not uncommon to hear women complain about being pressured to breastfeed. As one mother decries the imperative of "breast is best,"

> I thought I had to breastfeed. Everybody was pushing me saying, "It's natural, it's what the mother should do." So I just felt pressured into it. Then with my son, it was difficult. I was impatient, so I would resort to giving him a bottle, and then he did not want to breastfeed again. For weeks I pumped and fed him through the bottle because I couldn't get him to want to breastfeed. And I thought, "Well, I'm giving him my milk." Like I said, it's what I thought I had to do.[75]

The idea that breast is best has, at least in some circumstances, become a predominant norm that ignores and marginalizes women who are either unable or unwilling to go along with the command to breastfeed. These norms, however, sometimes ignore how real women make the best decisions for their children, families, and themselves, within the context of a variety of competing paradigms, in which the decision of whether or not to breastfeed is but one, regardless of its importance, competing concern. Some women are less likely to breastfeed because of operative assumptions and biases within the medical community that continues, for the most part, to play a supervisory role over the delivery and care of infants. Other women may choose not to breastfeed because of embedded cultural assumptions about the propriety of breastfeeding, the sexual nature of the breast, and about norms of what constitutes the proper space and body required for breastfeeding one's child.[76] Other women for whom breastfeeding may not be an optimal choice, who may, for example, face physiological challenges (cracked nipples, abcesses, breast lesions), whose milk has been contaminated by environmental realities, or by drugs in their system, or who may not choose to breastfeed for extended periods of time because of career or work obligations, find their self esteem, even their fitness as mothers, being challenged by an increasingly pervasive notion that good mothers breastfeed and those who do not are simply selfish. When women return to work remains the best predictor of how long a woman will breastfeed. This statistical insight reminds us that even though, where everything is equal, breastfeeding is clearly the optimal infant feeding method, other realities and choices can limit the feasibility of breastfeeding for extended periods of time.

Against the back drop of this complex terrain, we now turn to a more focused consideration of the how the public understands breastfeeding.

3

Breastfeeding in the Public Eye: Public Opinion and Media Coverage

Consider the following anecdotes, all taken from news coverage of women's experiences with breastfeeding:

- A manager of a Burger King restaurant in Utah asked Kate Geary to cover herself or move to the restroom when another customer complained that she was publicly breastfeeding. Burger King later apologized.[1]

- Emily Gillette was forced to disembark from an airplane in Burlington, Vermont because she refused to cover herself with a blanket while breastfeeding. A Freedom Airline official stated that breastfeeding mothers are expected to feed their children "in a discreet way."[2]

- *Baby Talk* magazine received over 700 letters in response to a cover photograph of a baby nursing at a breast, most expressing discomfort or revulsion.[3]

- In May 2006, a man was arrested in Myrtle Beach, South Carolina after he assaulted another beachgoer, whom he accused of ogling his wife while she breastfed in public.[4]

- In 2006, breastfeeding mothers protest in front of Victoria's Secret stores across the country to object to separate incidents in which customers were not permitted to breastfeed in stores in Wisconsin, South Carolina, and Massachusetts.[5]
- A photograph of actress Carrie-Anne Moss breastfeeding her child while strolling down the street appears in an issue of a celebrity magazine, under the caption "Not Normal."[6]

All of these anecdotes focus on the crux of this book: bringing the private act of breastfeeding into the public. They also appear to indicate a widespread discomfort with the biological function of an organ that has acquired sexual connotations in American culture. When one speaks with breastfeeding mothers, such anecdotes abound. Every breastfeeding mother seems to have a similar story to tell. For breastfeeding activists, these stories reflect systemic public hostility toward breastfeeding, and such attitudes complicate their efforts to encourage women to initiate and continue breastfeeding. From a social science perspective, however, anecdotes—even when numerous—fall short of providing solid evidence of widespread patterns. Consequently, in this chapter, we take breastfeeding advocates' assertion that the American public is hostile to breastfeeding and pose it as a question: Is the American public hostile to breastfeeding? In what circumstances is breastfeeding acceptable?

We use two approaches in our attempt to gauge breastfeeding attitudes. First, we examine public opinion by summarizing previous studies, and we present results of a survey conducted specifically for this book. Second, we conduct a comparison of breastfeeding stories in several women's magazines and several regional and national newspapers.

PUBLIC OPINION AND BREASTFEEDING

There are very few public opinion surveys about breastfeeding attitudes in the United States. Most study the attitudes of expectant parents or parents of young children. These studies, while limited by their target populations, do provide some insight into general social attitudes toward breastfeeding. These social attitudes appear linked to breasts' sexual connotation in American society, including their use for male sexual pleasure or fantasy. One way that the sexual role of the breast may impact the decision to breastfeed is reflective in the important role that fathers' support plays in that decision. One recent study revealed some 36 percent of mothers who chose bottle feeding did so because of the attitude of the baby's father, which was not supportive.[7] Similarly, other studies have found that a supportive father is highly correlated with a mother's decision to breastfeed.[8]

Even when fathers are aware of breastfeeding's health benefits, and supportive of their partners' decisions to breastfeed, ambivalence about public breastfeeding remains. A 1992 survey published in the journal *Pediatrics* found that 71 percent of fathers of breastfed infants believe that breastfeeding in public is not acceptable; 78 percent of fathers of formula-fed infants held the same opinion.[9] At the same time, however, a 1995 poll conducted by *Parenting* magazine and the Gallup organization found that 57 percent of parents (mothers and fathers) agreed that "a woman's right to breastfeed in public [should] be protected by law."[10]

Similarly, a baby who lives with both their mother and grandmother is less likely to be breastfed than a baby who does not share a home with a grandmother.[11] For example, a participant in a small study of low-income mothers reported that her mother discouraged her efforts with comments such as, "girl that thing hurts" and "you are not going to like that." The young mother's experience was typical of the women in this study.[12]

Finally, women also seem to perceive a social stigma to breastfeeding. One survey found that one-quarter of mothers who decided to bottle feed did so because breastfeeding is "embarrassing"[13]; a similar study of low-income mothers revealed that few had ever seen a mother breastfeed in public, and most of those who did perceived a negative reaction from those who witnessed it.[14] Another study of teenaged mothers attributed their low breastfeeding rates to a "greater concern for body image."[15]

While these studies of parents provide some insight into social attitudes about breastfeeding and how these attitudes may influence the decision to breastfeed, they are limited by the fact that they sample only parents of infants or small children. A more reliable measure of social attitudes needs to study society as a whole. Yet, few such studies exist. For example, the Henry J. Kaiser Family Foundation, on its *kaisernetwork.org* Web site, offers a search function of thousands of public opinion polls on health-related issues spanning several decades. Of these polls, only two asked questions relevant to breastfeeding, and neither assessed public attitudes.[16] The first study dates from 1979; it assessed public knowledge of breast cancer.[17] The second is a 1998 survey that assessed how closely the public followed health news.[18]

Two studies of college students attempt to measure attitudes toward breastfeeding and bottle feeding. They differ from the surveys of parents in several ways. First, many study participants are not parents themselves, and second, they have higher levels of education than the general population. However, the results of these studies indicate that social attitudes toward breastfeeding may be more supportive than what breastfeeding parents perceive. For example, a 1998 study of college students at a north-central public university found that 40 percent of the students had been breastfed themselves, and two-thirds had observed breastfeeding at some point. Moreover, they perceived breastfeeding as "natural," "healthy," and "pleasant." While 80 percent of the students thought that breastfeeding at home was a "natural setting," they were divided about whether breastfeeding in public parks, shopping malls, and restaurants was appropriate.[19] Another article published in 2003, reporting a study conducted at a Midwestern university, found that college students have more positive perceptions of mothers who breastfeed compared to those who bottle feed. Moreover, they found that attitudes toward breastfeeding were correlated with one's responses to sexual stimuli. Those students who responded negatively to sexual stimuli—and consequently sought to avoid such stimuli—viewed breastfeeding more negatively than the students who responded positively to sexual stimuli. In addition, men who held more traditional attitudes toward women's roles in the family tended to view breastfeeding more positively than other groups.[20]

A larger study of public attitudes toward breastfeeding was conducted by a group of public health professionals located in Atlanta, Georgia. They analyzed data from the 2001 Healthstyles survey, an annual, national mailed survey.[21] While 43 percent of all respondents supported a "woman's right to breastfeed in public places," 27 percent found breastfeeding "embarrassing," and 31 percent believed that a one-year-old should not be breastfed.[22] In addition, they found significant regional variations in attitudes toward breastfeeding in public. Respondents from the Central and Atlantic regions of the United States registered lower rates of approval of breastfeeding in public. By contrast, respondents from the Northeast and Western regions were more likely to accept breastfeeding in public. Respondents from Southeastern states were least likely to agree with the statement, "I believe women should have the right to breastfeed in public" (37%). Respondents in the Mountain states were most likely to agree with this statement (59%).[23]

Moreover, there were significant differences by age and level of education. Individuals with less education or who were 45 years old or older were less supportive of breastfeeding in public than respondents who were more educated or younger. In addition, men were more likely to support breastfeeding in public than were women.[24]

Defining the Socially Tolerable

These studies provide some insight into public attitudes toward breastfeeding. However, they do not probe the exact limits of what is considered socially tolerable. In an attempt to remedy this shortfall in existing studies, the Social and Behavioral Research Laboratory at Winthrop University conducted a telephone survey of 461 residents of Rock Hill, South Carolina and the surrounding areas of York County in fall 2004.[25] The survey included several questions geared toward measuring public attitudes toward breastfeeding. The survey used a quasi-experimental design, in which the respondents were randomly assigned to an experimental or a control group. The experimental group was asked a series of questions about witnessing breastfeeding in a restaurant, and the control group was asked a series of questions about witnessing breastfeeding in a museum. This was to ascertain whether there is a difference in attitudes toward public breastfeeding based upon the context. All other questions used the same language for all respondents.

The survey was designed to include a range of questions about breastfeeding and a possible *right* to breastfeed. A variety of scenarios were included, which go far beyond a general right to breastfeed. We deliberately included some "tough cases," such as exposing a breast and nipple while breastfeeding or whether incarcerated mothers should be allowed to breastfeed their babies while in prison. Such questions were included because they are a part of the policy conversation, and some breastfeeding advocates have asserted that breastfeeding should be an unconditional right.

About Rock Hill, York County, and South Carolina

Rock Hill, the largest city in York County, South Carolina is a city of 57,000 residents located about 25 miles south of Charlotte, North Carolina, and many of its residents work in Charlotte. Rock Hill's racial composition is approximately 58 percent white, 37 percent African American, and 2.5 percent Latino. Thus, Rock Hill's racial demographics are similar to those of South Carolina, but are not representative of the United States as a whole.[26] In addition, 75 percent of the adult population of Rock Hill (age 25 or higher) has a high school diploma, 24 percent hold a Bachelor's degree or higher; and median family income is $37,000. On these socioeconomic measures, Rock Hill compares favorably to both South Carolina and the United States.[27]

Politically, York County and Rock Hill are solidly Republican. Their state legislative delegations and the partisan County Council have strong Republican majorities. In the 2004 Presidential election, President George Bush (R) received 65 percent of the two-party vote cast in York County.[28] South Carolina is an ideologically conservative state and has a traditional political culture.[29] According to the Institute for Women's Policy Research (IWPR), South Carolina is the second worst state in the United States for women—second only to Mississippi—based on its measures of political representation and participation, economic status, health, and reproductive rights.[30] At the time of the survey, South Carolina did not have any breastfeeding rights articulated in its state code. Its breastfeeding rates are among the lowest in the country. According to the Centers for Disease Control and Prevention, only 50 percent of babies born in South Carolina are ever breastfed, compared to 70 percent nationwide.[31]

Respondents' Demographics

Respondents were identified using randomly generated telephone numbers. Trained callers used a computer-aided telephone interview system (CATI) to enter the data. The CATI system also randomly assigned respondents to the control or experimental groups. The respondents are disproportionately female (66%), white (76%) and are somewhat more educated than the population (94% reported having at least a high school diploma and 33% have at least a Bachelor's degree). Respondents' family income is higher than that of the typical Rock Hill family, with 50 percent reporting incomes over $40,000 per year. While these differences make the sample of respondents less like the demographics of the Rock Hill community, they are more consistent with the demographics of the United States. Thus, we are cautiously optimistic that our findings can be generalized to the U.S. population, even if they are less valid for the populations of Rock Hill or South Carolina.

Findings

Breastfeeding Is Uncommon

While 76 percent of respondents reported that they had children, a minority (47%) reported that their children were breastfed. Among those who could recall the duration of breastfeeding, the plurality of respondents reported that their children were breastfed for six months to a year (35 percent for first children; 23 percent for second children, and 11 percent for third children). Very few—less than four percent—reported that any child was breastfed more than one year. White women were slightly more likely to report that they breastfed their children than African American women (see Table 3.1). Reflecting national trends, reporting that one's children were breastfed was strongly correlated with education. Respondents with the highest levels of formal education were also those might likely to report their children were breastfed.[32]

Public Breastfeeding as a Contested Right

While many breastfeeding advocates and many public policies hold that women have a right to breastfeed in public, this idea does not enjoy widespread support among survey respondents. When asked whether women have a right to

Table 3.1
Respondents' Breastfeeding Behaviors

Question	Yes % (n)	No % (n)	DK/refused % (n)
Do you have children?	76.6 (353)	22.6 (104)	.2 (1)
Were your children breastfed?	47.2 (167)	51.4 (182)	1.1 (5)

Duration of breastfeeding	First Child	Second Child	Third Child
0–3 months	23.8 (41)	16.9 (29)	9.8 (13)
3–6 months	17.4 (30)	12.8 (22)	9.8 (13)
6 months–1 year	34.9 (60)	22.7 (39)	10.6 (14)
More than 1 year	7.6 (13)	7.0 (12)	4.5 (6)
Can't remember	4.1 (7)	2.3 (4)	2.3 (3)
Child not breastfed	6.4 (11)	9.9 (17)	11.4 (15)
No second/third child		8.7 (40)	43.9 (58)
DK/Refused	5.8 (10)	5.2 (9)	7.6 (10)

Were your children breastfed? **	Yes % (n)	No % (n)
Less than high school	26.6 (6)	73.9 (17)
High school diploma/GED	29.3 (27)	70.7 (65)
Some college	50.7 (37)	49.3 (36)
2-year technical college graduate	43.4 (23)	56.6 (30)
4-year college degree	71.2 (42)	28.8 (17)
Post graduate	65.3 (32)	34.7 (17)

Were your children breastfed? *	Yes % (n)	No % (n)
White	50.2 (135)	49.8 (134)
African American	37.5 (27)	62.5 (45)
All (total n = 361)	47.5	52.5

Source: Winthrop University Social and Behavioral Research Laboratory. Margin of error +/–4.4%.
* p < 0.037.
** p < 0.000.

breastfeed in public, a majority (55%) agreed or strongly agreed. This finding is somewhat higher than the results of the 2001 Healthstyles survey.[33] A smaller percentage, 28 percent, disagreed or strongly disagreed; and 16 percent responded that they neither agreed nor disagreed.

The overwhelming majority of respondents indicated that they would not be offended if they saw a woman breastfeeding an infant and her breast and nipple were covered by a blanket (87%); only 11 percent report they would be "offended" or "highly offended." Taken at face value, this indicates substantial tolerance for public breastfeeding. However, when parts of the woman's body are exposed or she is breastfeeding a toddler, support erodes. For example, 64 percent indicated they would be "offended" or "highly offended" if a woman's breast and nipple were covered but her "belly" was showing, and 69 percent report they would be "offended" or "highly offended" if a women's nipple and breast are showing. In addition, more than one-third (35%) report they would be "offended" or "highly offended" if the woman was breastfeeding a toddler (see Table 3.2).

There were no statistically significant differences between the experimental and the control groups in their responses to these questions. This indicates that respondents were not more squeamish about public breastfeeding in a restaurant setting, where presumably they would be eating, than in other public places.

Table 3.2
Attitudes toward Public Breastfeeding

Question	*Responses % (n)*				
	Strongly Agree	*Agree*	*Neither Agree nor Disagree*	*Disagree*	*Strongly Disagree*
Right to breastfeed in public	15.2 (70)	39.5 (182)	15.6 (72)	21.3 (98)	6.5 (30)
	Highly Offended		*Somewhat Offended*		*Not Offended*
BF woman covered by a blanket	3.5 (16)		7.8 (36)		87.0 (401)
BF woman w/ breast or nipple showing	29.3 (135)		39.5 (182)		29.3 (135)
BF woman w/ belly showing	32.3 (149)		31.7 (146)		31.7 (146)
BF woman nursing a toddler	13.4 (62)		21.5 (99)		61.8 (285)

Source: Winthrop University Social and Behavioral Research Laboratory.

Not surprisingly, respondents with the greatest amount of formal education were also the most supportive of a right to breastfeed in public[34] and were less like to be offended by witnessing an exposed breast and nipple on a breastfeeding woman.[35]

Accommodating "Deviant" Mothers

Other scholars have argued that the media valorizes mothers who ascribe to the traditional norms of "good mothers." These "good mothers" are middle-class, white, married, and not employed outside the home. Mothers who are racial minorities, poor, incarcerated, single or divorced, or employed outside the home are considered "deviants," and their parenting decisions are frequently called into question.[36] Public policies with respect to breastfeeding mirror these media depictions, where an expressed right to breastfeed does not often extend to policies that would enable so-called deviant mothers to easily exercise this right (see Chapters 4 and 5).

These patterns are reflected in this survey as well, implying that media coverage and the potpourri of sometimes conflicting breastfeeding policies reflect public opinion fairly accurately. There is a fair amount of support for accommodating breastfeeding among employed mothers. Over two-thirds (67%) agreed or strongly agreed that a coworker should "be allowed extra break time to breastfeed or to pump breast milk for her infant." Sixty percent agreed or strongly agreed that "your employer should be required to provide a clean, private place for your coworker to breastfeed" and nearly half (49%) agreed or strongly agreed that an employer should "be required to provide a refrigerator to store your coworker's breast milk."

As promising as these results appear, there is also a core of strong resistance to any accommodation for breastfeeding employees. For example, nearly a quarter of the respondents disagreed or strongly disagreed that a coworker should be allowed extra break time; 28 percent opposed providing a clean, private place to pump or nurse; and 39 percent opposed a requirement to provide a refrigerator.

Should other types of "deviant" mothers have a right to breastfeed? While there was some support (61%) for the statement, "courts should take into account whether a woman is breastfeeding her infant when making child custody and visitation decisions after a divorce," only a third (33%) agreed that "a woman who is jailed should be allowed to breastfeed her infant while in prison." There is little support for another type of "deviant" mothers—those who nurse their children more than one year—as demonstrated by the large percentage of people who reported they would be offended to see a woman nursing a toddler. Not surprisingly, those who supported a general "right to breastfeed" were also supportive

Table 3.3
Accommodating Breastfeeding Mothers

Question	Response % (n)					
	Strongly Agree	*Agree*	*Neither Agree nor Disagree*	*Disagree*	*Strongly Disagree*	*DK/ Refused*
Allowed extra break time at work	14.3 (66)	52.1 (240)	6.1 (28)	21.3 (98)	3.5 (16)	2.2 (10)
Clean private place at work to pump or breastfeed	11.9 (55)	47.7 (22)	8.5 (39)	24.1 (111)	4.1 (19)	3.0 (14)
Employer provides a refrigerator for breast milk	7.8 (36)	41.0 (189)	7.8 (36)	34.1 (157)	5.4 (25)	3.3 (15)
Take into account in child custody and visitation decisions	13.0 (60)	48.2 (222)	7.2 (33)	22.3 (103)	2.4 (11)	6.1 (28)
Jailed mothers allowed to breastfeed in prison	3.9 (18)	28.9 (133)	10.4 (48)	42.7 (197)	7.8 (36)	5.4 (25)

Source: Winthrop University Social and Behavioral Research Laboratory.

of all three employment accommodations and taking breastfeeding into account in divorce cases[37] (see Table 3.3).

Again, we find substantial opposition to either proposal. A quarter of respondents disagreed or strongly disagreed with the statement that breastfeeding should be taken into account in divorce cases, and about half of the respondents did not believe that incarcerated mothers should be allowed to breastfeed their babies in prison (see Table 3.3).

Breastfeeding Attitudes by Race and Sex

There was no difference in support for a right to breastfeed by race, nor were there many differences in their reported reactions to seeing women breastfeeding in public. Whites, however, were more likely to report they would be "offended" or "highly offended" by seeing a woman breastfeed a toddler in public.[38] African American respondents were also more likely than whites to favor break time for a coworker to nurse or pump,[39] but less likely to believe the employer should be required to provide a refrigerator.[40]

There was no statistically significant difference between men and women and their support for a right to breastfeed in public, and neither sex was more likely to be offended by public breastfeeding if the woman was covered by a blanket. However, women were more likely than men to respond that they would be "offended" or "highly offended" if they saw a woman's breast and nipple exposed while breastfeeding,[41] or her abdomen was showing,[42] or they saw a woman breastfeeding a toddler.[43] There was no difference by sex in terms of support for employment accommodations for breastfeeding mothers.

Interpretation

Boundaries of the Socially Acceptable

Our study, combined with the results of previous studies, provides some insight into public attitudes toward breastfeeding. First, the contradictory findings in our study indicate that there is considerable discomfort with public breastfeeding in part because people are unfamiliar with the realities of breastfeeding. For instance, many people report they are not offended by public breastfeeding that is done modestly; however, modesty is sometimes difficult to maintain. Babies may object to being covered by a blanket, or pull it off the mother while nursing, leaving her exposed. The breast and nipple are likely to be exposed when the baby is latching on, or has finished feeding and the mother is straightening her clothing. For these reasons, breastfeeding advocates routinely oppose any legislative language that requires that women be discreet when breastfeeding because such provisions could discourage, rather than encourage, breastfeeding.

Second, these findings demonstrate that, while there is some support for a *right* to breastfeed, particular applications of this right generate less support for women who deviate from the popular norm of "good mothers." In fact, there is a substantial minority—at least 25 percent—who oppose any accommodations for breastfeeding at all—even for mothers who are perhaps the "least deviant"—such as working mothers or divorcees. These findings are consistent with public opinion polls that find widespread support for constitutionally protected civil liberties (freedom of speech, for instance), but support erodes when those rights are exercised in a way that some people find offensive (flag burning, for instance).[44]

Third, these findings demonstrate a general lack of awareness of the biological realities of breastfeeding. First breast milk, like cow's milk, is perishable and can spoil without refrigeration. While there is support for working women to pump their breast milk at work, there is considerably less support for providing refrigeration for it. Inadequate refrigeration, of course, puts a baby at risk if they ingest spoiled milk. Similarly, because breastfeeding is demand-driven, nursing mothers must nurse or pump milk regularly in order to maintain their milk supplies. Lengthy interruptions—such as for an eight- or nine-hour work day, or a weekend visit to a father—can lead to painful engorgement, increased risk of infection, leaking breasts, and decreased milk supply.

Finally, these results imply that respondents believe that a "right to breastfeed" is one of those rights that a convicted criminal must sacrifice, along with others, upon incarceration. As such, it does not reach the status of, for example, right to counsel, which convicted criminals maintain even when incarcerated. What is different about a right to breastfeed, however, is that biologically, this right is one that only women can exercise. Thus, women who are incarcerated must sacrifice more rights than their male counterparts.[45] Depriving incarcerated women of this right, however, impacts other individuals besides the incarcerated women. Their infant children, and their interest in being breastfed, are ignored.

MEDIA COVERAGE OF BREAST MILK AND BREASTFEEDING

Mass media are another way to gauge public opinion, insofar as the mass media shape and reflect public attitudes. To date there are no studies of American media coverage of breast milk and breastfeeding. However, a few studies conducted in Canada, Australia, and the United Kingdom may provide some insight into possible patterns that may occur in the American context. Other insights may be gleaned from previous studies of media coverage of breast cancer, which deals with the same organ; and pregnancy and abortion, two other reproductive rights.

Studies of Breastfeeding in the Media

Women's magazines are an important source of information about health for women, and women's magazines frequently reinforce advice provided by other sources, such as medical professionals. Moreover, media consumers pick and choose the stories of most interest to them.[46] Studies of media coverage of breastfeeding and infant feeding provide a complex picture. For instance, in her study of Australian popular magazine articles published during 1996, Ann Henderson found that these media provided mixed messages about breastfeeding. While the coverage acknowledged that "breast is best," these same articles also noted that breastfeeding is problematic, requiring patience and time and risking embarrassment and frustration.[47] A similar study of British television programs and newspapers was completed by Lesley Henderson and colleagues. They found that bottle feeding was associated with "ordinary families," and breastfeeding was associated with middle-class and celebrity women. They also found that the mass media paid little attention to the health benefits of breastfeeding.[48]

By contrast, a study of Australian newspaper coverage over three years (1996–1999) found that the news stories presented a predominately neutral message about breastfeeding, and when stories were not neutral, they were positive toward breastfeeding.[49] Moreover, a study of Canadian teenagers found that exposure to television advertising promoting breastfeeding resulted in more positive attitudes toward breastfeeding.[50] At the same time, a study of infant feeding messages presented in *Chatelaine*, a Canadian women's magazine, over four decades, and an unrelated study of *Parents* magazine over 29 years, found that infant feeding messages comprised a relatively small percentage of the total coverage (3% in *Chatelaine* and 5–10% in *Parents*). The messages in *Chatelaine* reflected social trends; as breastfeeding became more common, messages became more supportive of the practice, but the messages declined in frequency. By contrast, *Parents* magazine tended to be supportive of breastfeeding over time, even if the infant feeding messages were also supportive of bottle feeding.[51]

Breast Cancer, Reproduction, and Motherhood in the Media

Because breast cancer, like breastfeeding, focuses on the breast, studies of mass media depictions of breast cancer may provide some insight into what to expect from media coverage of breastfeeding. Several studies found that media stories about breast cancer vary widely in their frames and accuracy. For example, Julie Andsager and Angela Powers found that news magazines (comparable to newspapers in our study) framed breast cancer as an economic issue while women's magazines focused on social concerns, such as diagnosis and recovery.[52] Women's magazines also tended to provide a distorted picture of women with breast cancer, focusing particularly on young women; a separate study of newspaper coverage had a similar finding.[53] Similarly, a study of magazine coverage of postpartum depression found that these articles, while few in number, contained inaccurate and conflicting information.[54]

There are surprisingly few studies of media coverage of pregnancy, other than when it is part of an analysis of media coverage of abortion. In 1979, Gaye Tuchman noted that in the 1950s, the words "pregnancy" and "rape" were taboo in news coverage. In their study of the sexual revolution's impact on mass circulation magazines, Joseph Scott and Jack Franklin noted that references to pregnancy and related topics, including abortion and birth control, increased over 100 percent from 1950 to 1970, and the articles became more accepting of abortion and birth control.[55] In the case of abortion specifically, Myra Marx Ferree documented how feminist frames that focus on individualism, personal autonomy, and women's right of self-determination dominated American media coverage. At the same time, in their study of several conflicts, including abortion, Frederick Fico and Michael Drager found that local newspapers were "generally fair" in their coverage. Perhaps most intriguing, however, is a study conducted by *Columbia Journalism Review,* which found that the 12 American women's magazines with the largest circulations generally avoided discussing abortion in their pages. These magazines published only about 100 stories collectively in 20 years, possibly out of concern for the issue's divisive nature.[56]

According to a recent study by Deirdre Johnston and Debra Swanson, women's magazines continue to perpetuate an image of idealized motherhood: This mother is white, middle class, happy, and proud. Interestingly, the most content mothers are those who work outside the home.[57] Yet, another study of magazine depictions of working mothers found that for white, middle-class women, any institutionalized child care was, by definition, inferior to that which could be provided by the mother. For black, low-income or working class women, however, any external type of child care, of any level of quality, is acceptable because it enables mothers to remain in the workforce.[58] These constructions thus imply that the best mothers are defined, in part, by race and socioeconomic status.

Other studies also demonstrate that the mass media tend to demonize women who deviate from ideal motherhood by abusing or killing their children, using illegal drugs while pregnant, or giving birth after menopause. These deviant mothers were depicted, variously, as cold-blooded killers, of low intelligence, poor, or "monstrous."[59] Thus, they deviated from the ideal mother in several ways, and in ways that are not necessarily related to a criminal act. By contrast, women who deviate from the ideal of motherhood by using fertility drugs and consequently undergoing multiple births, are valorized and considered heroic.[60]

Thus, these studies lead us to expect that media representations of breastfeeding may do little to support women's breastfeeding efforts. First, we expect to find little coverage of breastfeeding, given the paucity of coverage in other countries, and the paucity of coverage of topics related to reproduction in the United States. Similarly, we expect the media coverage may provide at best, mixed messages—and at worst, inaccurate messages—about breastfeeding. Moreover, the coverage may provide a distorted image of women who breastfeed, just as they provide a distorted image of women with breast cancer. Finally, we expect breastfeeding mothers to be depicted positively when they otherwise reinforce a stylized image of ideal motherhood. Those women who deviate from this ideal will be depicted negatively.

Media Content Analysis

We are interested in media depictions of breastfeeding because such depictions help shape the attitudes of the public and policy elites alike. We conducted a content analysis of news stories about breast milk or breastfeeding that appeared from 1990–2004 in a total of 18 media outlets. They include 4 newspapers, 3 television networks, and 11 women's magazines. The four newspapers are the *New York Times*, chosen because of its position as a media agenda setter and its wide readership among intellectuals and policy elites; *USA Today*, because of its position as a newspaper with a national circulation; *Columbus (OH) Dispatch*, as a newspaper with a statewide circulation in a state that did not have breastfeeding rights legislation at the time of the study; and the *Seattle (WA) Post Intelligencer*, a newspaper with a statewide circulation in a state that had passed breastfeeding rights legislation. The three networks are NBC, CBS, and ABC; and the women's magazines fall into three categories: magazines oriented to a general audience of women (*Good Housekeeping, Redbook, Better Homes and Gardens*, and *Ms*), magazines targeted to parents of young children (*Working Mother, Parenting, Baby Talk*, and *Parents*), and magazines targeted to African American women (*Jet, Essence*, and *Ebony*).[61]

Relevant newspaper articles were identified through the Lexis-Nexis database. Television network news stories were identified through the online abstracts provided by the Vanderbilt Television News Archive. Relevant magazine articles were identified through the *Reader's Guide to Periodical Literature* and the Infotrak electronic database. Articles were coded by medium,[62] whether the story was a "hard news" or "soft news" story;[63] tone,[64] whether the story profiled a breastfeeding mother; subject of story (up to three mentions); and story sources (up to three mentions). Statistical analysis was conducted using the SPSS statistical package. Quantitative content analysis is used to discern general patterns. However, for smaller subsets of the dataset (for example, articles in one particular medium or in a small cluster such as African American women's magazines) qualitative analysis is used, as appropriate.

A total of 270 articles were coded: 171 newspaper articles, 24 television stories, and 49 magazine articles. Of the newspaper articles, 100 appeared in the *New York Times*, 38 appeared in *USA Today*, 28 appeared in the *Columbus Dispatch*, and 22 appeared in the *Seattle Post Intelligencer*. In television, NBC carried 7 breastfeeding stories, ABC carried 10 and CBS carried 7. Of the magazines, *Parenting* published the most stories, with 20 articles. *Baby Talk* published 11; *Jet* published 6; *Working Mother* published 5; and *Redbook* published 4. The other magazines (*Better Homes and Gardens, Essence, Ebony, Good Housekeeping, Ms* and *Parents*) each published 2 articles (see Table 3.4).

Table 3.4
Breastfeeding Stories by Medium, 1990–2004

Medium Name	N (%)	Medium Type	N (%)
New York Times	100 (37.0)	Newspapers	188 (69.6)
USA Today	38 (14.0)		
Columbus Dispatch	28 (10.3)		
Seattle Post-Intelligencer	22 (8.1)		
ABC	10 (3.7)	Television	24 (8.9)
CBS	7 (2.6)		
NBC	7 (2.6)		
Baby Talk	11 (4.1)	Women's magazines	58 (21.5)
Better Homes and Gardens	2 (0.7)		
Ebony	2 (0.7)		
Essence	2 (0.7)		
Good Housekeeping	2 (0.7)		
Jet	6 (2.2)		
MS	2 (0.7)		
Parenting	20 (7.4)		
Parents	2 (0.7)		
Redbook	4 (1.5)		
Working Mother	5 (1.8)		
Total	270 (99.5)		270 (100)

Describing the Mass Media Coverage

A Dearth of Coverage

There is a general pattern of increasing coverage of breastfeeding from 1990–2004, although there is some variation (see Table 3.5). However, as we expected, our principal finding is that there is very little coverage of breastfeeding in these mass media. On average, only 18 items appeared in each outlet over a 15-year period, which translates to an average of one story per medium per year.

However, breastfeeding was not a story that appeared evenly across these media. Less than one-tenth of the stories appeared in network television newscasts (8.9%, or 24 stories). This finding is not surprising, given network television's small news hole. More surprising is that breastfeeding stories appeared more frequently in newspapers than in women's magazines. Nearly 70 percent (69.6%,

Table 3.5
Breastfeeding Stories by Year

Year	Number of Articles
1990	5
1991	6
1992	18
1993	7
1994	17
1995	10
1996	6
1997	18
1998	14
1999	24
2000	13
2001	34
2002	31
2003	25
2004	42
Total	270

or 188 articles) appeared in newspapers. Over half (51%, or 138 stories) of all stories appeared in just two newspapers: the *New York Times* and *USA Today*. By contrast only 58 articles appeared in the 11 women's magazines examined. Of these, 38 articles appeared in three magazines specifically targeted to mothers of young children: *Parenting, Baby Talk,* and *Working Mother*. Interestingly, several of the women's magazines studied here have little to no coverage of breastfeeding. Magazines as diverse as *Parents, Ms, Ebony, Better Homes and Gardens, Good Housekeeping,* and *Essence* share one thing in common: they published only two articles about breastfeeding in 15 years (see Table 3.4).

Of course, these data do not tell us the reason that reporters and editors for women's magazines did not publish many stories about breastfeeding. Perhaps, like abortion, the practice is considered too controversial or divisive. Alternatively, these journalists may not have perceived breastfeeding as an issue of general interest to women. The dearth of coverage in *Ms* magazine, the voicebox of mainstream feminism in the United States, also reinforces Galtry's argument about the concerns of NOW toward the question of breastfeeding (see Chapter 1).[65]

Mixed Messages: Miracle Milk and Sick Babies

Media coverage of breastfeeding and breast milk provided a mixed message to the public. On the one hand, among the most frequent stories were reports of breastfeeding rates and practices, indicating that breastfeeding is on the rise (26%) and that breastfeeding or breast milk is beneficial to infants (26%). For example, "Babies need to get most or all of their nutrition from the breast in the first six months," says the study in today's *American Journal of Public Health*.[66] Indeed "miracle milk" stories abounded. Over one-third (35%) of the media stories focused on the health benefits to babies and mothers, profiled children who were cured of illnesses when given breast milk, or reported other scientific findings, such as one that found consuming breast milk improves the conditions of elderly adults with cancer and another that discovered breast milk can cure warts (see Table 3.6).

Table 3.6
Subject Matter in Mass Media Stories about Breastfeeding and Breast Milk

Subject	%	N
Profile of mother	26.7	60
Benefits to baby	26.2	59
Breastfeeding rates and practices	26.2	59
Dangerous/bad for baby	17.8	40
Breastfed baby sickened or died	17.8	40
Public breastfeeding, positive	10.7	24
Balancing breastfeeding and employment	9.8	22
Benefits to mother	7.6	17
Infant formula, positive	7.1	16
Workplace discrimination against breastfeeding mother	4.0	9
Infant formula, negative	4.0	9
Pumping equipment/supplies	3.6	8
Public opinion about breastfeeding	3.1	7
Incarcerated breastfeeding mothers	2.7	6
Public breastfeeding, negative	1.3	3
Ill baby cured by breast milk	0.9	2
Dangerous/bad for mother	0.4	1
Other	8.4	19

Source: Data compiled by authors. Numbers total more than 100 percent because stories may be coded for up to three subjects.

Yet, nearly as prevalent were stories that focused on breastfeeding "mishaps"— women whose infants sickened or died in spite of being breastfed—and scientific evidence of toxins, viruses, or pollutants present in breast milk (36%; see Table 3.6). For example, the *New York Times* published five stories about the Tabatha Walrond case[67] and another three about similar cases involving babies dying or falling ill because of failed breastfeeding. All of these stories appeared in 1999, and comprised 34.7 percent of all breastfeeding coverage that year. Similar isolated stories are found in the *Seattle Post Intelligencer* and the *Columbus Dispatch*. In addition, an equal percentage of stories focused on how breast milk may be dangerous to the baby, because of toxins, viruses, or pollutants in the milk, or that the act of breastfeeding is somehow harmful. An example of the latter are problems associated with breastfeeding in the developing world, especially with respect to the spread of AIDS.

Breastfeeding in the Public Sphere

Another set of contradictory messages focused on breastfeeding in public. On the one hand, over 10 percent of media stories addressed breastfeeding in public in a supportive way, compared to only 3 percent of stories that presented public breastfeeding negatively (see Table 3.6). However, a nearly equal percentage of stories (9.6%) discussed the difficulties working women face in balancing breastfeeding with employment, or provided advice on the same; and another 4 percent of stories profiled cases of workplace discrimination against breastfeeding mothers (see Table 3.4).

News as Breastfeeding Advocacy?

In her study of Australian women's magazines, Ann Henderson found that breastfeeding was presented negatively: as demanding, draining, or even dangerous.[68] Our findings are significantly different. Of those articles that can be clearly coded as "positive" or "negative," positive frames outnumbered negative frames by more than two-to-one (110 positive articles [41%] compared to 47 negative articles [17.4%]). Only 21 articles (7.8% of newspaper and magazine articles) were coded as mixed.[69] Thus, while mixed messages do exist, generally the tone of the stories is positive or neutral.

Expert Knowledge vs. Personal Experience

The media coverage tended to use sources that focused on expert knowledge and de-emphasized individual experiences with breastfeeding. The three most commonly cited sources in stories about breastfeeding and breast milk were medical doctors or scientists (41%); government officials, including judges and police (34%)[70]; and medical journals (15.6%; see Table 3.7). Collectively, such "external experts" were cited far more frequently than those persons who are involved in the breastfeeding relationship (mothers [20%]; child [<1%]; father [<1%]), or breastfeeding advocates, including La Leche League (23%; see Table 3.7).[71] All articles relating to scientific findings cited either the medical journals where findings were published, the research facility that conducted the study, or both. Most articles, even those not specifically reporting scientific studies, cited at least once the American Academy of Pediatrics' recommendation to breast-feed. Coverage of AIDS-infected mothers cited the Centers for Disease Control and Prevention or the World Health Organization almost exclusively.

Important Differences in Newspaper Coverage

As noted previously, stories about breast milk and breastfeeding are more likely to appear in newspapers than on television or in women's magazines. Significantly more articles appeared in the *New York Times* (100, or 37%) than in any other newspaper. The reason for this is not entirely clear. One possible reason is that New York was one of the first states to enact breastfeeding protection laws. Consequently, *Times'* editors and reporters may believe that its readership is interested in breastfeeding stories. Alternatively, the *Times'* increase

Table 3.7
Sources Used in Mass Media Stories about Breastfeeding and Breast Milk

Source	%	N
Doctor or scientist	41.3	93
Government official	26.2	59
Mother	20.9	47
Medical Journal	15.6	35
Other breastfeeding advocate	8.9	20
La Leche League	8.0	18
American Academy of Pediatrics	5.8	13
Police	4.4	10
Judge	3.6	8
Child/baby	0.9	2
Father	0.4	1

Source: Data compiled by authors. Sources sum to more than 100 percent because news stories may cite more than one source.

in coverage reflects national trends of increasing breastfeeding rates and public awareness.

The *Times'* coverage had contradictory frames. For example, in 2003, a *Times'* article read, "The government should encourage women and girls to reduce the amount of meat, whole milk and other fatty foods as a way of protecting themselves and their children from dioxins... which can be passed through breast milk to an infant."[72] Yet, another article written the same year states, "Breast-feeding offers incomparable benefits to children. Among the benefits of breastfeeding are reduced risks of asthma, lymphoma, SIDS, meningitis, pneumonia, allergies, infections, diarrhea, and colds."[73]

The coverage in the other national newspaper in our study, *USA Today,* was similar. Its articles cover all of the same topics as the *New York Times*. The primary differences are a smaller number of articles (28, or 14% of the total), and *USA Today* did not cover protective breastfeeding legislation.

The two statewide newspapers had much different coverage than the papers with national circulations. While *USA Today* and the *New York Times* included a wide variety of topics and presented a mixed picture of the benefits and difficulties of breastfeeding, the coverage in the *Seattle Post Intelligencer* and the *Columbus Dispatch* focused almost entirely on the medical benefits of breast milk, to the exclusion of all other stories. However, the fact that Ohio lacked legislation to protect women's right to breastfeed in public did result in a difference in coverage between these two papers in 2004, when a U.S. Circuit court ruled that a Dayton, Ohio Wal-Mart store did not discriminate against women by banning public breastfeeding in its stores. No similar stories were found in the *Post Intelligencer,* where Washington state had breastfeeding rights laws in effect.

Differences between Television, Newspapers, and Women's Magazines

We conducted a number of analyses (cross-tabulations) to discern what differences, if any, there were by type of medium (television, newspaper, and women's magazine) and coverage of breastfeeding and breast milk. We found several interesting differences in coverage, in both story structure and content.

Differences in Structure

The first difference was along the hard news/soft news dichotomy. The vast majority of newspaper and television stories were classified as hard news (73% and 100%, respectively), while three-fourths (75%) of stories in women's magazines were classified as soft news. This difference reflects the differing audience for magazines, which are released less frequently (monthly rather than daily) and whose readership includes people who do not subscribe, but because of "pass along" readership, may read the articles months or even years after initial publication.[74]

Differences in Subject Matter

Damned If They Do and Damned If They Don't. One way that the content of the stories differs is by subject matter. First, newspapers were far more likely to carry stories about infants who sickened or died as a result of breastfeeding. Nearly one of every four newspaper stories (22%, or 42 newspaper stories), described such instances, while only two magazine articles (of 57, or 3%) and two television stories covered such cases. Some of this difference, although not all, is attributable to the Tabitha Walrond case.[75] Interestingly, newspapers were also more likely to include stories that cast infant formula in a negative light. Twenty-three of the 25 stories that discussed hazards associated with infant formula appeared in newspapers (12% of all newspaper articles). Apparently, women are "damned if they do and damned if they don't."[76]

Women's Experience Marginalized. On the other hand, women's magazines were more likely to include stories about breastfeeding rates and practices. Over half of all articles in women's magazines (54%, or 31 articles) discussed breastfeeding rates or practices. By contrast, there was no television coverage of this issue, and fewer than one in four newspaper articles (24%, or 46 articles) discussed breastfeeding rates and practices.[77] Similarly, breastfeeding women were far more likely to be profiled in women's magazines than in other media. Nearly a quarter of all articles about breastfeeding or breast milk in women's magazines included a profile of a breastfeeding mother (23%, or 13 of 57 stories). By contrast, only 1 television news story and only 25 newspaper stories (13%) profiled women.[78]

As noted previously, workplace discrimination was not a frequently occurring story. However, to the degree that it was covered at all, it was in women's magazines, namely *Working Mother.* Of the nine stories that highlighted workplace discrimination against breastfeeding mothers, five appeared in women's magazines. This comprised 10 percent of all breastfeeding stories in women's magazines.[79]

Marginalizing Advocates. Were there any differences in the sources that reporters for these different media use to authenticate their claims? Indeed there were. While all three types of media frequently cited medical doctors or scientists in their stories, these authorities appeared in 76 percent (19 of 25) of television stories, compared to 43 percent of newspaper stories (81 stories) and 52 percent of women's magazine articles (30 stories).[80] Newspapers were also more likely to cite government officials. A full third (73 of 188) of the newspaper articles cited a government official, compared to 24 percent of television stories (6 stories) and only 14 percent of the stories in women's magazines (8 of 57 articles).[81]

By contrast, women's magazines were more likely to use mothers, La Leche League representatives, or other breastfeeding advocates as sources.[82] For example, two-fifths of all women's magazine articles (42%, or 24 articles) included a breastfeeding mother as a source, compared to only two television stories (8%) and only 20 percent of newspaper stories (38 stories). La Leche League did not appear in any television stories and in only nine newspaper articles, but was cited in one-fifth of all stories in women's magazines. Finally, other breastfeeding advocates (neither La Leche League nor the American Academy of Pediatrics) were cited in one-fifth of the articles in women's magazines; none were cited in television news, and they appeared in only 10 percent of newspaper articles.

These findings imply that different media had vastly different interpretations of what types of individuals were considered authoritative sources. Other authors have argued that the lay women in La Leche League successfully challenged medical authority to provide women with alternative information about breastfeeding and have won the sometimes begrudging respect of medical doctors in the process.[83] However, our findings imply that reporters do not grant La Leche League advocates and mothers with the same credibility.

Disembodied Motherhood. Linda Blum, in *At the Breast: Ideologies of Breastfeeding and Motherhood in the United States,* discussed a notion of "disembodied motherhood." She argued that there is a dichotomy in American breastfeeding discourse that separates the act of nursing from the product of breast milk.[84] Similarly, Laura Woliver, in *The Political Geographies of Pregnancy,* argued that certain technologies, such as ultrasound and microscopic cameras, which provide images of a growing fetus *in utero,* serve to promote the fetus as a separate entity and to make the pregnant woman invisible.[85] While we are dealing with infants *ex utero,* we discern a pattern in the mass media coverage that contributes to both of these notions.

Two of the most frequently cited sources in our sample of news stories were doctors or scientists (41%) and mothers (21%). Yet, these sources rarely appeared in the *same* story. In fact, out of 174 stories (58% of the sample) that cited either a doctor/scientist and/or a mother, only 20 stories (7%) cited both a mother and a doctor/scientist.[86] Similarly, few articles cited both a medical journal and a mother.[87] Instead, medical journals and doctors/scientists were usually cited in news stories about the medical benefits of breast milk to babies or breastfeeding to women. In other words, the media coverage tends to frame breast milk as a *product*, without focusing on the physical mechanics of how this product is delivered. In other words, the mother is invisible. Because much of the coverage in newspapers and televisions focused on such health benefits, the media that men and opinion leaders were most likely to be exposed to (as opposed to women's magazines), presented a particularly disembodied view of breastfeeding.

On the other hand, women were cited in stories that focus on how women must negotiate breastfeeding in today's society. They were cited disproportionately in stories about breastfeeding rates and practices,[88] stories about breastfeeding in public,[89] public opinion about breastfeeding,[90] balancing breastfeeding with outside employment,[91] and discrimination faced by breastfeeding women in the workplace.[92] Moreover, as noted previously, many of these subjects are likely to be found in primarily women's magazines, indicating that citing breastfeeding mothers as authoritative sources is most acceptable when the audience is other women, specifically other mothers of young children. However, their particular form of expertise did not translate to other audiences.

Breastfeeding Through a Racial Lens

Given the significantly lower breastfeeding rates among African American women, we compared the coverage of breast milk and breastfeeding in three African American women's magazines (*Jet, Essence,* and *Ebony*), to that of other women's magazines (which have, presumably, a "whiter" readership). On the one hand, there was relatively little coverage of breastfeeding in African American women's magazines. There were only 10 articles over a 15-year period; 6 of these articles appeared in *Jet*. While this was miniscule coverage, it was comparable to the level of coverage in other (white) women's magazines that are not targeted to mothers of young children.

The coverage in the African American women's magazines did differ in some important ways from the coverage in other media. First, the stories are overwhelmingly positive. They were, in effect, persuasive pieces, attempting to convince African American mothers to breastfeed. There were no mixed messages. Rather the message was positive and clear: "Black women should breastfeed because it's good for their babies!" Indeed, the only article in a women's magazine that focused on a baby who was cured of an illness, or had a less severe illness because of breastfeeding, is in an African American women's magazine. Interestingly, only one article mentioned benefits that mothers accrue as a result of breastfeeding.

The sources cited in the African American women's magazines also differ. Like all other media analyzed here, the writers rely heavily on medical doctors or scientists as sources. Seven of the nine articles (77%) cited medical doctors/scientists in their analyses, compared to 32 percent of articles in other women's magazines.[93] However, they used mothers less frequently; only two of the nine articles cited mothers.

Also notably absent was La Leche League. None of the 10 articles provided information from La Leche League. These data, of course, do not tell us why La Leche League was ignored. However, this finding is very interesting and may be attributable to a culture clash between La Leche League adherents and African American women. First, the League was founded in the 1950s by seven white, Catholic, middle-class women who breastfed. Even today, League membership is predominately white and middle class.[94] Second, for many years, La Leche League urged breastfeeding women to forgo outside employment so they could breastfeed on demand and prolong the breastfeeding relationship. Only recently has La Leche League begun to provide advice and support to breastfeeding mothers who return to work. This philosophy, too, places the League culturally and socioeconomically at odds with African American women, who have always been more likely to be employed outside the home.

Implications of Media Coverage

These results indicate that breastfeeding was presented in a contradictory way in the mass media from 1990–2004. On one hand, a large number of articles about breastfeeding practices and the desirability of higher breastfeeding rates were positive in tone. On the other hand, a sizable subset of the articles and news pieces surveyed were negative in tone, focusing on the possible harm to infants from breastfeeding. It is important to note, however, that these negative articles did not attack the idea of breastfeeding per se, but rather talked about specific dangers from breastfeeding that arise in specific circumstances. One might argue, in fact, that these articles, rather than reflecting negativity toward breastfeeding, are a sign that the idea of breastfeeding in general is becoming a normatively desirable practice. The growing normative enthusiasm for this practice, these articles seem to suggest, needs to be curbed.

Alternatively, some of the articles with negative frames reflect that, in some circumstances, breast milk is not always "the best" food for babies, such as when breast milk may transmit disease. These stories, therefore, do not necessarily reflect social hostility to the practice of breastfeeding that advocates decry.

In terms of the media outlets that we have surveyed, we can say that there is no uniform hostility toward breastfeeding. Rather, the evidence suggests that breastfeeding is becoming increasingly accepted within our media-saturated consciousness. In fact, the stories that most immediately appear as negative in tone may be part of larger discursive assumptions about mothering based on socioeconomic circumstances, racial positioning, and norms of good mothering. Many of the negative stories can also be explained by the norms of the print or television media, which famously play on the pathological in order to attract readers and viewers.

We are particularly interested in how the coverage of breastfeeding varied across media outlets that are typically consumed by different kinds of audiences. The data suggest that particular frames and particular appeals to authority differ across these outlets, forming a hermetically sealed dyad between those particular outlets and their audiences. To take one example, we note that newspaper articles were much more likely to appeal to physicians, policy makers, and managers as authoritative sources, while women's magazines were more likely to entail testimonials from mothers themselves. In the small sample of African American women's magazines, the expert testimony of doctors and policy makers was more prevalent than the testimony of mothers.

Likewise, the subject matter of these articles varied across outlets. Newspaper articles were more likely to focus on possible health problems associated with breastfeeding, whereas women's magazines tended to focus on breastfeeding practices and rates. African American magazines tended to advocate for breastfeeding, urging African American mothers to breastfeed.

The more elite (including policy makers) and male audiences reading the *New York Times* (and, to a lesser extent, other papers and television news outlets) heard a lot from doctors and other experts about either the desirability or dangers of breastfeeding. As such, those stories contribute to the idea of an invisible, disembodied mother–feeder whose own experience was not necessarily relevant to the issue of whether or not to breastfeed. Though this does not invalidate the truthfulness of these pieces, it does resonate with the ongoing feminist concern that the trend toward the medicalization of health care practices tends to rob women of the autonomous choice that takes into account women's own perspectives about mothering and breastfeeding. Someone else, other than women themselves, is telling women what to do.

This same finding further reinforces the message that "we want you to do it, but we don't want to see it." Thus, women who conform to the media's norm of "good mothers"—well-educated, white, middle-class mothers, not employed outside the home—have fewer difficulties with the contradictory social expectations to breastfeed, but to do so in private. It is deviant mothers—the nonwhite, the ill, the polluted, the employed, and those who venture into shopping malls and restaurants—who encounter difficulties.

By way of contrast, the messages of women's magazines, often focused on the practice of breastfeeding as it is seen from the perspective of breastfeeding women themselves, contributes to an emerging norm of what constitutes good mothering. The white, educated readers of these magazines will likely accept, or have already accepted, breastfeeding as the norm for what good mothers will do in order to most fully care for their children. Though the health benefits accrued by both the mother and child suggest that this is a reasonable assumption, the normalization of breastfeeding as constitutive of good mothering runs the risk of stigmatizing those mothers who may not be able to breastfeed or who reasonably choose not to breastfeed. Given the success of conservative law makers in using the "unfit mother" as a rhetorical device in the pursuit of policies, this normalization, whatever its benefits, is not cost free.[95]

AMERICAN ATTITUDES ABOUT BREASTFEEDING IN THE PUBLIC EYE

Our central question in this chapter is: Is American society hostile to breast-feeding? We conclude that there is no uniform hostility to breastfeeding. Rather, there is some public support for breastfeeding and breastfeeding rights in the abstract, and breastfeeding and breast milk are covered positively by the media. The primary difficulty is incomplete information, which leads the general public and policy makers to have unrealistic or inaccurate expectations of what breast-feeding demands, and what public breastfeeding might entail.

First of all, these studies indicate that there is little awareness of the physical mechanics of breastfeeding. Not only do we lack personal experience with breastfeeding, there is little media coverage about it. What media coverage exists tends to separate breast milk from the act of suckling. Moreover, breastfeeding mothers themselves are fairly invisible in the mass media. Story sources are often those who have medical and scientific credentials, not the breastfeeding mothers speaking of their own experiences.

Second, while there is no uniform hostility to breastfeeding in the media, neither is there uniform support. Rather, as the opening epigraphs show, and as the analysis of media coverage documents, the media do report the difficulties women face when they breastfeed in public, go to work, or their babies sicken and die. Coupled with public opinion findings that demonstrate that there is considerable unease about breastfeeding in the workplace or in public when parts of the women's bodies are exposed, these factors could lead a woman to decide not to breastfeed, especially if her baby's father is hostile to the idea.

Negative stories are not necessarily detrimental to the aims of breastfeeding advocates. For instance, news stories about harassment breastfeeding women experienced have led to legislative changes. In Ohio, the experience of the women asked to leave Wal-Mart led Ohio to enact breastfeeding legislation. In South Carolina, breastfeeding rights legislation was passed after a woman publicized that she was turned away from a Victoria's Secret store where she asked to feed her baby in a dressing room (see Chapter 5).

Similarly, we do not think that the news media should shy away from stories about possible environmental contamination or illnesses that could be transmitted through breast milk, simply because they depict breastfeeding in a negative light. Rather, these are important public health stories that provide information to women.

4

Limited Rights: Breastfeeding Rights in Federal Law and Litigation

As breastfeeding advocates have gained strength in numbers and in political skill, they have worked to ensure that a mother's right to breastfeed is protected in federal and state laws, and in court cases. However, the texts of this legislation and these cases demonstrates forcefully that the field of breastfeeding rights is complex where the rights and interests of numerous entities—the mother, the father, the employer, the state, and the child—come into conflict.

Federal and state breastfeeding policy is comprised of disparate laws, administrative actions, and unrelated court cases. In 2006, they include some 46 state laws (see Chapter 5); several federal Treasury Appropriations laws; federal programs such as Temporary Assistance to Needy Families (TANF); the Women, Infants, and Children (WIC) food program; the Family and Medical Leave Act (FMLA); the Civil Rights Act and the Pregnancy Discrimination Act; and dozens of federal and state appeals court decisions in cases in which breastfeeding is a central issue.

Given that breastfeeding is addressed in a variety of policy venues, breastfeeding policy is, perhaps unsurprisingly, uncoordinated and conflicting. Laws and judicial decisions often leave gaps. Prescribed policy changes may be mismatched to the problem. In fact, as in the case of judges, breastfeeding policy may be made by individuals who are hostile to breastfeeding, or at the very least, indifferent to the biological realities of nursing.

The purpose of this chapter is to describe the various federal laws that might influence a women's decision to breastfeed, or to continue breastfeeding, and the various federal court cases that have breastfeeding as a central issue. This chapter then uses social construction theory to analyze disparate federal policies and to determine what changes might be made to protect women's right to breastfeed and children's interest in being breastfed.

We identified relevant federal legislation through reading court cases, secondary sources, and through a Lexis-Nexis search of the Federal Code and the Congressional database "Thomas," using the words "breast feeding," "breast-feeding," "breastfeeding" and "breastfed." Court cases were identified through Lexis-Nexis searches using the same key words. Other cases were identified through references in law review literature. All cases and laws are grouped by topic based upon the authors' reading and interpretation.

FEDERAL LEGISLATION AND REGULATIONS

Breastfeeding first came on the federal agenda in the 1980s, when activists instituted an international boycott of Nestlé Corporation to protest its marketing practices in the developing world. Nestlé's marketing practices included giving away free formula samples to women, often provided by employees dressed as medical workers. The mothers' own milk supply would then dry out, forcing them to purchase additional formula to feed their babies. Because formula was costly, the mothers often diluted the formula to make it last longer, leaving their babies malnourished. In addition, water supplies in many areas of the developing world were not safe, thus leaving these formula-fed babies susceptible to water-borne infections. The Nestlé boycott led to Senate hearings and other public disclosures. Eventually Nestlé and other formula manufacturers were forced to change their marketing practices.[1]

Promoting Breastfeeding through Public Health Initiatives

Breastfeeding practices in the United States, however, did not arrive on the federal agenda until 1984, when Surgeon General C. Everett Koop hosted the first Workshop on Breastfeeding and Human Lactation. Subsequent workshops were held in 1985 and 1991. One outcome of this initiative was the creation of the U.S. Breastfeeding Committee, which fulfills one of the goals in the United Nations' *Innocenti Declaration,* a document produced by a 1990 United Nations conference aimed at promoting breastfeeding worldwide.[2]

The Public Health Service, a division of the Department of Health and Human Services, began to emphasize increasing rates of breastfeeding rates in the 1990s. *Healthy People 2000* was the statement of public health goals generated by the Public Health Service, the Centers for Disease Control and Prevention (CDC), and the National Center for Health Statistics, issued in 1991. Among the Maternal and Infant Health goals is Objective 14.9, which sought to increase breastfeeding rates for all women, irrespective of race, ethnicity, or income, to 75 percent in the early postpartum period, and to 50 percent at six months. By 1999, no racial or ethnic group had met the 75 percent target for the early postpartum period, although all racial, ethnic, and income groups had experienced increases of 7 percent (for low income mothers) to 18 percent (for African American mothers).[3]

Increasing breastfeeding rates is also a priority in *Healthy People 2010*, the successor to *Healthy People 2000*. Its goals include: 75 percent of mothers will breastfeed in the early postpartum period, 50 percent at six months, and 25 percent at one year. In addition, *Healthy People 2010* set additional goals that 60 percent of mothers will be exclusively breastfeeding at three months and 25 percent exclusively breastfeeding at six months. The Public Health Service reported that by 1998, there was significant movement toward the *2010* targets, especially in increasing breastfeeding rates in the early postpartum period (at 55 percent of goal) and one year (at 44 percent of goal).[4]

In 2000, the Office on Women's Health (OWH) issued the *HHS Blueprint for Action on Breastfeeding,* which outlines an ambitious public health agenda. It includes advocating breastfeeding-friendly practices in hospitals and maternity centers, changes in the workplace to facilitate working mothers' efforts to continue to breastfeed and express milk, encouraging child care centers to accommodate breastfeeding mothers, and to enhance public education efforts.[5] Pursuant to these efforts, the OWH embarked on a National Breastfeeding Awareness Campaign in 2002, in which they worked with the Ad Council to create public service announcements for television and radio and print messages for newspapers, magazines, and outdoor billboards. One goal of the campaign was to communicate a consistent message that babies should be breastfed for six months and possible drawbacks of using formula. The OWH reports—based on a survey conducted after the campaign—that the campaign was successful in raising awareness of the importance of breastfeeding and the recommendation that babies be exclusively breastfed for the first six months of life. Moreover, the percentage of respondents who believed infant formula was as good as breast milk declined.[6]

Promoting Breastfeeding through Legislation

Since 1999, Representative Carolyn Maloney (D-NY) has ensured that the Treasury and General Government's Appropriations Acts have included the following identical language: "notwithstanding any other provision of law, a woman may breastfeed her child at any location in a Federal building or on Federal property, if the woman and her child are otherwise authorized to be present at the location." According to the Congressional Research Service, this law applies to both visitors and federal employees.[7] By implication then, federal employees may bring their infants to work to breastfeed.

The federal government also supports breastfeeding efforts through the Women, Infants and Children program (WIC). WIC was created as a pilot project in 1972 to provide nutritious food to pregnant, lactating, and postpartum women and their children. When the program was permanently authorized by Congress, the legislation specifically defined breastfeeding and allowed breastfeeding women to receive WIC benefits for up to one year postpartum, compared to six months for nonlactating, postpartum women. In the 1989 reauthorization, Congress built on its commitment to breastfeeding by implementing several measures, including requiring participating states to hire a breastfeeding coordinator and to spend a portion of their federal subsidy on breastfeeding promotion. By 1992, the WIC program was charged to develop and distribute educational materials promoting breastfeeding, and in 1998 Congress allowed women to use WIC food funds to purchase or rent breast pumps.[8] WIC was reauthorized in 2004. The legislation authorized the WIC program to use up to $14 million on special projects, including breastfeeding promotion, and another $20 million for special education programs, to include breastfeeding peer counselors.[9]

As of Fiscal Year 2007, women and children in families up to 185 percent of the federal poverty guideline were eligible to receive WIC benefits. For the 48 contiguous states, this translates to a family income of about $24,000 per year for a family of two, and $30,000 for a family of three. Approximately half of all babies born in the United States are eligible for WIC benefits.[10]

Employment Legislation

Numerous studies have documented that one of the primary predictors of the duration of breastfeeding is when a woman returns to work.[11] Aside from the protection given to women on federal property, federal law provides little by way of employment law that would enable women to breastfeed for the year recommended by the American Academy of Pediatrics. For example, the most relevant federal law is the Family and Medical Leave Act (FMLA), enacted in 1993. The FMLA entitles eligible employees to take up to 12 weeks of unpaid leave upon the birth or adoption of a child, or the placement of a foster child; to care for a sick family member; or because of one's own illness or medical condition. As such, the FMLA supports breastfeeding for up to 12 weeks, if the employee is eligible for leave and the employee can afford to take all or part of this leave without pay.[12]

As explained in detail later, working women who have encountered some difficulty managing breastfeeding and work have filed lawsuits under the Pregnancy Discrimination Act, the Americans with Disabilities Act and Title VII of the Civil Rights Act of 1964. The Pregnancy Discrimination Act, passed in 1978, states that discrimination against women who are pregnant is sex discrimination and forbids discrimination against women on the basis of pregnancy or any related medical condition. The Americans with Disabilities Act was passed in 1990. It prohibits employers from discriminating against applicants and employees on the basis of a physical or mental impairment that inhibits some "major life activity."[13] The Civil Rights Act of 1964 was a landmark piece of legislation designed to eliminate employment discrimination on the basis of race. It also protects against discrimination on the basis of sex.[14]

LIMITATIONS IN FEDERAL LEGISLATION AND REGULATIONS

While this list of federal initiatives appears to be supportive of breastfeeding, federal support of breastfeeding remains limited. In fact, other legislation and regulations operate at cross-purposes with the goals of some of these efforts.

First, in the wake of the foiled terrorist plot to smuggle explosive materials aboard aircraft in common containers such as shampoo bottles in 2006, the Transportation Safety Administration imposed strict regulations regarding what foods, liquids, and prescription drugs could be carried on aircraft. In September, these regulations stipulated that passengers could carry expressed breast milk or infant formula only if they are traveling with an infant.[15] As La Leche League International pointed out, this policy is particularly burdensome for employed breastfeeding women who travel on business without their infants and express their milk while away from home. Thus, these mothers can no longer bring their breast pumps, with their expressed milk tucked between cold packs in the carrying cases, on the airplane. They must either include the milk in their checked baggage, where it might spill or spoil, or ship frozen milk to their homes.[16] Either alternative could present a significant incentive to wean rather than pump and throw away spoiled milk, or incur the expense of shipping.

Similarly, notwithstanding the encouraging results of the National Breastfeeding Awareness Campaign, the federal campaign has engendered criticism. Jacqueline Wolf documents how the messages of the public education campaign were diluted under pressure from the American Academy of Pediatrics and lobbyists for the formula and dairy industries. The Ad Council, known for its rather provocative public service announcements (PSAs), such as "friends don't let friends drive drunk," had produced a series of ads focusing on risky behavior: pregnant women engaged in a log rolling competition or riding a mechanical bull at a bar. The tag line, "You wouldn't take risks before your baby's born...Why start after," was initially followed by a series of statistics citing formula-fed infants' increased risk of developing various diseases, including cancer. After significant pressure, these statistics were eliminated, and the final line of the PSA stated simply, "Breastfeed exclusively for 6 months," with an announcer's voice stating: "Recent studies show babies who are breastfed are less likely to develop ear infections, respiratory illnesses and diarrhea. Babies were born to be breastfed."[17]

Rebecca Kukla criticized the ad campaign for being too abstract and for not targeting its intended population well. For instance, she notes that the magazine ads do not include photographs of women and babies, but rather use images of flowers or an ice cream sundae, which only obliquely represent breasts. Few of those women who are depicted are women of color, subtly communicating, Kukla believes, that breastfeeding is a white woman's practice. Her most damning criticism, however, is that the Public Health Service ignored the data that indicated that pregnant women knew that breastfeeding was best for their babies. The Public Health Service's response to low breastfeeding rates was not to enact policies that would help women negotiate their public and private lives, but to continue to tell women what they already know, that they should breastfeed. In her words:

> DHHS itself admits, "Research has shown that many women know that breastfeeding is the best nutrition for babies. This knowledge has not translated into changed behaviors, and breastfeeding rates have hit a plateau. . ." In light of this, their chosen strategy of looking for a more compelling slogan is especially remarkable. It utterly fails to examine or address the *reason* for this gap between message and behavior, insistently keeping the focus on changing women's choices and insistently maintaining the background assumption that these choices are best treated as the products of isolated free wills that can be understood and manipulated in abstraction from the social and material conditions that constrain, position, and shape them.[18]

The WIC program has come in for criticism from breastfeeding advocates as well. Despite the fact that it has many efforts underway to promote breastfeeding among the mothers receiving WIC benefits, few of these mothers breastfeed, or if they initiate breastfeeding, do not continue for long. The CDC noted that WIC-eligible mothers who did not receive WIC benefits were more likely to breastfeed than mothers receiving WIC benefits. The difference was particularly pronounced among low-income, white women. Nearly 75 percent of the

WIC-eligible white women had "ever breastfed" compared to only 60 percent of WIC recipients. Slightly more than half (51%) of African American mothers who were WIC-eligible reported that they had "ever breastfed" compared to 46 percent of African American WIC recipients.[19]

The reasons for these trends are unclear, although these data suggest that there is something about participation in the WIC program that discourages breastfeeding. Many breastfeeding advocates believe that WIC mothers are less likely to breastfeed because they are exposed to marketing by formula manufacturers. This advertising can be through the mass media, or in the form of samples and other promotional items given to new mothers while still in the hospital. In addition, some formula manufacturers use the WIC logo on their labels, which appears to imply that WIC endorses the product. U.S. Department of Agriculture regulations forbid such practices, but in 2005, only 17 states included these limitations in their WIC formula contracts. The U.S. Government Accountability Office (GAO) found that formula manufacturers do not specifically target mothers in the WIC program, although these women are exposed to the same marketing as the non-WIC population.[20]

An alternate explanation may be that the women who receive WIC benefits are somehow different from WIC-eligible women who do not receive WIC benefits. Exposure to formula marketing campaigns may explain why some women do not breastfeed, but they do not explain why mothers receiving WIC benefits breastfeed at lower rates than WIC-eligible women who do not receive benefits. As of 2006, no study has satisfactorily answered this question. However, we can speculate. Perhaps the WIC-eligible mothers who do not receive benefits are more likely to be recent immigrants. Recent immigrants may be less likely to understand and access government social welfare benefits and are also more likely to breastfeed their infants, especially if they come from countries with strong breastfeeding traditions. In fact, immigrant women receiving WIC benefits report longer breastfeeding durations.[21] Moreover, no analysis of breastfeeding practices has examined the WIC-eligible population to determine if they are somehow categorically different from the WIC beneficiaries. Perhaps the WIC-eligible population is more likely to be married, older, or high school graduates, all of which would make them more likely to breastfeed.[22] They may also be less likely to be employed, which could also affect breastfeeding practices.

Moreover, the WIC program's own financial mandates set it at odds with its pro-breastfeeding mission. The single most expensive food item in the WIC program is infant formula; WIC accounts for as much as half of the infant formula purchased in the United States. Beginning in 1989, in response to rapidly increasing infant formula costs, state WIC programs were required to implement cost containment policies. Most states have implemented "sole-source" contracts with a formula manufacturer; this manufacturer then has an exclusive contract to sell its infant formula to WIC mothers, who use their WIC vouchers to purchase qualified food items. Under these contracts, state WIC programs receive a rebate from the formula manufacturer on all cans of formula sold to WIC participants. This dramatically reduced the costs of the program; the GAO estimates that the formula company rebates totaled $1.2 billion in Fiscal Year 1996 (the most recent data available), and enabled WIC programs to provide benefits to 1.7 million additional women and children monthly. The GAO concluded that rebates for any other foods purchased by the WIC program would not generate as much savings. Thus, in a sense, WIC is financially dependent upon formula use. If more WIC mothers breastfeed, then program costs will decrease significantly. However, none of the breastfeeding mothers' food costs are eligible for rebates.[23]

Employment Limitations

Just as efforts to promote breastfeeding through federal public health and food programs have some serious drawbacks, so do various employment laws. The Family and Medical Leave Act provides valuable opportunities for parents to spend time with their newborn children. Mothers can use this leave to establish breastfeeding. However, FMLA only applies to organizations with 50 or more employees and does not provide paid leave. Taking leave without pay is a serious detriment to most workers. Only well-paid workers are likely to be able to take full advantage of this program. Recognizing this, the U.S. Department of Labor under the Clinton Administration created a voluntary program whereby states could opt to pay unemployment benefits to workers taking leave under the FMLA upon the birth or adoption of a child. However, no state implemented this provision, and the Department of Labor under the G. W. Bush Administration rescinded it in 2002.[24]

Moreover, even for those able to take full advantage of the Family and Medical Leave Act, workers can take only three months of leave. This period is only half as long as the period of time that the AAP recommends for exclusive breastfeeding. The most privileged middle-class families may be able to have the father take three months of leave after the mother returns to work, but unless the mother can nurse or pump at work, this does not necessarily allow mothers to breastfeed exclusively for the full six months recommended.

Similarly, the federal government's breastfeeding promotion efforts target low-income women especially. Another program that serves this same population is the modern incarnation of the welfare program, Temporary Assistance to Needy Families (TANF). First created in 1996, TANF was reauthorized in 2005. Neither the 1996 program description nor the legislation that reauthorized it specifically mentioned breastfeeding or nursing.[25] However, numerous provisions could discourage women receiving TANF benefits from breastfeeding. Of greatest concern are the program's emphases on seeking and finding employment and the limitations on how long a woman may receive benefits. Studies of employed women find that those with the most professional autonomy are best able to balance the competing needs of breastfeeding and outside employment.[26] Women at the end of their time limits to receive benefits may be forced into the workforce, regardless of the age of their youngest child, or whether they are breastfeeding. Finally, women moving from welfare to work are unlikely to be in high-status positions that would allow them the flexibility to breastfeed or express milk on the job.

FEDERAL LITIGATION

Since the first federal case involving a breastfeeding mother was decided in 1981, approximately 20 lawsuits have been filed in federal courts that involve breastfeeding mothers, or breastfeeding as a secondary issue. Most involve employed mothers and varying interpretations of federal civil rights laws, although a few deal with other issues. This section will describe and analyze these cases.

The first, precedent-setting case was decided in 1981, by the Fifth Circuit Court of Appeals in *Dike v. School Board of Orange County*. The court ruled in a wrongful dismissal case that breastfeeding is a constitutional right. In this case, Janice Dike, a kindergarten teacher, sued her employer, the Orange County School Board, because her employer would neither allow her to breastfeed her child on campus, nor to leave campus for brief periods to breastfeed, when her child refused to nurse from a bottle. In the words of Chief Judge Godbold, who wrote the Court's opinion, "we conclude that the Constitution protects from excessive state interference a woman's decision respecting breastfeeding." In this respect, the Court built upon a long legal tradition of recognizing parental authority and extending the right to privacy to parents' decisions about their children's education and welfare.[27] However, the Court also ruled that the school board's competing interests in preventing disruptions of the educational process and limiting liability were equally valid.[28]

This case has been the basis for a variety of subsequent lawsuits involving breastfeeding mothers. No other court has backed away from the essential premise in *Dike*, that breastfeeding is a constitutionally protected right. Yet, the qualified judgment has allowed subsequent courts to rule against breastfeeding mothers without contradicting the central finding in *Dike*.

EMPLOYMENT LITIGATION

As women have faced difficulties combining work, breastfeeding, and/or breast pumping, they have turned to the federal courts. Women have claimed discrimination under, variously, Title VII of the Civil Rights Act, the Americans with Disabilities Act, the Pregnancy Discrimination Act, and the Family and Medical Leave Act.

Title VII of the Civil Rights Act

Title VII of the Civil Rights Act of 1964 forbids employment discrimination on the basis of race, color, religion, sex, or national origin. The courts have used two theories to determine discrimination under this statute: disparate treatment and disparate impact. Disparate impact involves a "factually neutral employment criterion that has an unequal effect on members of the protected class."[29] This provision was used directly in the lawsuits filed by two breastfeeding women. The first was Alicia Martinez. Martinez was an associate producer, and later a producer, at MSNBC. In her suit, she argued that MSNBC discriminated against her on the basis of a "sex plus" criterion: in her case, her sex and her need to pump breast milk. The federal court for the Southern District of New York rejected Martinez's claim, arguing that the "sex plus" criterion is based upon a comparison of women to similarly situated men. Because men cannot lactate, there is no similarly situated group of men upon which to base this claim.[30]

The second was Kimberlie Bloise Jacobson, who sued her former employer, Regent Assisted Living, in 1999. Jacobson encountered a variety of difficulties in her job as Controller, such as failing to meet reporting deadlines, even prior to the birth of her child in 1996. Upon the birth of her child, she began to work part-time, and these difficulties worsened. Jacobson noted two incidents in which her direct supervisor was insensitive to her needs to pump breast milk or nurse her child, and she began to leak breast milk. In one instance, she related, she was "forced to sit on [an airplane], drenched in breast milk. This caused her humiliation and pain." These incidents were used by Jacobson as evidence of disparate treatment under Title VII. The District Court of Oregon ruled against Jacobson, citing among other reasons, that disparate treatment claims are contingent upon an employee performing their job satisfactorily.

Americans with Disabilities Act

Two women have attempted to file employment discrimination lawsuits based on the Americans with Disabilities Act (ADA). The first case occurred in 1998. Christine Bond filed a discrimination case against her employer, Sterling, Inc. and Kay Jewelers, under the New York Human Rights Law, portions of which are based on the definition of disability found in the ADA. Bond faced some hostility to her pregnancy and her decision to breastfeed from her employer. For instance, the personnel officer at the firm informed her, "we are not a family oriented company, we are a business." Shortly after her son was born, Bond was ordered to attend a training seminar. Because her son was only five weeks old and Bond was breastfeeding, Bond requested that she be allowed to bring her son to the seminar, or be excused from attendance. Both requests were denied. Bond did not attend the seminar, and consequently, she was terminated.[31]

Bond claimed that as a breastfeeding mother she was disabled, because when she is nursing, a mother is prohibited from performing various "normal bodily functions" including walking, bending over, moving things, or operating a motor vehicle. The federal court for the Northern District of New York ruled against Bond, arguing, "common sense suggests no impairment associated with the status of being a breastfeeding mother," and concluded, "It is simply preposterous to contend that a woman's body is functioning abnormally because she is lactating." The court further asserted that anyone who is bottle feeding an infant is also prohibited from walking, bending over, and the like.[32]

Details in the *Martinez v. MSNBC* case are similar. Martinez would pump breast milk in empty editing rooms, and on at least three occasions, coworkers attempted to enter the room while she was pumping, seemingly unaware that she was in the room. Martinez refused human resources' suggestion that she post a "do not disturb" sign when pumping her milk. After a series of conflicts regarding scheduling and child care concerns, Martinez resigned from MSNBC. According to the court, she then filed suit claiming under the Americans with Disabilities Act, "(1) discrimination in violation of the ADA on the theory that lactation is a disability, (2) retaliation under the ADA for complaining of the allegedly inadequate facilities for her breast pumping." The court ruled that lactation is not a disability because pregnancy and related conditions are not disabilities, and quoted the "preposterous" language used in the *Bond* decision. Consequently, the court ruled that the claim of inadequate accommodations for a disability moot, although the court did acknowledge in a footnote, "This of course is not to say that a statute requiring employers to afford reasonable accommodations to women engaged in breast feeding or breast pumping would be undesirable."[33]

Arguably, the courts are correct in their assertion that breastfeeding is not a disability. Indeed, it is the full fruition of the female body's reproductive abilities. Consequently, one might then think that an inability to breastfeed is a disability. This is exactly the argument made by Ann Tozzi in 2001. She sued her former employer, Advanced Medical Management, for wrongful termination under the ADA and the FMLA. Tozzi was diagnosed with breast cancer at age 27 and underwent bilateral mastectomies and reconstructive surgery. Her recuperation was slow and she experienced significant fatigue and difficulty when she returned to work. Tozzi argued that she qualified for the designation as disabled because the surgery left her unable to complete various functions, including the ability to breastfeed. Tozzi defended this proposition by connecting breastfeeding to the reproductive function, which had been previously defined as a "major life activity." The U.S. District Court of Maryland rejected this argument, stating:

> An interpretation of the language of "reproduction and the sexual dynamics surrounding it" to include breastfeeding would be unreasonably broad and expand the ADA well beyond its intended scope. Although this court acknowledges the importance of breastfeeding and the special relationship it establishes between a mother and child, this Court declines to expand the outer margins of the ADA by holding that it is a major life activity for the purposes of that statute.[34]

If these conflicting court decisions were not sufficient to leave breastfeeding in legal limbo, the case *Toyota v. Williams* (2002) is. In this case, Ella Williams sued her employer, Toyota, under the ADA. She claimed that her carpal tunnel injuries were a disability for which Toyota failed to make appropriate accommodations. The Supreme Court ruled against Williams, stating that "the impairment's impact must be permanent or long term."[35] The Supreme Court did not expressly define "long term" in its opinion, and the Department of Labor's definition of disability under the ADA does not specify a minimum duration for any covered impairment. However, the Social Security Administration defines a disability for the purposes of receiving disability benefits as "a severe disability (or combination of disabilities) that has lasted, or is expected to last, at least 12 months or result in death."[36] By these standards, breastfeeding is unlikely to be considered a disability by the government. It is not a permanent condition, does not result in death, and the AAP's recommended duration for exclusive breastfeeding (six months) is less than the minimum required by the Social Security Administration, and consequently, is unlikely to meet the "long-term" standard articulated in the *Toyota* case. The AAP's recommended period for breastfeeding (at least 12 months) does meet the Social Security Administration's standard for duration. However, breastfeeding for one year can be considered a disability only if courts find that breastfeeding also limits major life activities, which is unlikely in light of the *Tozzi* decision.

Family and Medical Leave Act

Just as women suing under Title VII or the ADA were unsuccessful, any claims for additional leave to breastfeed under the Family and Medical Leave Act (FMLA) were denied by the court. Christine Bond (in *Bond v. Sterling*), in addition to her ADA claim, also argued that she suffered a violation of the FMLA. Bond developed complications in the latter months of her pregnancy that led to her working reduced hours in June and taking full-time leave beginning in July, a full month before the birth of her son. Consequently, her leave expired shortly after she gave birth and Bond returned to work when her child was barely one month old. Bond charged that her termination was in retaliation for taking leave under FMLA. The district court again ruled against her, stating that she was terminated for failing to attend the managers' meeting.[37]

Kellie Gallegos filed a similar complaint against the Department of Interior in 2000. She had requested a three-month extension of her leave, after the 12 weeks allowed under the FMLA expired, so that she could continue to breastfeed her child. Her request was denied, yet Gallegos did not return to work for another three months, and consequently was terminated. This decision was upheld by a U.S. Circuit Court for the Federal Circuit in 2001, stating that Gallegos "made no efforts to resolve the situation with her supervisor by seeking workplace accommodations, which could have permitted her to continue breastfeeding, nor did she submit medical documentation for her asserted medical inability to return."[38]

Pregnancy Discrimination Act

Several breastfeeding mothers have attempted to sue their former employers under the Pregnancy Discrimination Act, which prohibits discrimination on the basis of pregnancy and related medical conditions. However, these efforts, too, were unsuccessful. A key case, often cited in subsequent decisions, is *Wallace v. Pyro Mining Company*.[39] Martha Wallace was an accounting clerk employed by Pyro Mining Company. She took disability leave beginning in January 1987 and gave birth to a daughter in February. She was scheduled to return to work in March. As her date to return to work approached, Wallace asked for an additional six weeks of leave because her infant, then six weeks old, refused a bottle, and would only breastfeed. When Wallace did not return to work on the appointed date, she was fired. In this case, the Sixth Circuit Court ruled in 1990 that breastfeeding was not covered by the PDA because breastfeeding is not a "medical condition" related to pregnancy or childbirth. The Court stated:

> While it may be that breastfeeding and weaning are natural concomitants of pregnancy and childbirth, they are not "medical conditions" related thereto . . . We believe . . . Congress' intent that "related medical conditions" be limited to incapacitating conditions for which medical care or treatment is usual and normal. Neither breastfeeding and weaning, nor difficulties arising therefrom, constitute such conditions.

Moreover, the Court added, "Nothing in the Pregnancy Discrimination Act or Title VII, obliges employers who accommodate child-care concerns of breast-feeding female workers by providing additional breast-feeding leave not available to male workers."[40]

This case was cited as precedent in subsequent rulings, including *Martinez v. MSNBC* and *McNill v. New York City Department of Correction* (1996). In the latter case, Michele McNill faced some employment sanctions due to "excessive absences" following her maternity leave. McNill responded that these absences were due to her need to breastfeed her infant because her child had a cleft palate. She asserted that breastfeeding should be covered under the PDA because of her infant's medical condition. The judge for the District Court for Southern New York decided that the PDA did not cover McNill's claim because "conditions related to pregnancy or childbirth would directly involve the condition of the mother . . . An infant's malformed palate and lip does not directly affect the condition of the mother."[41]

Rona Barrash's case, decided in 1988, is one that many breastfeeding legal advocates cite as an example of courts and judges that are hostile to a woman's decision to breastfeed.[42] In this case, Barrash, a Social Security Administration employee, sued for wrongful dismissal. Barrash, who had been granted six months' administrative leave after the birth of her first child in 1982, was granted only six weeks of leave after the birth of her second child in 1984, because the Social Security Administration had been ordered to reduce its grants of administrative leave without pay. Barrash continuously requested six months' leave, endorsed by her pediatrician, because she was breastfeeding her baby. While Barrash's leave requests were routinely denied, her scheduled date to return to work was changed repeatedly. Eventually Barrash was granted six months of leave, as a result of these delays. When she failed to return to work on her final deadline, Barrash's supervisor began the termination process.

Barrash claimed sex discrimination on the basis that several men in the Social Security Administration had been granted sick leaves of six months or longer, while her requests for maternity leave without pay, so that she could breastfeed, were not granted. She argued this was a violation of the PDA. The U.S. Appeals Court rejected this claim, arguing that the PDA protected pregnancy and related medical conditions only when they were incapacitating. In the words of the opinion: "One can draw no valid comparison between people, male and female, suffering extended incapacity from illness or injury and young mothers wishing to nurse little babies." Moreover, the Court continued, echoing but not directly referencing *Dike*:

> She [Barrash] may have a constitutional right to nurse her baby for six months, or even longer, that would inhibit government interference with

it, but the plaintiff here asserts a right to be let alone while she cares for her baby in the matter she thinks best. Her claim is one of entitlement to maternity leave because she demanded it. A public employer may have some duty to take reasonable steps to accommodate the needs of young mothers and their babies, but the measure of any duty of responsible accommodation is not the same as the measure of the mother's right to care for her child as she pleases.[43]

In one particularly complex case, a husband and wife couple both claimed wrongful dismissal under the Pregnancy Discrimination Act. The wife, Kristen Fortier, claimed she was fired because of her stated intention to breastfeed her child after birth. Her husband, Michael Fortier, claimed he was fired later because he knew his wife intended to sue the company over her dismissal. In a rather convoluted argument, the District Court for Western Pennsylvania ruled that Ms. Fortier could not claim discrimination on the basis of her stated intention to breastfeed while she was still pregnant, because she was not yet a breastfeeding mother. Both claims were dismissed.[44]

Sexual Harassment

Sexual harassment is a particular form of employment discrimination. Four unrelated cases decided between 1995 and 2000 included comments about breastfeeding in sexual harassment lawsuits. These comments were included as evidence of a hostile environment. For instance, comments included a supervisor's statement made in response to an employee's request for a private room to express breast milk. He allegedly responded, "She doesn't need the pump; I'll take care of her."[45] Similar comments include: "It's too bad [she] wasn't breastfeeding anymore because her breasts were so much more prominent before."[46] Only one case did not specifically allude to the breast as a sexual object, a comment allegedly made by a supervisor stating that the breastfeeding employee "smelled like curdled milk."[47] Two of these cases were successful, at least in part, and two were dismissed. In no case did the reasons for the judgment specifically involve the comments about breastfeeding.

BREASTFEEDING AS A CONSTITUTIONAL RIGHT

Incarcerated Mothers

Three federal cases have addressed breastfeeding among incarcerated mothers. The courts have ruled against the incarcerated women. The first case involved Diane Southerland, who was pregnant when she pled guilty to embezzlement and was sentenced. After she gave birth and was scheduled to return to prison,

Southerland filed an injunction, stating that she had a constitutional right to breastfeed and that her son was at risk of developing diabetes and allergies. She asserted that she wanted to keep the infant, Matthew, with her in prison. The Fifth Circuit Court ruled that a woman's right to breastfeed, as articulated in *Dike*, does not extend to incarcerated women, especially when "allowing Southerland to breast-feed would impair legitimate goals of the penal system. The state's interest in deterrence and retribution would be undermined by allowing temporary suspensions for female prisoners who choose to breast-feed or by attempting to house nursing infants."[48]

In an unusual twist, the court actually took into account the infant's interest in this case; typically the infants' interests are ignored in federal cases. The court ruled against infant Matthew's "protected interest" in being breastfed, stating, "plaintiffs presented extensive evidence concerning the desirability of breast-feeding generally and in this instance. However, they did not establish that cessation of breast-feeding posed a really substantial and serious health risk to Matthew." Moreover, the court asserted:

> There was no testimony that Matthew would more likely than not avoid diabetes if he were breast-fed and would more likely than not have diabetes if he were formula-fed, or that breast-feeding was his only meaningful chance to avoid diabetes. Nor was there any testimony that other sources of human milk were not available.[49]

In 1996, the Circuit Court of Appeals for the District of Columbia ruled that the District Court had erred in delaying sentencing because a mother convicted of crack cocaine possession was breastfeeding.[50] Finally, a third court, the District Court of Kentucky, ruled that, while lactating women are not guaranteed a right to express milk with a pump while imprisoned, they must be allowed to breastfeed during visitation, because other incarcerated mothers are permitted to formula feed their babies during visitation. The prison, however, is not obligated to provide storage for expressed breast milk, or allow a prisoner to bring a breast pump into the prison.[51]

In Social Welfare Context

The child's best interest, however, does come into play more obviously in various social welfare cases. While family law and child protection are under the jurisdiction of the states, two women have sued their states' social welfare agencies in federal court after they were forbidden to breastfeed because of risks to their infants. For instance in 1999, Kathleen Tyson, who is HIV-positive, gave birth to a healthy son, Felix. When Tyson indicated that she intended to breast-feed, with her husband's support, the state of Oregon removed Felix from the Tysons' legal custody and ordered that she stop breastfeeding. Tyson's unsuccessful defense depended upon the finding in *Dike* and her claims of parental rights.[52] In another case, a social worker told hospital officials to throw away Catherine Ploski's breast milk and to keep her separated from her newborn infant, because Ploski appeared to be mentally unstable. The concern was that Ploski may have tampered with her breast milk. Ploski sued on behalf of herself and her infant son, stating, among other claims, that her constitutional right to breastfeed under *Dike* was violated. The U.S. District Court of Northern California ruled against Ploski, stating that, under the circumstances, Ploski had not "clearly established [her] constitutional right to ensure her child was receiving her breast."[53]

Disability Claims

Breastfeeding was relevant in two cases where women were denied Social Security Disability benefits. In the first case, decided in 2001, Heather Giguere claimed that she was disabled and unable to work because she suffered from fibromyalgia. She was unable to take various medications because she was breastfeeding her infant. The U.S. District Court of Maine upheld the Social Security Administration's (SSA) decision to deny Giguere's disability claim, in part because her disability was not permanent. Once she ceased breastfeeding, Giguere could resume taking medication to relieve pain caused by fibromyalgia.[54] In a 2002 case, Patricia Walls appealed the SSA's decision not to grant her disability benefits, in part because she was not taking medication to treat her bipolar disorder. The District Court judge for the Eastern District of Pennsylvania ordered that the SSA reconsider Walls' application, in part because courts have allowed disability benefit applicants to refuse treatment "for reasons much less dire" than Walls' determination to breastfeed her infant.[55]

PROBLEMS IN FEDERAL LITIGATION

Women's efforts to use the federal courts to protect their breastfeeding rights have failed in nearly every circumstance. One part of the problem is akin to fitting a square peg into a round hole: Women have sought court protection of their efforts to breastfeed at work by using laws that arguably were not intended to include breastfeeding. Certainly, breastfeeding is not a "medical condition" protected by the PDA, although it is a biological consequence related to pregnancy and childbirth. Arguably, it is not a disability, protected under the ADA, but the fulfillment of the organ's *ability*. Yet, the courts have not recognized how the biological reality of lactation completely dominates one's life by protecting it under any civil rights legislation.[56]

Certainly, these cases also point out the severe limitations of the Family and Medical Leave Act. The period of time that a worker may take unpaid leave from a job is very short—12 weeks. The FMLA by itself is simply inadequate to allow women to breastfeed exclusively for six months as recommended by the AAP. When women encounter complications in their pregnancies that prohibit them from working until delivery, then these women have even shorter periods postpartum to breastfeed, wean, or to make child care arrangements that would enable them to continue to breastfeed. Moreover, the FMLA would have been inadequate to help Michele McNill care for her infant born with a cleft palate. Her child required breastfeeding until he was able to have corrective surgery, which was not until he was over six months old.[57]

The Title VII claims were generally rejected based upon the courts' use of the precedent set in *Gilbert v. General Electric*.[58] In this case, the Supreme Court ruled that General Electric's corporate practices that discriminated against pregnant women were not sex discrimination because the corporation did not differentiate between women and men, but pregnant and nonpregnant employees. The latter category included both women and men. This case led Congress to pass the Pregnancy Discrimination Act. While pregnant women are now a "protected class," breastfeeding mothers are not. The courts in *Martinez v. MSNBC* and *Wallace v. Pyro Mining*, two critical precedents, use the same argument laid out by the Supreme Court in *Gilbert*: that failing to accommodate breastfeeding women is not sex discrimination because not all women breastfeed. Moreover, the courts took pains to differentiate breastfeeding from pregnancy, which is protected under the PDA.[59]

The provisions protecting women's rights to breastfeed on federal property, especially the federal Treasury Appropriations laws, arguably may have assisted Rona Barrash had this provision been in place when her child was born. Even if she could not receive additional leave under FMLA or administrative rules, as a federal employee Barrash could have brought her infant to work to breastfeed. Interestingly, Kelly Gallegos was also a federal employee whose child was born after this language was inserted in the 1999 Treasury Appropriations Act. Yet, she did not ask to bring her child to work so that she could breastfed, and one cannot discern whether Gallegos or her agency were even aware of this provision.[60]

The discussion of Matthew Southerland in *Southerland v. Thigpen* also highlights another potential difficulty for breastfeeding advocates: that science and the judicial system use different standards of evidence. Scientific evidence is based on probabilities: Breastfed infants have lower risk of developing diabetes. However, the Court appears to want evidence that a particular infant, Matthew

Southerland in this case, would not develop diabetes if he were breastfed and would develop diabetes if he were not.[61] Such questions are impossible to answer, and if broadly applied, become an insurmountable obstacle for breastfeeding advocates.

UNDERSTANDING FEDERAL POLICY USING SOCIAL CONSTRUCTION THEORY

According to Anne Schneider and Helen Ingram, the social construction of target populations "has a powerful influence on public officials and shapes the actual design of policy."[62] All public policies have some sort of "target population"—the population that the policy is designed to impact either positively or negatively. However, the way that target populations are treated by policies varies dramatically. Schneider and Ingram divide target populations into four types based upon two variables: whether the target population is positively or negatively constructed and the power the target population holds in the public arena. The benefits they receive and the level of burdens each are asked to bear also vary according to their social construction.[63]

According to Schneider and Ingram, "advantaged" groups are positively constructed, politically powerful groups. They typically include the elderly, veterans, and scientists. These groups receive a large number of benefits and bear few administrative burdens. "Contenders" are negatively constructed, but politically powerful; they include big business and labor unions. Benefits for these groups are present but hidden, and their administrative burdens are light. "Dependents," including mothers and children, are positively constructed but politically weak. These groups receive only symbolic benefits and find that they face a large number of administrative burdens to realize their benefits. The fourth group, "deviants" such as welfare mothers and criminals, receive few benefits, have little control over their lives, and confront numerous social burdens.

Social construction of target populations has been used in previous policy analyses of AIDS policy and the war on drugs.[64] By using breastfeeding as a lens through which to understand the various experiences of breastfeeding mothers, social construction theory is a powerful tool to understand the limited nature of federal breastfeeding rights policy in the United States and helps us envision how federal breastfeeding policy can be improved.[65]

Target Populations

Given that federal breastfeeding policy is a potpourri, there are several target populations that are variously situated, depending upon the particular policy, and whether one is discussing legislation or litigation. However, we discern several patterns among them.

Breastfeeding Mothers as Dependents in Legislation

In federal law, breastfeeding mothers generally fall into the dependent category of target populations: positively constructed but politically weak. The mother–child dyad is protected by laws that provide symbolic protections—a right to breastfeed on federal property, as employees who take unpaid leave from work, as targets of federal campaigns to increase breastfeeding rates, or as participants in the WIC program. These women are targets of a variety of messages on the importance of breastfeeding, which, as Rebecca Kukla noted, often ignore the realities they face that make breastfeeding difficult or impossible. Indeed, lactating women must bear all of the burdens of breastfeeding, whether they are managing the physical demands of breastfeeding, negotiating family leave, or pumping and storing breast milk while at work. Even the Treasury Appropriations' language is largely symbolic, because it has no bearing on women who are not on federal property when their babies get hungry. Even those who work on federal property and wish to breastfeed their babies on site carry the burdens of bringing their children to work and arranging accessible child care between feedings.

Breastfeeding Mothers as Deviants in the Courts

Breastfeeding mothers who appear to deviate from a traditional "good mother" paradigm by being employed outside the home, or being incarcerated, or ill, are treated as deviants by the courts. For instance, employed lactating women are deviants because of their difficulties combining their public lives in the workplace and their private lives as mothers, and their burdens are heavy. As Alicia Martinez's experience indicates, breastfeeding mothers must try to find a private place to nurse or pump and may be expected to post "do not disturb" signs. Other women have endured inappropriate comments from their fellow employees. Michele McNill had perhaps the greatest burden to bear: She had to choose between her job and breastfeeding her baby, whose need to breastfeed was medically indicated. Moreover, the mothers' biological need to breastfeed or to pump was not recognized by employers or the courts. The case of Kimberly Jacobson and her leaking breasts, and Christine Bond's request to bring her infant son on a business trip, illustrate these needs.

Thus, employed breastfeeding mothers find themselves in legal limbo insofar as their biological trait, lactation, is not recognized nor protected by law as are other biological traits, such as race, sex, physical disability, and pregnancy.

Rather, the courts treat breastfeeding as a personal choice and one that employers are not obligated to accommodate, even if the choice has public health consequences, and the employers stand to benefit from lower health care costs. In this respect, breastfeeding falls in the same category as purchasing automobiles with safety features or joining a gym. In so doing, however, the courts have not backed away from the fundamental ruling in *Dike*. They simply change the subject. For example, the issue was not that Kellie Gallegos or Martha Wallace was breastfeeding. The issue was their absences from work.

Incarcerated mothers who sought to breastfeed or express milk in prison are another group of deviants. Generally, their right to or interest in breastfeeding was not recognized by the state. Even Luz Berrios-Berrios, who won the right to breastfeed her infant during visitation, won an incomplete victory, because she was not allowed to pump her breast milk between visits.[66] Lactation is demand driven. Lactating women must nurse or pump regularly and without interruption in order to maintain their supply of breast milk. The infrequent feedings in which Ms. Berrios-Berrios was permitted were unlikely to be sufficient to sustain her milk supply.

Breastfed Children as an Invisible Target Population

By and large, children do not appear to be the target population in the corpus of breastfeeding policies. Their absence is telling and further reinforces the limited support for breastfeeding in public policy. For example, the Treasury Appropriations Act and *Dike* focus on the *mother's* right to breastfeed. They do not focus on whether a *child* has a right to, or interest in being, breastfed. Similarly, public health messages often refer to babies only in the abstract, and occasionally in photographs.

Similarly, the courts rarely appear to consider the infants' perspective in any breastfeeding decision. For example, in the cases involving incarcerated mothers, the courts ruled against the mothers because of the burden it would pose to the *state*, not out of any concern for the rights of children who would be incarcerated unjustly.[67] Similarly, courts usually have dismissed arguments about the health benefits of breastfeeding, even when there was compelling evidence that a particular child needed to breastfeed. Presumably Michele McNill's infant had an interest in being breastfed, given his cleft palate. Yet, the Court ruled that existing legislation does not accommodate disabled children of working parents.

Judges also have not taken into account infants' preferences in their decision making. While infants cannot talk, and they lack adults' decision-making ability, anyone who spends time with infants will attest that they can communicate their preferences, and often do so forcefully and loudly. In two instances, infants did express their preference for breastfeeding and did so by refusing a bottle. In no case did the judges take the infants' perspective or preferences into account. Rather, the judges merely dismissed these phenomena as inadequate parenting.[68] Martha Wallace was dismissed from her position, and Janice Dike was forced to take a leave of absence from her teaching position.

Employers and the State as Contenders

In this analysis, two groups stand out as contenders—negatively constructed but powerful target populations—employers and the state. According to Schneider and Ingram, contenders must comply with few burdens in policy, and their benefits are hidden. Such is certainly true with breastfeeding policy.

To date, federal policy makers have sought to increase breastfeeding rates only through public health campaigns. The federal government has not asked employers to share the burden of increasing breastfeeding rates by providing wage replacement or unemployment benefits for mothers taking leave under the FMLA, providing longer and/or paid maternity leaves, or accommodating breastfeeding or milk expression in the workplace. Moreover, the state has not assumed any burdens by extending TANF time limits or providing other public assistance.

The state has other roles that are negatively constructed and place it in the contender category: its powers to incarcerate criminals. In these cases, the state's power to deprive people of rights without considering the potential benefits of breastfeeding demonstrates the tenuous nature of breastfeeding rights and further illustrates mothers' and children's positions as policy dependents or deviants. In fact, the language used by the courts is illustrative. In the rulings with respect to two incarcerated mothers, the court specifically discussed the "burdens" placed upon the state if it were asked to accommodate breastfeeding or milk expression.[69] Similarly, the state has the power to take children from their parents if they see evidence of abuse or neglect. In this respect, the state has the very power to determine when breast milk is healthy and life-giving and when it is dangerous.

Moreover, the state has the power to legally define breastfeeding as a consequence of pregnancy. Arguably, Congress chose to place breastfeeding outside the scope of the Pregnancy Discrimination Act (PDA) in 1978 by using the phrase "medical condition." As noted previously, arguably breastfeeding is *not* a medical condition, but a biological one. Moreover, various federal courts have interpreted the PDA to exclude breastfeeding, further demonstrating the state's role in defining lactation. Congress has the power to change this legal definition, even though it has not done so by 2007.

Fathers Are Advantaged

If there is one target population that is advantaged in federal breastfeeding policy, it may be the fathers. Advantaged populations are positively constructed and politically powerful. They receive benefits with few administrative burdens. Fathers are generally missing in this discussion of federal breastfeeding policy. Where they are found is as a target population in the WIC program. There appears to be some implicit acknowledgement that the (male) sexual partners of the mothers—rightly or wrongly—play a role in their decisions to breastfeed. Some men may discourage their female partners from breastfeeding because of a perception that they "own" or "claim" women's breasts as their sexual property.[70] In response to these dynamics, WIC developed a series of posters and brochures aimed at African American men, gently persuading them to support their part-ners' decisions to breastfeed.

POSSIBLE CHANGES TO FEDERAL POLICY

While social construction analysis does reduce women to a single characteristic, lactation, it does provide some insight into the nature of policy. Specifically, it highlights that federal breastfeeding policy is heavy on symbolic expressions of sup-port, but weak in terms of actual support for women wishing to breastfeed. Telling women to breastfeed is similar to the "miracle milk" stories found in the media (Chapter 3), and like miracle milk stories, there is little or no discussion of the bio-logical realities that come along with lactation. In this respect, federal policy reflects the ambivalence to breastfeeding found in public opinion and media coverage.

What would effective breastfeeding rights policy look like? Certainly, the law needs to recognize that lactation is a logical, biological consequence of childbirth, and federal policy needs to demonstrate that breastfeeding is encouraged and sup-ported. Because breastfeeding is the optimal choice for most women and for most children, especially during the first year of life, public officials and employers need to recognize their common interests in enabling breastfeeding, and public policy needs to recognize the child's interest in being breastfed. However, the health and psychological benefits of breastfeeding do not accrue at the same rate over time. For both mothers and infants, the benefits of breastfeeding are greatest in the first few months postpartum and considerable for the first year. Therefore, optimal breastfeeding policy would recognize and protect breastfeeding for the first year and then begin to balance concerns of others, such as employers and the state, against those of the mother and child.

Thus, as a first step, and one that all breastfeeding advocates would support, Maloney's language in the Transportation Appropriations laws should be passed in a form that does not require reenactment and recodification each year. Another step would be to restructure the WIC program to include rebates for other food items besides infant formula. While the GAO acknowledges that other rebates would be unlikely to produce as much revenue as the infant formula rebates,[71] the program's financial structure would be less closely tied to formula use.

However, any other changes to federal policy would need to deal with mothers who are somehow "deviant," such as being employed outside the home. Consequently, breastfeeding and expressing breast milk should be protected in the same way as "other medical conditions" related to pregnancy are currently. Representative Carolyn Maloney (D-NY) introduced the Breastfeeding Promotion Act of 2007 in the 110th Congress (2007–2008). This legislation would amend the Civil Rights Act of 1964 to stipulate that lactation is a protected condition related to childbirth and further defines lactation as including feeding a child at the breast, or expression of milk. This legislation also includes standards for the manufacture and production of breast pumps, defines breastfeeding services and equipment as covered medical services, and includes tax incentives to employers that provide breast pumps to their employees or provide a private location for the use of their lactating employees to breastfeed or express milk.[72] Legislation like this would negate the courts' dependence upon the *Gilbert* precedent, because breastfeeding mothers would be a protected class just as pregnant women are today.

However, amending the PDA alone is not sufficient to help mothers negotiate their private lives and public roles in the workplace. If the federal government is serious about meeting its breastfeeding goals for *Healthy People 2010*, then the Family and Medical Leave Act needs to be expanded. Another bill introduced by Representative Carolyn Maloney in the 110th Congress (2007–2008) titled the "Family and Medical Leave Expansion Act" is a prototype. It would expand the FMLA to include employers with at least 25 employees, directs the federal government to provide at least six weeks of paid leave to federal employees upon the birth or adoption of a child, and expands unemployment eligibility to include workers taking leave under the FMLA.[73]

Similarly, in the 109th Congress (2005–2006), Senator Tom Harkin (D-IA) introduced S. 1074, the "Healthy Lifestyles and Prevention Act America," or the HeLP America Act. Among its provisions, this proposal would have expanded the FMLA to require employers to provide break times for lactating women so they could breastfeed or pump milk and provide a facility dedicated to this purpose, unless providing this space posed "an undue hardship" on the employer.[74]

While the Maloney and Harkin proposals would shift some of the burdens of breastfeeding from the women to the state and the employer, they do not offer complete protection to breastfeeding women. While the expansion of the FMLA would cover millions of women who currently are not covered by the legislation, women who work for companies with fewer than 25 employees would still not be eligible. Second, the guarantee of some paid leave after the birth of a child is laudable, but the six weeks included in Maloney's bill falls short of the AAP recommendation for six months of exclusive breastfeeding and a minimum of 12 months. Moreover, Maloney's bill would not increase the total number of weeks available for family leave, and there is no discussion of extending the time limits under TANF to enable new mothers to breastfeed their babies.

Another possibility, and one that should shift even more burdens to employers, is to amend the Americans with Disabilities Act to include breastfeeding as a protected disability. This proposed expansion is paradoxical; it would define a normally, fully functioning organ as somehow *impaired*. Yet, such an amendment would recognize the potentially long-term duration of breastfeeding (6 months, 12 months, or longer) advocated by the AAP and the Public Health Service. Moreover, such an amendment would recognize, and expect, employers to accommodate the physiological demands of lactation by providing "reasonable accommodations." Such accommodations would be, presumably, adequate break time, an appropriate place to nurse or express milk, and adequate storage for expressed milk.

Without doubt, the government will continue its efforts to encourage women to breastfeed. There are few arguments against breastfeeding public awareness campaigns, insofar as they are low cost, and they can be effective.[75] Moreover, they are classic tools used in the field of public health and can lead to changes in behaviors. Harkin's HeLP America Act included a provision to place warning labels on cans of formula that are similar to the warning labels on cigarettes or alcoholic beverages. Yet, Harkin's proposal and the other breastfeeding awareness campaigns fail to understand the biological limits of choice in the matter of breastfeeding. Unlike other "risks" one might take—such as failing to secure a child in a car seat, or smoking cigarettes—a mother cannot simply decide to start breastfeeding after several months of reading warning labels on cans of formula. Breastfeeding is demand-driven. If she does not establish breastfeeding in the early postpartum period, a mother will not have a supply of breast milk in later months. Consequently, such efforts are unlikely to increase breastfeeding rates.

A final piece of legislation introduced into the 109th Congress by Senator Richard Durbin (D-IL) was a resolution to recognize the value of breastfeeding and called for state legislation to remove barriers faced by breastfeeding women. While encased in supportive language, this resolution did not require the federal government to take any action to remove these barriers, or to ease the burdens of breastfeeding faced by women.

Barriers to Federal Policy Changes

One needs to keep in mind that introducing legislation does not imply that policy changes are simple to enact. The legislative process is convoluted, and most bills fail to pass in any given Congress. Moreover, even if enacted, these policy changes would not necessarily lead to a dramatic increase in breastfeeding rates.

Breastfeeding rights advocates lack an effective public face. Indeed, many of the women who have attempted to expand breastfeeding rights through the courts are somehow flawed: They did not show up for work; they performed poorly on the job; or they were involved in some conflict with their co-workers. Still others are convicted felons, or their decision to breastfeed may endanger their children. None is a famous or a completely sympathetic champion for the cause.

Any legislation that might help mothers manage the competing demands of the private sphere of breastfeeding and the public sphere of work will require a coalition between breastfeeding advocates who espouse an "intensive mothering model" that frowns upon working mothers and feminists who have traditionally eschewed breastfeeding as a feminist issue because of their preference toward shared parenting. This coalition may be difficult to create and sustain over the long term and may be one reason that federal policy has to date focused on symbolic protections.

Finally, breastfeeding advocates and feminists alike must accept the possibility that, even with enhanced employment protections and more information about the benefits of breastfeeding, women may decide not to breastfeed. Perhaps the most difficult barrier to success of public health campaigns is that infant formula is an acceptable choice, if not a preferable choice, for many women. While there are documented health benefits to using breast milk, millions of Americans have been fed formula and led healthy lives and enjoyed successful careers.

5

Uneven and Competing Rights: Breastfeeding Rights and State Policy

Given that the federal government has done little to protect rights and interests of breastfeeding women and their children at the federal level, states have been free to innovate. States have developed breastfeeding rights policies through laws and judicial rulings. Compared to federal policy, state policies are more sweeping in scope, including employment regulations, insurance provisions, family law, child abuse protection, and jury duty, to name a few issue areas. This range of policy areas reflects states' traditional jurisdictions in the American federal system. However, unlike federal policy, which is binding over the entire country, state laws and judicial rulings are binding only upon the state in which they are enacted or decided.

Taken together, this panoply of state laws and policies embodies two different, but not conflicting, realities. First, nursing mothers and their infants have different legal protections depending upon the state in which they reside and work. This situation will remain unchanged as long as there are few federal policies in place to protect breastfeeding rights.[1] Second, diverse laws and court cases demonstrate how the question of breastfeeding rights is an area where several rights-bearing entities collide—mothers, fathers, infants, and employers. Moreover, the rights of breastfeeding mothers and their infants also encounter the powers of the state and of employers.

This chapter will describe and analyze the various state laws designed to protect and encourage breastfeeding and state court decisions in which breastfeeding is a central issue. One of us was actively involved in the South Carolina Breastfeeding Action Committee (SCBAC) in 2006, which successfully lobbied the South Carolina state legislature to pass a bill to allow women to breastfeed in public. This experience also informs our analysis and provides insights. As in our analysis of federal policy, we use social construction theory to tease out the relative power of each target population of state policies, and we use these insights to determine our idea of optimal state breastfeeding policy.

UNEVEN RIGHTS: STATE BREASTFEEDING LAWS

We identified the relevant state laws from lists compiled by La Leche League International (LLLI), the National Conference of State Legislatures (NCSL), and our own searches of state legislative code. Table 5.1 is a summary of the provisions passed by the 50 state legislatures as of December 2006. Because our inventory includes laws that do not explicitly mention breastfeeding, especially in terms of jury service, that also apply to breastfeeding mothers, our inventory differs from those compiled by these other organizations. Also, unlike material compiled by the LLLI or the NCSL, Table 5.1 includes details that describe the political environment of the state when breastfeeding laws were passed.

As of December 2006, 46 states had enacted some sort of breastfeeding rights legislation. The exceptions were Arkansas, Massachusetts, Pennsylvania, and West Virginia. The first state to recognize the importance of breastfeeding legislatively was Michigan, which in 1970 passed a law requiring judges to consider whether a child is nursing when making child custody decisions in divorce cases.[2] The vast majority of states, however, passed their legislation since the 1990s. The current trend began in 1993 when Florida passed legislation guaranteeing a woman's right to breastfeed in public and exempting breastfeeding from various definitions of criminal sexual conduct. Florida law also allows pregnant women and parents who are not employed full time and have custody of a child who is less than six years old to be excused from jury duty.[3] The year 1999 was the busiest for breastfeeding advocates because nine states passed legislation in that year; 2006 also saw a lot of activity, with five states enacting breastfeeding rights laws.

A flurry of legislative activity does not imply that these laws have extensive provisions. Over half of the states (17 of 46) that have enacted breastfeeding rights laws have only one or two provisions in their codes.

Table 5.1
State Laws and Regulations Related to Breastfeeding, December 2006

State	Year Enacted	Public BF	Indecency Exemption	Fines for Violations	Workplace	Jury Duty	Awareness Campaign	Child Care	Divorce and Visitation	Other	Women's Caucus	% Women	Party Control
AL	2006	✓										10.0	D
AK	1998	✓	✓			✓					✓	13.3	R
AZ	2006	✓	✓									27.8	R
AR						✓					✓	16.3	D
CA	1995	✓		✓	✓	✓	✓				✓	20.8	D
	1996									Milk distribution		20.0	R/D
	1997											22.5	D
	1999											25.8	D
	2000											25.8	D
	2001											28.3	D
CO	2004	✓										33.0	D
CT	1997	✓		✓								28.9	D
	2001				✓							28.8	R
DE	1997	✓										25.8	R/D
FL	1993	✓	✓									17.5	D/even
	1994						✓					18.1	even/D

(Continued)

Table 5.1 (*Continued*)

State	Year Enacted	Public BF	Indecency Exemption	Fines for Violations	Workplace	Jury Duty	Awareness Campaign	Child Care	Divorce and Visitation	Other	Women's Caucus	% Women	Party Control
GA	1999	✓			✓							18.6	D
	2002											20.8	D/R
HI	1999	✓		✓	✓					Civil rights study	✓	22.6	D
ID	1996					✓						27.6	R
IL	1995	✓	✓		✓	✓	✓					23.2	R
	1997											26.0	R/D
	2001											26.6	R/D
	2004											28.2	R/D
	2005											27.7	D
IN	2002	✓					✓					18.0	D
	2004											18.0	D/R
IA	1994	✓				✓						20.7	R
	2002											15.3	R/D
KS	2005	✓				✓						32.7	R
KY	2006	✓	✓									11.6	R
LA	2001	✓						✓		Insurance coverage	✓	16	D
	2002											16	D
ME	1999	✓										28	D
	2001								✓			30.1	D

State	Year	Sales tax exemption	Car seat exemption	Mercury alert	Incarcerated mothers	%	Party
MD	2003	✓				29.3	D
						33.0	D
MA		✓				24.5	D
MI	1970		✓			4.7	D/R
	1981					10.8	D
	1994					20.9	D
MN	1998					18.4	D
	2000					30.8	D
MS	2006					13.8	R
MO	1999					28.7	D
MT	1999					24.7	R
NE	2004					18.4	NP
NV	1995					34.9	D/R
NH	1999					31.8	D
NJ	1997			✓		15	D
NM	1999	✓				27.7	D
NY	1994					18.5	D/R
NC	1993					18.2	D/R
ND	2005					16.3	R
OH	2005					19.7	R

(Continued)

Table 5.1 (*Continued*)

State	Year Enacted	Public BF	Indecency Exemption	Fines for Violations	Workplace	Jury Duty	Awareness Campaign	Child Care	Divorce and Visitation	Other	Women's Caucus	% Women	Party Control
OK	2004	✓	✓		✓	✓				Rates reports		11.4	D
	2006											14.8	D
OR	1999	✓				✓						30.0	R
PA												14.6	R
RI	1998		✓		✓					Mercury alert	✓	26.0	D
	2001											22.7	D
	2003											19.5	D
SC	2006	✓	✓			✓						8.8	R
SD	2002		✓									15.2	R
TE	1999	✓	✓		✓	✓						16.7	D
	2006											17.4	R
TX	1995	✓			✓	✓			✓	Milk distribution post-partum care		22.2	D
	2001											22.9	D
	2003											24.8	R
UT	1995	✓	✓									16.3	R
VT	2002	✓					✓					27.8	R/D

					BF is medical condition related to childbirth		
VA	1994	✓	✓			11.4	D
	2002					15.0	R
	2005					15.0	R
WA	2001		✓			38.8	R
WV						15.7	D
WI	1995			✓		24.2	R
WY	2003				Recognizes importance ✓	17.8	R

Sources: National Conference of State Legislatures, La Leche League International, Center for the American Woman in Politics, individual state codes, telephone interviews, and various state legislative Web sites.

Description of Laws

As detailed in Table 5.1, state breastfeeding laws vary considerably. Yet, they fall into the following general categories.

Right to Breastfeed in Public

Almost all states—37 out of 46 (or 80% of those states with breastfeeding laws)—guarantee an explicit right for women to breastfeed in any public location. Some states expand this right even further. Alabama, for instance, states that women have a right to breastfeed in any "public and private location"; Colorado's language simply states a woman may breastfeed "any place she has a right to be."[4] There are some exceptions to these expansive definitions. California law stipulates that a woman's right to breastfeed does not include "the private home or residence of another." In Illinois, the law stipulates that women breastfeeding in a "place of worship" must follow "appropriate norms" while inside this place of worship. The Georgia legislation passed in 1999 required that breastfeeding mothers act in a "discreet way"; this provision was eliminated in 2002. Missouri's law, which was passed in 1999 but has not been amended, also requires that women be discreet when nursing. Virginia's law applies only to land owned or leased by the state. By implication then, women's right to breastfeed in Virginia does not apply to private property, or to public property owned by local governments.[5]

Indecency Exemptions

Another common provision in state breastfeeding laws is to exempt breastfeeding from definitions of indecency, obscenity, sexual conduct, and/or public nudity in state codes. Eighteen states (39% of those with breastfeeding rights laws) include this provision in the state code. These laws vary in detail. The legislation passed in Florida and Kentucky are the most sweeping. Florida stipulates in its obscenity codes that breastfeeding is exempted from its definition of child sexual abuse and obscenity. Kentucky stipulates that breastfeeding is exempted from criminal definitions of lewd touching, obscenity, indecent exposure, and sexual conduct. Other states, such as Michigan, simply exclude breastfeeding from the definition of public nudity.[6]

Employment Rights Issues

Presumably, any state laws that guarantee a woman's right to breastfeed in any public or private place, or any public or private place where she is otherwise authorized to be, would include the workplace. However, in practice, this right may be difficult or impractical to enforce. Imagine a woman attempting to nurse or express milk while serving customers at a fast food restaurant, or while working on an automobile assembly line. Consequently, 13 states (28% of those with breastfeeding rights legislation) recognize that for such rights to be meaningful, lactating women employed outside the home need additional protections. Eight states stipulate that employers must provide break time, usually unpaid break time, for their employees to breastfeed or express milk.[7] Seven states require employers to provide a place for women to nurse or pump milk. Three of these states—Illinois, Minnesota, and Tennessee—stipulate that the space cannot be a toilet stall. California calls for "adequate facilities"; Rhode Island stipulates "a safe private place."[8] Five states simply "encourage" employers to accommodate lactating employees' need to express milk.[9] If employers adopt these practices in Texas or Washington, they may earn a "mother friendly" or "infant friendly" designation that they may advertise to potential employees.[10]

Two states have related provisions that address child care facilities, in particular. Louisiana prohibits any child care facility from discriminating against children who are breastfed. Mississippi's child care regulations require that licensed child care facilities accommodate mothers by providing a private place to nurse with an outlet, chair, and running water; provide a refrigerator to store breast milk; train staff on the proper handling of human milk; and provide breastfeeding information on site.[11]

Jury Duty Exemptions

Ten states explicitly exempt breastfeeding women from jury duty upon request. Most of these laws carry no stipulations. California's law, however, states that a breastfeeding mother may be excused for up to one year, unless she submits a written request for an extension.[12] However, six additional states have some sort of jury duty exemption for individuals who have primary responsibility to care for young children. Presumably these provisions would extend to breastfeeding mothers. They include Alaska's clause to exempt a juror if that individual's service would jeopardize "the health or proper care of the person's family."[13] New Jersey allows a prospective juror to be excused if the individual has an obligation to care for a minor child.[14] South Carolina allows women with custody and "duty of care" of children under the age of seven to be excused from jury service if she signs an affidavit to that effect.[15] Tennessee allows individuals caring for family members, including children, to be excused if jury service poses an "undue hardship,"[16] and Texas excuses persons responsible for caring for children under age 18.[17]

Divorce, Child Custody, and Visitation

Three states allow breastfeeding to be considered in child custody and visitation arrangements after a divorce. Michigan's Child Custody Act of 1970 provides that the court may consider whether a child up to one year old is nursing when making decisions with respect to child custody and visitation.[18] Maine's law stipulates that the court's determination of the "best interests of the child" in child custody and visitation orders should include whether a child under the age of one is breastfed, and more generally, "the physical and psychological well being of the child."[19] Finally, Utah's child visitation guidelines lay out specific visitation schedules for children under age five that gradually increase as the child ages. However, the law also stipulates that the court may deviate from these recommendations if there is "a lack of reasonable alternatives to the needs of a nursing child."[20]

Breastfeeding and Health Provisions

Six states have instituted breastfeeding awareness campaigns of various types, and in 2003, Wyoming passed a resolution recognizing the benefits of breastfeeding. Texas and California have regulations about the sale and distribution of human milk. Two states, Rhode Island and New Jersey, mandate that breastfeeding mothers be warned about possible mercury contamination of fish caught in the state's lakes or rivers.[21]

Miscellaneous Provisions. In addition, Maryland exempts breast pumps from state sales tax; Louisiana has ordered a study of the implications of insurance coverage of breastfeeding education. Virginia defines breastfeeding as a "medical condition" related to childbirth. New York allows incarcerated breastfeeding women to care for their infants in prison under certain circumstances, and Michigan allows nursing infants to ride in automobiles unrestrained.[22]

Uneven Rights

Given that nearly all states had passed breastfeeding rights legislation by 2006, this lengthy and varied list of state legislation appears to provide rather extensive protections of breastfeeding mothers. Yet, only four states provide any specific legal remedies for women whose breastfeeding rights are violated. Connecticut provides fines of $25–$100 and up to 30 days in jail for those who interfere with a woman's right to breastfeed in public. Hawaii provides for fines of up to $100, plus court costs and attorney's fees in cases where women's right to breastfeed in public are violated, and New Jersey provides graduated fines of $25–$200 for the same. Employers who do not comply with California's law to accommodate breastfeeding in the workplace may be subject to a $100 fine. Women in New York may claim damages if they are harassed for breastfeeding as a violation of their civil rights.[23]

Consequently, legal scholars argue that state breastfeeding policies fall short of providing meaningful protections to nursing mothers. One scholar states that breastfeeding is a "right that is no right."[24] Others claim that, in general, these laws specify rights but do not provide remedies for the women when their rights might be violated.[25]

Certainly, breastfeeding women have different rights depending upon the state in which they reside or work. The most frequently articulated right is to breastfeed in public, although the language "in public" could possibly be interpreted as excluding private homes, clubs, and worship spaces. Moreover, 17 states that guarantee a right to breastfeed in public do not exempt breastfeeding from public nudity, sexual misconduct, or indecency laws. Women breastfeeding in public in these states may still find themselves running afoul of such laws. Durmeriss Cruver-Smith sees this as a manifestation of the breast as a sexual object, not as a functional organ, in Western culture. She comments:

> Criminalizing the mere exposure of women's breasts, yet allowing men to expose theirs, sends the wrong message to both women and men as to how they should feel about women's bodies. Women end up believing that their bodies are to remain covered and hidden in public, even for breast-feeding.[26]

Cruver-Smith argues that the criminalization of women's breasts is the primary way that breastfeeding mothers have been harassed for breastfeeding in public. Moreover, some states have failed to enact breastfeeding laws because the proposed legislation offered women remedies if their right to breastfeed was violated.[27]

The same concern explains the reason that some breastfeeding rights legislation is weakened with language stipulating that a woman be "discreet" when nursing. The push to require discretion arose in the legislative debate surrounding legislation in South Carolina on two occasions. When the legislation was first introduced in 1997, it was referred back to committee because it did not include language requiring women to be discreet. The legislation then died in committee. The bill was not reintroduced until 2006, and the idea that women should be discreet became an issue again, but was kept out of the legislation.[28] A similar scenario played out in Kansas. The bill, passed in 2006, was introduced without the word "discreet." The word "discreet" was added as an amendment in the Kansas House of Representatives. The Kansas Senate voted on a "clean" bill, but succeeded only when it scheduled the floor vote when the bill's primary opponent was absent and unable to introduce an amendment mandating that women be "discreet."[29]

However, the uneven nature of these laws does not end with the conflict between guaranteeing rights but offering no remedy, or encouraging women to breastfeed while continuing to criminalize exposure of the breast. The laws in most states do not help women balance the competing demands of work and breastfeeding. In fact, these laws appear to encourage breastfeeding "in one place but not the other."[30] Only women who work in the 13 states that provide some sort of employment provisions have any legal protection as they try to balance the demands of work and lactation. However, even these protections are fairly limited, usually only guaranteeing unpaid break time to nurse or express milk. Yet, these women enjoy protections of their right to breastfeed that women in other states do not.

From our perspective, even the presumably supportive language exempting breastfeeding women from jury duty is a mixed blessing. Surely the long hours that one might be in court, or waiting for sessions to begin or resume, could be problematic for women who need to pump or nurse regularly. Similarly, court buildings may be ill-equipped to provide breastfeeding jurors child care or a private place to nurse or express milk. Yet, at the same time, such provisions seem to be a throwback to a time—not so long ago—when women were excluded from jury service altogether. Women fought to exercise this particular right of citizenship, and it should not be readily sacrificed.

As weak as breastfeeding rights legislation might be, such laws do provide women some protection. The 2005 Ohio law was the result of a federal court decision against a group of breastfeeding mothers.[31] In 2004, a U.S. Appeals Court ruled against three mother–infant pairs who sued Wal-Mart stores for violating Ohio's sex and age discrimination laws when these women were not permitted to breastfeed in Wal-Mart stores. On separate occasions and at different Wal-Mart stores, these women were told by Wal-Mart employees to either stop breastfeeding in the store, or to continue nursing in the restroom. In *Derungs v. Wal-Mart Stores, Inc.*, the U.S. Appeals Court upheld a lower court ruling that concluded that Ohio's civil rights legislation prohibiting sex discrimination in public accommodations did not include breastfeeding in public.[32]

Explaining Uneven Rights

What explains these differences between states? Why does California have such sweeping breastfeeding legislation on the books, while Massachusetts has none, for instance? Variations in state policy are not unique to breastfeeding policy. In fact, in most policy areas not under the jurisdiction of the federal government, states have very different policies in place. Reproductive rights policy is no different; think of the various state laws with respect to waiting periods for abortion, parental consent, or crossing state lines with a minor for the purpose of securing an abortion.[33] Scholars of state-level politics in the United States have several possible explanations for this phenomenon, including the influence of women in the state legislature, political culture, and competitiveness of the two major political parties in each state.[34] We examine these hypotheses in the context of breastfeeding rights legislation. Because almost all states have passed breastfeeding rights legislation, we sought to explain *when* states first passed these laws and *how many provisions* each state incorporated into its code. We also looked for any association between these variables and breastfeeding rates.[35]

Women in the State Legislature

A growing body of scholarship finds that female elected officials have an impact on public policy. Numerous scholars of women state legislators have found that women are interested in pursuing a different set of issues than their male counterparts. While previous measures of "women's issues" have not usually included breastfeeding legislation, it is a logical extension of women's traditional interests in reproductive rights and children's welfare. Moreover, as more women join a legislature, the greater the chance that such legislation will be passed, especially if there is also a women's caucus within the legislature.[36] We analyzed the year that the first breastfeeding bill was passed, and the number of provisions in the state's legislation, by the percentage of women in the state legislature, by whether a woman's caucus existed, and whether a woman was the principal sponsor of the bill. We expected all of these variables to lead to earlier passage of breastfeeding rights legislation and laws with more numerous provisions.

Indeed, women were the primary sponsors of breastfeeding rights legislation in half the states—23 of the 46 states with breastfeeding rights laws. Given that women constituted between 20–22 percent of all state legislators in the country from 1990–2006, this finding is an important one.[37] However, the year that the legislation was passed and the number of provisions in state law are not associated with the presence of a women's caucus, or the percentage of women in the state legislature.

This discovery demonstrates that women legislators take a leadership role in promoting breastfeeding rights legislation, even if they are a small minority of members, or do not have the support of an organized women's caucus. This finding reinforces previous observations that women elected officials matter. They bring issues to the agenda, especially issues of particular relevance to women and children that would otherwise be ignored. Moreover, as Jocelyn Elise Crowley found, having large percentages of women in office is not necessary to meaningful policy change. Rather, even token women can be very influential.[38]

Political Culture[39]

Daniel J. Elazar, in his landmark study of American state politics, found three dominant political cultures in the United States: Individualistic, moralistic and traditionalistic. The individualistic political culture focuses on individual rights. The government is utilitarian, present to provide services demanded by the citizenry, but the government is not concerned with moral issues or with creating a good society. With the focus on individual achievement and gain, politics becomes another means for individuals to achieve, whether they seek power or material gain. Moralistic political culture is based on the notion that government is a tool for the common good, to create a good society. Government is a means to assist those who need help and to better the community. Traditionalistic political cultures are elitist; social and family ties, rather than merit, are important for advancement. Government exists to maintain current power relationships, thus the bureaucracy plays a rather conservative role.

While elements of all three political cultures are found throughout the United States, there is some significant regional variation. The individualistic political culture dominates in the middle-Atlantic states, those states immediately along the Mason-Dixon line, and the interior West. States such as Montana, Wyoming, and Alaska typify the individualistic political culture. The moralistic political culture dominates in New England and the upper Midwest and influences states along the Pacific coast and Hawaii and Utah. The traditionalistic political culture dominates in the states of the Southeast, and influences neighboring areas, including Oklahoma, Texas, Tennessee, Florida, and New Mexico. Many states fall into two categories because their population is dominated by two of these three political cultures.[40]

While political culture is an important means to explain variations in state policy in terms of education funding, economic policy, and even family policy,[41] it does not predict a great deal in terms of breastfeeding rights legislation. We expected that moralistic political cultures would be more likely to pass breastfeeding rights legislation, given their interest in a "good society," and traditionalistic political cultures to pass less legislation, given their concern for maintaining the status quo. Yet, political culture failed to predict when a state would pass breastfeeding rights legislation. Among the states whose political culture includes moralistic influences are North Dakota and Massachusetts, two states that had not passed breastfeeding rights legislation by December 2006. The 19 states most influenced by individualistic political culture enacted breastfeeding rights legislation slightly later (in 1999, on average) than did those with moralistic or traditionalistic political cultures (in 1998, on average). However, this difference is not large, and the relationship only approaches statistical significance.[42] Interestingly, Florida, which has an individualistic/traditionalistic political culture, was the first state to enact breastfeeding rights legislation since 1990.

Political Variables and Breastfeeding Rates

Finally, we analyzed the breastfeeding legislation against two political variables—Democratic control of the state legislature[43] and the Democratic share of the two-party vote in the 2000 presidential election—and the state's breastfeeding rates, as reported by the Centers for Disease Control and Prevention. In terms of the political variables, we found an association between Democratic control of the state legislature and when the state's first breastfeeding rights bill was passed. States under Democratic control enacted their first breastfeeding rights bills slightly later (1999 on average) than those with a Republican-controlled or shared-control of the state legislature (1998 on average); however, this difference is not large.[44] Moreover, partisan control of the legislature does not predict how many provisions are in state law.

In addition, the Democratic share of the two-party vote, which indicates party competitiveness in each state, was not related to when breastfeeding rights legislation was first passed, or how many provisions the law includes. Interestingly, states' breastfeeding rates also were not associated with when a state enacted breastfeeding rights legislation, or how many provisions are in state code.

Explaining State Breastfeeding Legislation

What do we make of these disparate findings? Political culture, citizens' political party preferences, and even breastfeeding rates have little or no impact. Instead, we find ourselves turning to the importance of women and their willingness to take up legislation of consequence to other women. Certainly, men are supportive of breastfeeding rights, or such legislation would not be passed. Yet, women seem to be key legislative advocates for such laws.

However, ambivalence to breastfeeding is also evident here. It took a long time for this issue to reach the policy agenda. Many landmark women's rights laws were passed decades before breastfeeding rights laws were enacted in any large measure. We do not exactly know the reason for this phenomenon, but we can speculate. Women elected to state legislatures are probably comfortable operating outside traditional gender roles, and they are more likely to be Democrats than Republicans.[45] One reason that breastfeeding took so long to come onto the agenda may be due to its historical link to more traditional forms of mothering, making Democratic, liberal, feminist women less likely to focus on the issue. Moreover, conservative men and women, who are more likely to be comfortable with the traditional forms of parenting espoused by many breastfeeding advocates, may have shied away from promoting breastfeeding rights because of the breast's position as a sexual object. Notably, the primary advocates for adding the word "discreet" to the Kansas legislation were conservative women.[46]

COMPETING RIGHTS AND INTERESTS: STATE COURT CASES

As of this writing, dozens of state appeals courts have ruled on cases where breastfeeding is an issue. These cases cover a wide range of subjects, but most fall into the following categories: family law, including divorce, child custody and visitation; child abuse or neglect; employment issues; medical malpractice; incarcerated mothers; and harassment or trauma.

Description of Cases

Family Law

Breastfeeding was an issue in approximately 20 cases involving divorce, child custody, child support, or visitation. Notably, the majority of these cases (15) ruled against the breastfeeding mother. In every case that dealt with extended breastfeeding (breastfeeding more than one year), the courts have ruled against the mother. Generally, the courts have ruled that the breastfed child's best interest was served by having a relationship with the child's father, which was also in the father's best interest. These rulings are consistent with the precedents in the cases of "Baby Jessica" and "Baby Richard," both of which occurred in the early 1990s. These children were put up for adoption by their birth mothers who did not inform the children's biological fathers of the children's existence. The biological fathers asserted their parental rights after the children had been living with their adoptive families for years. In both cases, the state courts involved ruled on behalf of the biological fathers, despite the risk of emotional distress on the part of the children, putting the fathers' rights above the children's interests.[47] While the breastfeeding visitation and custody disputes are less extreme than these two adoption cases, the courts did tend to defer to fathers' parental rights over arguments of the children's best interests. The following summary of a 1996 Pennsylvania trial court decision is typical of the sentiments expressed:

> The courts said it found no evidence to support the mother's position that the best interests of the child would be served by allowing [mother] unlimited control of visitation by [father] to indulge her belief in the need for breast-feeding up to the child's age of two.[48] (brackets in original)

The cases that ruled in favor of the breastfeeding mother included one Ohio case in which the mother's child support obligations were suspended while she took leave from work to breastfeed her newborn.[49] In a 1981 Colorado case, trial court judges awarded custody of an infant to a breastfeeding mother, apparently out of respect for the breastfeeding relationship. The father appealed, charging that such a consideration constituted sex bias on the part of the judge. In this case, the appellate court ruled against the father.[50] In three other appellate court cases, trial court decisions that failed to take into consideration breastfeeding, or used breastfeeding as a reason to rule against the mother, were overturned or remanded. These last three cases were all cited in an article by a family law specialist, who argued that fathers must fight to "win the weaning war" in child custody and visitation cases. [51]

The opposite perspective is argued by Kristen Hofheimer, who concludes that family law judges tend to rule against breastfeeding mothers and children because the judges fall into a "generation gap."[52] The judges typically are unaware of the health and psychological benefits of breastfeeding for children and make decisions that are consistent with Blum's concept of the "disembodied mother." As Hofheimer describes one visitation schedule:

> The . . . court viewed lactating breasts as faucets, implying that the mother can simply pump and store milk indefinitely so that the child has a ready supply of breast milk for as long as she is away from the mother. Not only is this biologically unsound, it also erroneously assumes that only the product and not the process of breastfeeding benefits the child.[53]

In these decisions, the court usually ignored the biological demands of breastfeeding, other than to mention that the mother can nurse when the child is with her. However, this trend may be changing since Hofheimer wrote her analysis in 1998. In a 2004 Delaware case, the court recommended that the mother express her breast milk so that the father could feed it to the child when he had overnight visits.[54] A more complex case, *Stelluto v. Stelluto,* was decided in Louisiana in 2005. The biological and nurturing functions of breastfeeding played a central role in the state Supreme Court's final ruling. In this case, Becky Stelluto left her home in California suddenly in 2001, presumably to visit her mother in Louisiana, when her daughter Anna was only five weeks old. Ms. Stelluto filed for divorce in Louisiana one week later. Her husband, Donald Stelluto, sued for divorce and child custody in California. These competing lawsuits led to a dispute between Louisiana and California over which state would have jurisdiction over the child custody and visitation decisions regarding Anna. The Louisiana Supreme Court eventually ruled that Anna was too young to have any "home state" because she lived in California only for the first five weeks of her life and Louisiana for the sixth week of her life. However, the Court ruled that Anna did have a "significant connection" to Louisiana through her mother, who in a separate decision, successfully argued that she was a Louisiana resident. In the language of the opinion:

> Anna's entire experience of the world at such a young age was filtered through her primary caregiver, her mother. Moreover, Anna's connection to her mother was quite literal, as Anna was still breast-feeding at the time Ms. Stelluto brought her to Louisiana. This relationship, combined with Anna's one-week residence in the state . . . suffices to establish a significant connection to Louisiana.[55]

The importance of the breastfeeding relationship in the case is further expressed in the Louisiana Supreme Court's later comment, "Anna's infancy and the primacy of her relationship to her primary caregiver, her mother, render Anna's connection to Louisiana based on living here one week more significant than it would in the case of an older child."[56]

Child Abuse or Neglect

Twenty-three cases involved charges of child abuse or neglect where breastfeeding was one of many reasons for the charges. In most of these cases, the mother was charged with abuse or neglect in part because she was breastfeeding while taking illegal drugs (seven cases), while extremely intoxicated,[57] had high lead levels in her blood and breast milk,[58] was HIV-positive,[59] breastfed a severely disabled child who could not breathe properly while nursing,[60] or took prescription medications that caused adverse reactions in the breastfed infant (three cases). In addition, two cases involved severely undernourished breastfed babies,[61] and three cases concerned breastfeeding mothers who refused to take medications to treat their mental illnesses. These women refused their medications because they did not want to transfer the medications to their infants through their breast milk. They consequently suffered psychotic episodes and lost custody of their children as a result.[62]

In at least three cases, the courts or social service agencies appear to have based their decisions upon the idea that the breast is a sexual object, without regard to its biological function. One mother was charged with sexual abuse because she breastfed her infant in front of her older son.[63] Another mother was charged with neglect because she continued to see an estranged, abusive partner and to breastfeed in front of him.[64] The most notorious case is that of Karen Carter (later revealed to be Denise Perrigo), a young mother who was disturbed by feelings of arousal when breastfeeding her child, who was nearly two. Unaware that such feelings are normal during breastfeeding, Ms. Carter called a local hot line looking for a La Leche League contact. Instead, she was referred to a rape crisis center. The rape crisis center turned her in to the police, who arrested her on child sex abuse charges. The Department of Social Services in Carter's state placed Carter's daughter into protective custody, and Carter was not able to regain custody of her daughter for a year, after a lengthy investigation in which all child sexual abuse charges were found to be groundless.[65]

Employment Issues

Two cases involved women who applied for worker's compensation or disability benefits resulting from their breastfeeding decisions. In the first case,

Melissa Kallir applied for temporary disability leave from her employer, Friendly Ice Cream, because her child developed allergies and required breast milk. The court ruled that the child's medical condition was covered under New York employment law because the child's condition was "biologically and realistically inextricably connected to the pregnancy" and was therefore covered under the disability law, even though the disability was the child's, not the employee's.[66] In the second case, Colleen Curran refused steroid injections and surgery to treat a back problem so she could breastfeed her infant. Her injury prevented her from returning to work. Her employer, the American Red Cross, petitioned to terminate or suspend her workers' compensation benefits until Curran agreed to either the steroid treatments or surgery. The Pennsylvania Appeals Court ruled on Curran's behalf, arguing that her refusal of treatment was appropriate because she was nursing.[67]

While these first two cases are victories for breastfeeding mothers, two other cases ruled against the breastfeeding women. In 1979, the Pennsylvania Appeals Court overturned a lower court ruling involving Cheryl Rossetti, a nursing mother whose infant son refused to nurse from a bottle. Rossetti asked for an extension in maternity leave benefits in order to breastfeed her child. The school district that employed her refused and dismissed Rossetti when she failed to return to work. The appeals court ruled Rossetti's "failure to return to work was without any legal justification [therefore] her dismissal by the Board was for proper cause."[68]

More recently, Jolie Perdrix-Wang was denied unemployment compensation benefits after she quit her job as a chemist. Perdrix-Wang asked her employer to limit her exposure to potentially hazardous chemicals while she was breastfeeding. Her employer refused her request. They offered her a choice of a lower-level position at lower pay, or weaning her daughter. Perdrix-Wang resigned, and the state of Arkansas refused her application for unemployment benefits. The administrative appeals court concurred, stating that Perdrix-Wang's decision to breastfeed was a "matter of personal choice."[69]

A final case, one that again calls to mind the breast as a sexual object, is an employment discrimination case filed by a male nurse, Michael Slivka, against a hospital in West Virginia. Slivka had applied for a job as an obstetrical nurse and was informed that the hospital's policy was to hire only female nurses in obstetrics "out of concern for patient privacy, staffing and quality of care." Noting that many obstetric nurses' tasks are invasive, or "sensitive or intimate," including assisting new mothers with breastfeeding, the court nonetheless ruled that gender is not a *bona fide* occupational qualification (BFOQ) for obstetric nurses. The West Virginia court held that the hospital did not substantiate its claims of protecting patient privacy, noting that the patients surveyed indicated greater concern about being cared for by student nurses, rather than male obstetrical nurses.[70]

Medical Malpractice Cases

Three cases involved medical malpractice or negligence. Two cases were resolved in favor of the plaintiffs, the nursing mothers. The first case involved a hospital in which hospital personnel gave a newborn baby to the wrong mother, who then breastfed the child.[71] The second was a case in which a woman contracted hepatitis from a blood transfusion given during delivery, leaving her unable to breastfeed. Her child consequently developed allergies to formula.[72] The final case, involving a misdiagnosis of breast cancer in a nursing mother, was resolved in favor of the defendant.[73]

Incarcerated Mothers

Two cases involved incarcerated mothers who wished to breastfeed their children. One wanted temporary leave from jail to breastfeed her child outside of prison. The other wanted to breastfeed her child while incarcerated. Both requests were refused by the courts. In the latter case the plaintiff, Debra Bailey, was incarcerated in New York, and this decision predated New York's legislation permitting incarcerated mothers to keep their infants with them while breast-feeding.[74]

Harassment or Trauma

Six cases involved some sort of harassment or trauma. One was a sexual harassment lawsuit, another involved harassment of a witness, and a third charged a violation of a family court decree by an estranged spouse who videotaped his former wife breastfeeding. A fourth case involved a harassment dispute between neighbors, where the plaintiff accused the defendant of hiding in the bushes to watch the plaintiff's wife breastfeed.[75] Another case charged that witnessing a traffic accident so traumatized a nursing mother that she was no longer able to breastfeed her child. The resolutions of these cases are mixed. The judges who ruled against the women did so due to legal technicalities unrelated to the breast-feeding issue.[76] In the case of trauma due to witnessing a traffic accident, the Appeals Court ruled that the driver was negligent, but did not rule on the woman's claim that she could no longer breastfeed, nor attach a value to this loss.[77] With the exception of the trauma case, all of these cases clearly frame the breast as a sexual object and intimate that breastfeeding is a sexual act.

Competing Rights

The state courts clearly demonstrate that breastfeeding is a legal domain that is characterized by competing rights. If a woman has a right to breastfeed based on *Dike*, which predated many of these cases, how is this right balanced against other competing interests? In most cases, the courts have ruled that a woman's right to breastfeed is secondary to other considerations. One of these considerations is a father's parental rights and a child's interest in having a relationship with both parents. Most child custody disputes in which breastfeeding was an issue ruled against the mother. The exceptions appear to be in cases of very young infants. Certainly, the courts have consistently ruled against extended breastfeeding as a reason to curtail or deny fathers' visitation rights.

The cases of child neglect or abuse also demonstrate how breastfeeding involves competing rights. When a mother's milk is potentially harmful to her child, because of the presence of illegal drugs, alcohol, medications, pollutants or viruses, it ceases to be the "best" food for babies. Rather, the child's best interest then indicates that the child should be fed formula, and in the most extreme cases, continued breastfeeding could be considered child abuse. It is important to note that in the vast majority of cases of child neglect or abuse, breastfeeding was only one reason that a parent was considered unfit.

The most tragic cases are perhaps those cases of mothers who are mentally ill and, in their desire to provide their children with the best care, stop taking their medications in order to breastfeed, and suffer mental breakdowns as a result. Breastfeeding was short sighted in these cases. A suffering, delusional mother cannot adequately care for her child, even if she is breastfeeding, and may even lose custody of her child.

The major exception, of course, is the Carter (Perrigo) case. Not only were the sexual abuse charges against her baseless, they were the result of considerable ignorance—on Carter's part and on the part of various authorities—of the physiology of breastfeeding. Carter and her daughter suffered emotionally and saw their rights abridged as a result.

Employers' rights also appear to supersede women's right to breastfeed. The Perdrix-Wang case is particularly germane, because it is subsequent to the *Dike* decision. The courts did not find Perdrix-Wang's claim of discrimination convincing and trivialized it by calling breastfeeding "a personal choice." Similarly, the state assumed no burdens of accommodating breastfeeding in the cases of incarcerated mothers.

STATE POLICY AND SOCIAL CONSTRUCTION THEORY

As in the case of federal laws and cases, social construction theory is a powerful lens through which we can understand the impact of state breastfeeding policy on target populations. As in the case of federal policy, we find that state policy has the same target populations: mothers, fathers, children, employers, and the state.

Fathers as Advantaged

Advantaged target populations are politically powerful groups that are positively constructed. In the case of federal policy, we saw that some men were advantaged because their claim of "ownership" of women's breasts went largely unchallenged. The advantaged position of fathers also is very clear in the area of family law. In most cases involving breastfeeding, and in every case involving extended breastfeeding, the father's parental rights supersede the mother's right to breastfeed and the child's interest in being breastfed. In fact, the mother's constitutional right and the child's interests are rarely even acknowledged by the courts. Fathers are "winning the weaning war" and have solid legal footing to demand favorable visitation schedules. Martha Fineman has documented many ways in which the father enjoys legal advantages in family law.[78] "Winning the weaning war" is yet another example of fathers' legal dominance. Moreover, fathers are rarely asked to bear any burdens of breastfeeding in terms of child custody or visitation schedules, other than in a few cases involving very young infants.

Employers and the State as Contenders

As in the case of federal law, employers are contenders, negatively constructed but politically powerful. Only in a few states are employers expected to accommodate the needs of their lactating employees. Even then, the burdens placed upon them are few: unpaid break time, a private place to express milk, and perhaps access to a refrigerator. Some states have a provision to opt out of providing even these modest accommodations if they pose an "undue burden." In two states, the employer provisions are voluntary, which actually impose no burdens on businesses, but use incentives.

Likewise, the policy burdens imposed on employers are slight—only a small degree of lost productivity and providing a private space for brief periods during the work day. Yet, at the same time, employers stand to benefit from increased breastfeeding rates, in the form of lower absenteeism and lower health care costs. One scholar argued the cost of accommodating break time for milk expression in the workplace was comparable to providing employees unpaid breaks to smoke. She noted the irony that allowing breastfeeding breaks are likely to save employers health care costs, while adapting to smokers' unhealthy habits will generate higher health care costs.[79] Yet, burdensome accommodations, such as requiring longer or paid maternity leaves, paid break time to nurse or express milk, allowing infants on-site to nurse, or providing on-site day care if the workplace is dangerous for children, are not required of employers in any state.

The powerful position of employers is also found in some of the debates surrounding even the weakest breastfeeding rights legislation. For instance, one key senator in the South Carolina legislature threatened to oppose the bill because he "didn't like to tell businesses what to do." The irony, of course, is that the South Carolina law imposed no burdens on businesses. In fact, advocates argued in response that the legislation required employers to do nothing; they just had to leave breastfeeding mothers alone.[80]

As in federal legislation, the state also is a contender. States have imposed few burdens upon themselves even as they pass breastfeeding rights laws. Consider breastfeeding awareness campaigns: These efforts only require the state to talk about the importance of breastfeeding, but not to support it in any material way. By the same token, many breastfeeding rights laws lack a specific remedy for women whose rights are violated. States are not responsible for enforcing or adjudicating any violations of these rights. Similarly, states have assumed few burdens to make courts a friendly place for lactating women. Rather, these women are simply excused from jury service. Other than New York, states do not accommodate incarcerated breastfeeding mothers. Perhaps most importantly, through their enforcement of child abuse and neglect laws, states define when breastfeeding is benevolent and when it is dangerous. Women are encouraged to breastfeed by the state, and yet this very act may be used against them later. The exception, of course, is New York. New York accepted some of the breastfeeding burden when it extended its disability benefits to a mother whose child had a cleft palate and allows some incarcerated women to breastfeed in jail.

Mothers and Children as Dependents

Dependent target populations are positively constructed, but politically weak. Their benefits are symbolic, and their burdens are heavy. As in the case of federal policy, state breastfeeding policy places mothers in a position as a dependent. Most of the breastfeeding rights legislation offers symbolic benefits to women. Women have to defend their right to breastfeed in public, if it is challenged, and are rarely provided remedies. In Missouri, women have to worry about being "discreet." Working mothers have to use unpaid break time at work to nurse or express breast milk. Arguably, mothers called for jury duty have to forgo some of their rights of citizenship in order to breastfeed in an uninterrupted fashion.

Children are primarily dependents in the context of state policy, positively constructed and politically weak. The courts and state welfare agencies purport to act in their defense or best interests, yet, the children are largely without voice. Certainly, determining a child's "best interest" can be difficult and requires courts to balance, in the words of one commentator, "psychiatry against constitutional law."[81] In custody and visitation cases, the "best interest" of the breastfed child usually appears to be defined as having a relationship with the father. This definition respects the child's relationship with its father. However, there appears little attempt to redefine the child's interest to take into account the possible health and psychological benefits of breastfeeding. The balance of "psychiatry and constitutional law" does not appear to have room for a third variable: breastfeeding. Some recent cases, *Stelluto* in particular, may indicate that breastfeeding is assuming a more important position in the field of family law, but no trend is yet apparent. Similarly, children appear to have little input into the neglect and child abuse cases, even those children who might be old enough to speak for themselves.

The New York law that allows incarcerated mothers to breastfeed their children while in jail also places children in the position of dependents. The design of the program is benign; its intent is to give children a healthy dose of breast milk during infancy and to forge a bond between mother and child. Certainly both are in the child's best interest. However, this policy benefit is small compared to the burden imposed: jail time. Presumably, these infants have committed no crime; yet they are placed in prison.

Notable exceptions are the Louisiana law, which prohibits discrimination against breastfeeding children, and the Mississippi law, which requires child care centers to accommodate breastfeeding mothers. In Louisiana, the child's civil rights are explicitly protected, and in Mississippi, some of the burden of breastfeeding is shifted from the mother to the child care center.

Deviant Mothers

Some mothers are deviant target populations: negatively constructed and politically weak. Deviants' benefits are under prescribed and their burdens are over prescribed. Among the deviant mothers are those declared incompetent parents who are drug addicted, alcoholic, or ill. Rather than receiving the benefit of drug or medical treatment, these mothers bear a heavy burden: losing custody of their children and their right to breastfeed them. In this group are also those who breastfeed for more than one year. Courts ruled against these mothers in every child custody case, and Karen Carter (Denise Perrigo) paid a terrible price because of a normal physiological reaction to breastfeeding. State authorities defined the very practice of extended breastfeeding as perversity and sought to terminate her parental rights as a consequence.

RECOMMENDATIONS

State policy, like federal policy, reflects the contradictory nature of public opinion about breastfeeding. By December 2006, most states had enacted laws supporting general breastfeeding rights, an idea that appears to have widespread support. Fewer states have imposed remedies, guarantees for employed women or other provisions, reflecting less widespread support for these provisions. Few courts have accommodated breastfeeding in child custody and visitation cases, reflecting public ambivalence on this issue. By shining a light on the act of breastfeeding and the many actors in the relationship, social construction theory helps us discern what ideal state breastfeeding policy should include to more equitably distribute benefits and burdens.

First, we advocate for greater burden sharing with fathers, employers, and the state. For instance, states should enact remedies for women whose breastfeeding rights are violated by other parties. Second, the state should ensure that breastfeeding is exempt from all laws against public nudity, obscenity, and child sexual abuse. Moreover, the state needs to publicize women's breastfeeding rights and the appropriate application of these rights.

We particularly like the strong language in Hawaii's state code. The entire package of Hawaiian breastfeeding rights laws defines breastfeeding as a civil right, subject to enforcement by the Civil Rights Commission. In the process, Hawaii does not *require* employers to *provide* break time. Rather it *prohibits* employers from *forbidding* its employees from expressing breast milk. This subtle difference in language implies that breastfeeding is something that is presumed, not given permission for one to do. Similarly, we support the Louisiana provision that prohibits discrimination against breastfed children in child care settings. This law couches a child's "best interest" in constitutional terms, rather than in public health or psychological terms. Moreover, it is perhaps the only law that expressly recognizes that the child, too, is a rights-bearing individual. Similarly, out of respect of the child's rights, we also oppose legislation that allows incarcerated women to breastfeed their babies in prison.

Third, employers stand to benefit enormously from increased breastfeeding rates for many reasons. One is that these companies have more satisfied employees. One study found that employees, especially female employees, found companies that accommodated breastfeeding in the workplace to be more fair and attractive employers. The respondents in this study also reported that they would be more likely to apply to, and accept an employment offer from, companies with workplace lactation programs.[82] Because breastfed babies are less prone to illnesses, and develop illnesses of shorter duration and severity when they do fall ill, employers will experience less employee absenteeism if they accommodate their breastfeeding employees. Moreover, these healthier babies will have lower health care costs, which are passed on to the employers through health insurance claims. Consequently, we advocate that employers assume more of the burdens of breastfeeding, by providing longer, paid maternity leaves, paid break time for nursing or milk expression, a private place for nursing or expression, suitable storage for expressed milk, and on-site child care for lactating mothers. Some of these burdens could be subsidized by the state. For example, the state could subsidize the cost of paid maternity leave by permitting women to file for unemployment compensation during their leaves, or provide tax breaks to employers to offset the costs of accommodating breastfeeding mothers.

Third, we support the Mississippi legislation as a model, whereby some of the burdens of breastfeeding are shifted from the mother to the child care center. This law does help working mothers balance their private and public lives.

Fourth, breastfed babies need their fathers to share the burdens of breastfeeding in child custody and visitation decisions. Given that breastfeeding benefits are greatest for infants, we believe that breastfeeding should be accommodated in child custody and visitation arrangements, especially during the first year. Possible arrangements include multiple short visits during a week, rather than lengthy overnight or weekend visits, or visits accompanied by the mother to enable her to nurse the infant. After one year, custody and visitation arrangements can be adjusted to accommodate the child's legitimate interest in having a relationship with its father and the father's parental rights. The Utah law, which recommends gradually increasing the duration of visits with the noncustodial parent as the child ages, is a possible model.

Of course, we do not believe that breastfeeding is an unlimited right. As in any other case, rights are curtailed when the exercise of those rights endangers another person. Consequently, we agree with current practices that curtail women's right to breastfeed when they might infect their children with diseases, or pass along pollutants, illegal drugs, or dangerous medications through their breast milk. Similarly, Michigan should repeal its provision that exempts nursing babies from being restrained in a car seat.

Our final point is the most obvious, however. Absent federal legislation that establishes breastfeeding rights at the national level, breastfeeding rights will be legally protected by an uneven patchwork of state laws. Consequently, some women continue to enjoy more legal protections for their right to breastfeed, simply by accident of location, than many of their sisters in other states.

6

A Democratic, Feminist Approach to Breastfeeding Rights

As we have developed our discussion of breastfeeding rights, we have carefully surveyed the legislative and judicial status of those rights at both the state and federal levels, and we expanded our analysis by looking at the "targeting biases" that pervade breastfeeding policy. This attentiveness to the material effects of policy—who gets what, when, and how—helps avoid an oversimplifying focus on the formal promises of both legislative and judicial articulations of breastfeeding.

We have also begun to take a look at how the politics of breastfeeding operates below and beyond the level of government institutions. To this end, Chapter 3 analyzed how breastfeeding is portrayed in the media and what the public's attitudes about breastfeeding are like. By looking at how breastfeeding is communicated and understood by the public at large, we were able to explore the contexts in which breastfeeding rights are contested by norms of social expectation. To the degree that the realization of rights is always dependent on a supporting culture, the continuing possibility of breastfeeding rights cannot be disentangled from what they mean in the day to day consciousness of various actors who affect decisions of whether or not to breastfeed.

We now turn to take a look at how a right to breastfeed might be approached, in terms of political coherence, by the variously situated women making the breastfeeding decision. This focus on women does not preclude the important role that men play in the success (or the failure) of breastfeeding practices, but given that it is women who breastfeed, and given their centrality in making the decision to breastfeed, a women-centered approach is appropriate. The decision of whether or not to breastfeed, as well as the decision about how long to continue breastfeeding, is always entwined in the specific socioeconomic experiences of women's lives. Given the different constellations of interests that distinguish women's lives, women will make different, but still reasonable, decisions about the role that breastfeeding will play in their child rearing practices.

Our concluding analysis privileges the perspectives of women. Thus, it is, if in a minimal sense, a feminist analysis.[1] It begins with, and thus gives primacy to, the women whose labor, in every sense of the word, is still typically responsible for the great majority of child rearing in American society. Taken as a set of policies that give women more choice about how they can best feed their children, the right to breastfeed is an issue about women's real material and pragmatic interests. By approaching breastfeeding issues from the materially situated contexts of different women's lives, we can get the best picture of what the right to breastfeed should look like. From such a perspective, breastfeeding rights create a field of opportunity for women that maximizes their ability to raise their children in a reasonable way, but it also marks out important limits of what that right should entail. It is important to note that the claim for a right to breastfeed is not entirely dependent upon the scientific case that breast is best, or any moral obligation that might arise on the basis of that evidence.

Though the scientific and moral cases for breastfeeding offer persuasive reasons for why women should breastfeed, our analyses make it clear that breastfeeding, even if it is "right" for many women and many children, is not the best choice for all women or all children. Certainly, much of the impetus for gains made in achieving this right is dependent upon the weight of the scientific consensus that breastfeeding optimizes the health of both mother and child; but the right to make this decision within the larger contexts of their lives has been established as, and should remain, the right of individual women. The right to breastfeed, a reflection on women's broader circumstances suggests, should not be transformed into a duty to breastfeed. Rather we think of this as women's right to choose to breastfeed.

This feminist approach presumes that there are plenty of bases for women's solidarity about this right. The decision of whether or not to breastfeed, after all, involves a decision about women's bodies and whether or not women will have the ability to autonomously control them. Furthermore, women, despite crucial differences in their circumstances, can recognize how they are similarly affected by social realities. In Western societies such as the United States, for example, the way the breast functions as a sexual object within a predominant understanding of heterosexual eroticism seems to crucially underlie a great deal of the anxiety about public breastfeeding.

Despite the similarities that draw together a women-centered perspective on breastfeeding rights, however, it remains crucial to think about differences in the way different actors experience the choice and act of breastfeeding. This attentiveness to difference makes it difficult to articulate a simple picture of what a feminist, or a woman-centered, response to the question of breastfeeding should look like. As our picture of how different women make the choice of whether or not to breastfeed suggests, there are a wide range of attitudes about breastfeeding among women. Despite those differences, we believe that feminism can develop a coherent, inclusive response to the question of breastfeeding. In fact, we want to suggest that the diversity of women's specific circumstances regarding the question of breastfeeding is ultimately a strength that can be utilized by a broad feminist response to the question of breastfeeding rights. In that important sense, the perspective that begins to emerge here can be called a *democratic*, feminist perspective. We hope to suggest how differences between women, particularly in the context of breastfeeding decisions, might move toward a politically actionable consensus that maintains some flexibility. As we shall see, this flexibility is particularly important in the many ways that we understand "good mothering."

Though we often use the terms *women, woman,* and *feminist* as if all women are the same, they clearly are not, and, certainly, not all women make breastfeeding decisions in the same context. Women's backgrounds, particular experiences, race, ethnicity, and class status are all variables that complicate the decision of whether or not to breastfeed. Some women have the opportunity and desire to choose intensive, exclusive forms of mothering; they are able to stay at home with their young children. These women can feed and care for their children following the prescribed method espoused by some breastfeeding advocacy groups such as La Leche League.

Other women do not have this economic option and must work to support themselves and their families. Many women also see their careers as an important dimension of who they are, and breastfeeding over extended periods of time can interfere with those commitments. Employment outside the home for any reason can clearly make breastfeeding more difficult for these mothers, particularly over extended periods of time. In first world situations, where potable water, access to excellent medical care, plentiful supplies of pasteurized cow's milk formula, and sanitary living conditions are available, these women can reasonably conclude that using infant formula is safe, and the health benefits of breastfeeding are relatively marginal. Moreover, using formula provides benefits to their careers, both for themselves and as an example for their children, about how adults should shape the meaning of their lives. African American women, in particular,[2] have inherited breastfeeding patterns that emerged in earlier generations, and those learned behaviors have led African American women to breastfeed at lower rates than the rest of the population. Clearly, the decision of whether or not to breast-feed is not precisely the same for all women.

An attentiveness to the way in which different actors understand breastfeed-ing also helps us understand that the politics of breastfeeding is about much more than breastfeeding. Attitudes about breastfeeding are, in fact, typically part of a larger constellation of assumptions or ideas about the world, and those assump-tions are themselves nested within specific economic and social contexts that forcefully shape women's behavior. Those contexts entail a typically complex set of relationships, some of them highly intimate, to a variety of actors affected by the decision of whether or not to breastfeed. These relationships with family, employers, and even strangers, are themselves nested in a variety of social pat-terns, such as the expectations of patriarchy and heterosexuality.

Part of feminism's critical project must continue to demystify how those systems contour women's self-understandings. In the context of breastfeeding rights, a feminist analysis would investigate how those systems, and the self-understandings that they engender, influence women's decisions about breast-feeding. The legal recognition of breastfeeding rights, however, is a practical achievement for women that can operate within the assumptions of these patri-archal and heterosexual patterns. Even as a feminist approach to breastfeeding rights seeks to uncover the ways in which heterosexual and patriarchal systems discourage breastfeeding, an inclusive, democratic, feminist approach to breast-feeding rights would remain open to how women who live within these systems struggle to make choices about what is best for themselves and their children.

ASSESSING BREASTFEEDING RIGHTS: JUSTICE, PRAGMATISM, AND TACTICS

As the legal precedents we have examined make clear, the right to breastfeed has been articulated within the established legal presumption that parents have the right to make reasonable judgments about how to raise their children. In the language of Chief Judge Godbold's opinion in *Dike*, "the Constitution protects from excessive state interference a woman's decision respecting breastfeeding."[3] In centering the right to breastfeed on the woman's *decision*, this language echoes the established lineage of parents' rights cases stretching back to *Pierce v. Society of Sisters* (1925) and *Meyer v. Nebraska* (1923), but it also seems to lean on the expectation of intimate privacy established in cases such as *Griswold v. Connecticut* (1965) and *Lawrence v. Texas* (2003). In focusing on the woman's decision, in fact, Godbold's ruling veers toward the holding in *Roe v. Wade* that a woman's individual choice about matters pertaining to her body and the child that she bears cannot be contravened by state regulation. In state and federal law, the right to breastfeed has also been articulated as a women's right to breastfeed, to the near total exclusion of other actors.

This positively articulated right, then, is consonant with our women-centered approach. It specifies that it is the woman's decision that merits protection. Pragmatically, the way that the right has been articulated continues to ground efforts to expand that right, and that articulation is also consonant with the feminist approach that we are pursuing in this chapter. The feminist approach that we are endorsing, however, should not be limited to the adversarial language of "gaining ground"; a feminist approach, in fact, can benefit by entering into the broader social conversation in which rights are contested and implemented.

Given that rights claims, like claims about breastfeeding rights, often entail some strategy for balancing a cluster of competing rights (and, at the level of their social enactment, competing interests) of different actors, the socially complex scene revealed by different women's breastfeeding circumstances reminds us that the breastfeeding decision is made within definite social and relational contexts. Our analysis, while giving primacy to women's perspectives, seeks to further expand the conversation about breastfeeding rights by maintaining the space to listen to the concerns and interests of other affected actors. To contextualize the breastfeeding choice, we need to consider the interests and rights of fathers and husbands, the impact of breastfeeding on the community at large, and, perhaps most compellingly, the interests of infants and young children.

Taking this broader set of interests into consideration, our optimal, women-centered vision of breastfeeding rights and policy can build on more explicit policy recommendations discussed in Chapters 4 and 5. Women should be able to expect:

- A social atmosphere that is conducive to breastfeeding and that is protected by law. This right should be unqualified, and it should apply to both public and private spaces.

- A reasonable chance of balancing breastfeeding and work. This requires at least some protection from the courts where breastfeeding can be accommodated at minimal costs, but it may also require governmental incentives.

- That breastfeeding will be taken into account in visitation and child custody cases during the infant's first year.

- That public awareness campaigns should target fathers and the public at large, not only expectant women. Given the important role that men can play in the success or failure of breastfeeding, and given the indifference, ignorance, and hostility many people feel toward breastfeeding, the educative impact of these campaigns could have a crucial effect in establishing the normalcy of breastfeeding.

Nonetheless, we do not advocate for an absolute right to breastfeed. We take this position for two reasons. First, though breastfeeding is typically best for most children and most mothers in most cases, this is clearly not always the case. In situations where a mother's drug addiction, or her exposure to environmental toxins, or her status as a carrier of the HIV-virus risks passing along those pollutants or diseases through her breast milk, for example, breastfeeding is not in children's best interest. The state is entirely right in not endorsing a women's right to breastfeed in these situations. Likewise, when a mother is on medication to control a psychological or physiological illness, not taking her medication in order to breastfeed may not be in the child's best interest. This is clearly the case when ceasing to take medication leads to severe psychological disability.

Second, a women's right to breastfeed should not be absolute with respect to the parental rights of the father, and women should not be allowed to use breastfeeding as a weapon to deprive men of their parental rights, particularly after the child's first year. Moreover, arguing that breastfeeding is an absolute right could also deprive children of having a loving relationship with their fathers, which is clearly in children's interests.

Opening up this conversation between rights-bearing actors, however, does not mean that breastfeeding advocates should compromise their belief that "breast is best." When we consider the rights of fathers, for example, we are not endorsing claims that fathers' rights as parents trump a women's right to breastfeed. Legally, we are confident that policymakers can strike a reasonable balance between a right that protects the mother and child's interest in breastfeeding and the parental rights of fathers. We want to move beyond the current jurisprudence that rarely considers breastfeeding in custody cases and visitation decisions. We argue that due consideration of breastfeeding should be given throughout the first year of the infant's life.

At a social level, a triumph of the women's rights movement has been its insistence that fathers are parents, too, and that they should share the primary burdens of child rearing, so the compromise achieved at a legal level can be translated into an ethic of parental responsibility deployed at a cultural and social level. Groups such as La Leche League recognize that fathers can offer important support for breastfeeding mothers, but male attitudes remain one of the most important sites for breastfeeding advocacy work.[4] Broader efforts to educate fathers about the importance of breastfeeding could encourage fathers to compromise on questions of visitation during the early postpartum period, when the benefits of breastfeeding are highest. Such a series of compromises may, in fact, be in the best interest of the child, preserving the child's interest in being breastfed in the crucial postpartum period, but they might also help stabilize relations between the child and the child's parents despite the separations of divorce.

Likewise, children's interest in receiving breast milk and being nurtured at the breast suggests that employers should share the burden of creating breastfeeding opportunities for their employees. Private businesses that are able to give women the space and time to breastfeed combine pragmatic business sense with good corporate citizenship. Sound breastfeeding policy could entail mandates—or at the very least various incentives such as tax breaks—that would encourage employers to materially assist women with their efforts to breastfeed. Businesses would also reap the benefits of less absenteeism resulting from the need to care for sick children, not to mention the well being that allowing women to breastfeed would promote. For more competitive professional jobs, breastfeeding flexibility can even be included as part of the package used to attract workers.

While our analysis demands an alertness to the ways in which an emphasis on the interests of children can be wielded perniciously, as part of strategies for labeling certain mothers as somehow less fit mothers, those interests should not be ignored, and, in many respects, they should be paramount. We believe that the right to breastfeed gives women a choice about how to feed their children, and we believe that it is important to recognize that some women might make a rational choice that, all things on balance, breastfeeding—or at least the intensive breastfeeding idealized by many breastfeeding advocates—is not the right choice in their situation. Nonetheless, given the unquestionable, myriad benefits conferred to infants by breastfeeding, the persistence of barriers to being able to breastfeed—barriers created by the different working conditions of different sectors of jobs (professional v. working class) and by the failure to give women break time to nurse or to pump milk—our failure to take breastfeeding rights seriously discriminates against children along class, and by extension racial, lines.

Finally, the community at large has breastfeeding-related obligations as well; the courts and policy should recognize these obligations. In particular, given that women will be more likely to initiate and continue breastfeeding if they do not have to worry about being arrested under obscenity laws, it is important that breastfeeding rights laws and policies not be attached to provisions that mothers be discreet when breastfeeding and that obscenity exemptions be codified into law. If we think of the role that infants play in these conversations, their lack of consciousness about norms of decency and discretion, their impatient tugging away of the blanket that covers the women's breast, for example, reminds us of the breast's primary biological function in these contexts.

Considering the rights and claims of a broader group of actors certainly complicates the smooth story told by breastfeeding advocates, but it also allows us to pragmatically assess the best ways of optimizing women's ability to breastfeed. Considering the interests of fathers and children pushes questions of breastfeeding in terms of the competing obligations and concerns women must negotiate in the concrete experience of their social relations.

At the same time, remembering the broader context in which the struggle for breastfeeding rights occurs prevents us from trivializing the real experiences of women who have legitimate difficulties mastering breastfeeding, or who cannot produce enough milk to successfully breastfeed, or who make considered judgments that, taking the full sweep of their circumstances into balance, breastfeeding is not the best option for themselves or their children. Moreover, women who choose to use formula should not be separated into categories of "good mothers," who made this choice for a "good" reason, such as fear of passing along poisons or pathogens to their babies, and "bad mothers," who use formula because they selfishly want to go back to work or who are emotionally distant from their progeny. This in no way suggests that breastfeeding advocates should not work as hard as possible to help women overcome barriers to breastfeeding, but women who do not breastfeed should not be marginalized in the conversation about breastfeeding rights.

BREASTFEEDING RIGHTS AND FEMINISM

When we look at the history of breastfeeding over the last 50 years, we find that the split between pro-breastfeeding discourses and alternative feeding discourses map onto recognizable factions within and in proximity to feminism. Many breastfeeding advocates have invoked and continue to invoke arguments about women's unique nature and about the naturalness of breast feeding, discourses that dovetail nicely with scientific data supporting the health benefits of breastfeeding. This language seems to hook into the rationales of a difference feminism that celebrates that which is unique to women. Conversely, those who supported alternative feeding methods appealed to the freedom from breastfeeding as freedom for otherwise impossible ways of life, such as the ability to participate fully in the public sphere. This emphasis on women's ability to compete with men as equals in the public sphere echoes the aims of liberal feminism.

Though this is a useful way to begin thinking about the relationship between different attitudes about breastfeeding and different factions within feminism, it oversimplifies those relationships. Of course, the way actual women integrate their attitudes toward breastfeeding into their broader views (feminist or otherwise) does not arise in an economic vacuum, and the way in which these general positions on breastfeeding intersect with the interests and self-understandings of women occupying different economic realities is an important part of the story of feminism's relation to breastfeeding. In any case, it is not clear that liberal and difference feminist attitudes, themselves oversimplifying ideal types, can sufficiently map the range of attitudes toward breastfeeding.

As the benefits of breastfeeding have gained scientific support, liberal feminists have increasingly joined difference feminists in advocating for an expansion of breastfeeding rights. Even within this pro-breastfeeding alliance, there remain important differences in orientation and commitment to the idea and practice of breastfeeding. Whereas difference feminists remain wedded to advocating and preserving the unique qualities of women, liberal feminist advocates of breastfeeding rights can frame those rights as an essential part of their ability to balance their duties as mothers with their professional responsibilities and opportunities. The position and activity of pro-breastfeeding groups such as La Leche League go beyond advocating the health benefits of breast milk to include a valorization of the bonding contact between the mother and infant. Liberal feminist discourse, recognizing the limitation on this kind of contact in some professional circumstances, focuses on the health benefits for the children themselves and is more amenable to pumping strategies.

In fact, the improved breast pumping technology that allows women to express and store their milk has been an important consideration in the promulgation and interpretation of breastfeeding rights. Some analysts have argued that liberal feminist discourse, with its emphasis on moving women into the public sphere, fails to recognize the language of empowerment that characterizes La Leche League discourse.[5] Nonetheless, the rhetoric of liberal feminist breastfeeding advocacy does not preclude a commitment to the well-being of the mother. Pumping technology has contributed to the rhetorical construction of the mother who might possibly bridge the gap between participation in the public sphere and the time and labor-intensive requirements of regular breastfeeding. In fact, one increasingly encounters advocates who help mothers deal with the dual demands of career and infant feeding. As one Web site specifically designed to help mothers with the multiple demands of career and breastfeeding implores, "Don't wean just because you work! Find ample help and support with these online and offline resources."[6]

Nonetheless, not all women are likely to flourish under the demanding regimen that such "double duty" requires, even with advances in pumping technology. Furthermore, liberal and difference feminists' rhetoric occlude the realities that face lower income, working mothers who are unlikely to benefit from an increasing tendency of professional employers to grant breastfeeding privileges without legal coercion. They both also underemphasize the physical difficulties that some mothers continue to experience when breastfeeding (even when they've been carefully coached by experts to overcome these difficulties) and those situations in which the best interests of the child indicate foregoing breastfeeding. There is a growing consensus that the effects of breastfeeding are, all things being equal, best for the child, and the evidence collected in this volume overwhelmingly reflects that consensus. Against this backdrop, mothers who choose not to breastfeed, in the various conditions when *things are not equal*, are often stigmatized for their decision as "bad mothers." The pressure of this norm, in fact, might motivate some women to breastfeed even when it is not the right decision for the child and the mother, as seen in the cases of HIV-positive women, or mentally ill women who forgo their medication. As the testimony and reported circumstances of these women's lives suggests, the increasing sense among various kinds of feminists that breastfeeding fits within a feminist framework should not be allowed to become an unproblematic consensus. At the very least, an inclusive kind of feminism must find a language that respects the autonomy of women and children for whom breastfeeding is not an optimal choice.

WOMEN'S IDENTITY AND RIGHTS

This kind of feminist response to the question of breastfeeding gives particular shape to what one means by breastfeeding rights. How does thinking of breastfeeding as a "right" frame the way people negotiate a public understanding of breastfeeding? Is the language of rights a profitable way of developing our public attitude toward breastfeeding?

Ultimately, adopting a rights-based strategy continues to make sense for breastfeeding advocates, but the ultimate success of that strategy entails refining and extending the logic of rights beyond their formulation and application within the formal legal sphere. Rights also need to be understood in terms of their extra-legal effects. Advocates need some sense of how deploying the language of rights has effects that go beyond their strict legal definition and implementation.

One important extra-legal consequence of talking about breastfeeding in terms of rights is that this idea can serve as a practical organizing tool for breastfeeding advocates, on two distinct but importantly related levels. The language of rights is used by particular groups as a strategic choice within a democratic conversation. At the same time, that language also informs our sense of what constitutes a democratic conversation in the first place. An identifiable right to breastfeed can help advocates clarify their voice and sharpen the aim of their political activity, and it also importantly identifies the preserve of a democratic conversation where this rights claim can be heard.

In an important ideal sense, *rights* are uniquely connected to that historically-specific understanding of what constitutes a democratic conversation, both underwriting *who* is allowed to participate in that conversation and *what* that conversation should look like. In fact, these two dimensions of rights—the *who* and the *what* that they articulate and protect—are logically connected. Rights serve as at least a formal declaration that one *is*, that one has standing within some definable community (even if that community is broadly conceived, as in "all of humanity" or "all sentient creatures"). Rights, in other words, serve to articulate and preserve our identities, at least in particular contexts. Especially for groups who have been denied a viable political and social voice, the language of rights can play an important role in the cultivation of that voice. Rights serve to articulate the greater empowerment that such groups seek, and they provide an organizing focus that promotes group solidarity at important points in the development of a group's political and social consciousness. One might think, for example, of how the struggle for the right to vote galvanized both the feminist movement of the late nineteenth and early twentieth centuries and the civil rights movement of the late 1950s and early 1960s.

This moment of recognition conferred by rights, in turn, underwrites an ethic of equal respect that would ideally govern our interaction with other rights-bearing agents in a democratic society. Rights carry with them a sense of the inviolability of ourselves and those that we encounter; as Patricia Williams has put it, rights imply a "regard for another's fragile mysterious autonomy."[7] In our ideal of contemporary democratic politics, rights thus function as a hinge, joining the individual and group identities that they affirm with the more broadly conceived identity of the democratic community. The logic of rights suggests, therefore, that the identity of the community necessarily remains open to a plurality of identities. We can best become who we are, best fill our potentials and realize our identities, in a world in which we agree to let others become who they are. As Jürgen Habermas has argued, in defending his communicative underpinnings for a democratically-imagined society,

> Equal respect for *everyone* is not limited to those who are like us; it extends to the person of the other in his or her otherness. And solidarity with the other *as one of us* refers to the flexible "we" of a community that resists all substantive determinations and extends its permeable boundaries ever further.[8]

We argue that the identity-constituting force of rights has been instrumental in the achievements of feminism over the last century-and-a-half, but we argue that a simple adoption of a prorights posture on a cross-cutting issue such as breastfeeding carries certain risks. Thus, we want to endorse a more complex, and perhaps more cautious, understanding of breastfeeding rights.

This stance does not abandon the language of rights. Rights serve an important organizing purpose for their advocates, and their legal achievement can create a materially better world. Furthermore, we endorse the idea of rights as principles that should be afforded to all human beings. Even if we agree that those rights are the product of ongoing social negotiation rather than a transcendentally or naturally conferred essence, those rights embody a legitimate effort to reflectively define what it means to be a human being. And, generally speaking, we endorse women's right to be able to breastfeed in as broad a set of circumstances as possible, a practice that indisputably benefits both mother and child, in both physiological and psychological ways.

That endorsement of rights, however, points to a broader set of assumptions about the kind of democratic society in which rights might meaningfully be enacted. That broader democratic notion, and the plurality of voices that it encompasses, complicate the connection between breastfeeding as a right and breastfeeding as a marker of what constitutes good motherhood. We endorse a women's right to breastfeed, but it is not her duty. We want to avoid too strong a connection between the right to breastfeed and "good mothering." This is a particularly important consideration given the ways in which the icon of the good mother has been defined as white, middle class, nonworking, and nursing. The right to be heard entails an openness to the perspectives of all women, and it implies the broader conversation that women must negotiate to achieve their aims; a commitment to that kind of conversation cannot abridge or denounce, in advance, the decision not to breastfeed. It cannot, in any a priori way, claim to trump other rights that we endorse and with which a right to breastfeed must necessarily collide.

Thus, the rights approach that we are willing to endorse emphasizes the relational, inclusive dimension of rights and informs the inclusive picture of a democratic feminism that we sketched previously, opening the ongoing construction of its identity to others not currently included within its self-understanding. Ultimately, we argue, an identity burnished by its engagement in a broader democratic conversation can more fruitfully inform feminism's contribution to a broader social conversation about breastfeeding. Within the terms of feminism's self-understanding, a relational, inclusive focus is a fruitful diagnostic tool; it can help highlight, for example, the ways in which the decision to breastfeed occurs at the intersection of a variety of economic and social forces, and it reminds us that the decision to breastfeed impacts a number of rights-bearing actors. This descriptive power, however, is suggestive for feminism's normative orientation, grounding feminism's demand for equity in an ethic of relation and inclusion. As such, feminism can serve as a model for the larger democratic conversation and social world that it seeks to realize.

DANGEROUS RIGHTS? BREASTFEEDING RIGHTS AND BEYOND

The very strength of couching the struggle for a political objective in a discourse of rights is what makes that strategy dangerous. Why would we call such a framing strategy dangerous? Why do we think that it is dangerous for feminism? First, we want to reiterate that we are not disavowing a language of rights, nor claiming that a language of rights is incompatible with or inadvisable for feminism in general or its relationship to breastfeeding in particular. What we worry about, and what we want to insist upon in our general advocacy for breastfeeding rights, are the way rights, in terms of their very power and importance, risk fixing identities. In our effort to imagine an admirable feminist response to economically, politically, and socially constructed barriers to breastfeeding, we want to pause to remember that this fixing of identities has complex political consequences. At the very least, feminist politics should be alert to the possibilities of rights becoming burdens for some women.

Rights carry a strange set of paradoxes. As Wendy Brown suggests, rights, like all classical liberal institutions, "cease to be liberal as soon as they are attained."[9] We worry that a "right to breastfeed" will evolve into an obligation to breastfeed, irrespective of a woman's medical, social, or economic circumstances. Given the politically proven discursive strategies of isolating the "bad mother" as a socially undesirable category to be regulated and denied economic assistance,[10] we worry that the demand for breastfeeding rights carries with it an ideal of proper motherhood that would stigmatize women who choose not to breastfeed as "bad mothers."

Given the current reluctance of the courts to rule in favor of breastfeeding mothers, we are particularly worried that the dominant discursive strategies in favor of breastfeeding carry a class bias that is inattentive to the needs of lower-class, working mothers. Thus, though one strategy for realizing women's preference for breastfeeding is to appeal to private businesses, we worry that breastfeeding will devolve into a privilege reserved for middle-class and upper middle-class women whose particular skills are more in demand in a given labor market. By contrast, women from lower economic strata will be denied access to breastfeeding in the workplace and have to face an increasing social stigma associated with being a nonbreastfeeding mother. Likewise, as we have previously noted, some women should not breastfeed because of medical reasons. Some women may make reasonable choices not to breastfeed based on their career or public ambition. Breastfeeding rights can only be considered empowering for women when they are considered with reference to the specific contexts in which they are being applied. As Wendy Brown has said about rights in general, "it makes little sense to argue for them or against them separately from an analysis of the historical conditions, social powers and political discourses with which they converge or which they interdict."[11]

Furthermore, an analysis of breastfeeding rights reveals that questions about breastfeeding law and policy cannot be disentangled from the broader social, political, cultural, and natural environment in which those policies are initiated, contested, and implemented. Ultimately, for example, advocacy for breastfeeding rights is entwined with the broader struggles of the environmental justice movement. If, as the preponderance of evidence overwhelmingly indicates, "breast is best" for both the short-term and long-term health of the child and the mother, then the problem of environmental toxins contaminating breast milk becomes a question of justice, particularly for poorer women and women of color who are more likely to live in environmentally contaminated areas.

Recasting the demand for a right to breastfeed in these terms, as the child's right to receive the optimal developmental feeding option available, links the struggle for breastfeeding rights to a larger effort to ensure the rights of children to full access to opportunities for healthy development. As Maia Boswell-Penc argues, the zeal of some breastfeeding advocates to promote breastfeeding has made them hesitant to address the health risks associated with environmental toxins.[12] Though reasonable arguments can be made that breast milk, considered in balance, remains the best feeding option for the children of mothers whose milk has been contaminated, this should not prevent breastfeeding advocates from joining the fight for environmental justice. Especially if particular populations are systematically more likely to be exposed to these types of toxins than others, then the push for the right to breastfeed must be accompanied by efforts to secure environmental justice.[13]

From the perspective of the kind of inclusive, democratic feminism that we endorse, the right to breastfeed would be the right to choose to breastfeed, but this entails working to create the conditions in which women would really have the capacity to make a real choice in the practical contexts of their lives. Too often, *choice* has been used against the ability of women to autonomously control their lives; in our free market economy, for example, exhortations that women can choose their profession in a sphere of equal competition ignores the way in which work has been traditionally gendered, precluding women from a whole range of career opportunities. In the context of breastfeeding rights, we pursue a woman's right to make this important child-rearing choice. Yet, we need to remain critically vigilant about the ways the language of choice can constrain women's ability to make the most informed decision in the full context of their lives. In the courts, for instance, breastfeeding is trivialized as a choice that merely reflects women's preferences, not an important dimension of optimizing the health of the mother and child. On the other hand, the language of choice can be used to condemn mothers who choose not to breastfeed. And yet, today, we see that some women are not able to make the choice to breastfeed because of their economic circumstances.

From a feminist perspective, then, the right to breastfeed, while not absolute and not a duty, is a right that women should fight to win, as part of their broader effort to protect the space of choice that preserves their autonomous control of their bodies—which they give, in numerous ways, to nurture their children.

Notes

CHAPTER 1

1. Betty Friedan, *Feminine Mystique* (1963; repr., New York: W. W. Norton, 1997). The "first wave" was the women's suffrage movement of the nineteenth and early twentieth centuries.

2. See Sheryl Burt Ruzek, *The Women's Health Movement: Feminist Alternatives to Medical Control* (New York: Praeger, 1978).

3. Barbara Ehrenreich and Deirdre English, *For Her Own Good: Two Centuries of Experts' Advice to Women*, rev. ed. (New York: Anchor Books, 2005).

4. Ruzek, *Women's Health Movement*.

5. Cynthia Costello and Anne J. Stone, eds., *The American Woman 1994–1995: Where We Stand, Women and Health* (New York: W. W. Norton, 1994); Karen M. Kedrowski and Marilyn Stine Sarow, *Cancer Activism: Gender, Media and Public Policy* (Champaign: University of Illinois Press, 2007).

6. Bernice L. Hausman, *Mother's Milk: Breastfeeding Controversies in American Culture* (New York: Routledge, 2003).

7. Judith Galtry, "Extending the 'Bright Line': Feminism, Breastfeeding and the Workplace in the United States," *Gender and Society* 14 (2000): 295–317. See also Julia DeJager Ward, *La Leche League: At the Crossroads of Medicine, Feminism and Religion* (Raleigh: University of North Carolina Press, 2000).

8. Barbara Downs, "Fertility of American Women: June 2002," U.S. Census Bureau, Current Population Survey, 2003, http://www.census.gov/prod/2003pubs/p20–548.pdf (accessed November 28, 2006).

9. The World Health Organization, *The World Health Report 2002: Reducing Risks, Promoting Healthy Life* (2002), http://www.who.int/whr/2002/en/ (accessed November 14, 2006).

10. Mary Grace Kovar and others, "Review of Epidemiologic Evidence for an Association Between Infant Feeding and Infant Health," *Pediatrics* 74 (1984): 615–38.

11. American Academy of Pediatrics (AAP), "Breastfeeding and the Use of Human Milk," *Pediatrics* 100 (2005): 496–506.

12. Isabelle De Plaen and Michael Caplan, "Necrotizing Entercolitis," http://www.pediatrie.be/NECROT_%20ENTEROCOL.htm (accessed August 30, 2006).

13. Jon Weimar, *The Economic Benefits of Breastfeeding: A Review and Analysis*, U.S. Department of Agriculture, Food Assistance and Nutrition Research Report No. 13 (Washington, D.C.: U.S. Department of Agriculture, 2001).

14. American Liver Foundation, "Alpha-1 Antitrypsin Deficiency," http://www.liverfoundation.org/cgi-bin/dbs/articles.cgi?db=articles&uid=default&ID=1044&view_records=1 (accessed September 7, 2006). We estimate the number of affected infants based upon total number of births from the Centers for Disease Control and Prevention (CDC), National Center for Health Statistics (NCHS), "Birth/Natality (2004)" (Washington, D.C., 2006) http://www.cdc.gov/nchs/faststas/births.htm (accessed September 7, 2006).

15. John N. Udall and others, "Liver Disease in alpha-1 Antitrypsin Deficiency: A Retrospective Analysis of Early Breast- vs. Bottle-feeding," JAMA: *Journal of the American Medical Association* 253 (1985): 2679–82.

16. "Crohn's Disease in Children" (2006). Available at: http://digestive-disorders.health-cares.net/crohns-disease-children.php (accessed August 30, 2006).

17. S. Koletzko and others, "Role of Infant Feeding Practices in Development of Crohn's Disease in Childhood," *British Medical Journal* 298 (1989): 1617–18.

18. National Institutes of Health (NIH), National Institute of Diabetes and Digestive and Kidney Diseases (NIDDKD), National Digestive Diseases Clearinghouse, "What is Celiac Disease?" http://digestive.niddk.nih.gov/ddiseases/pubs/celiac/#1 (accessed December 19, 2006).

19. L. Greco and others, "Case Control Study on Nutritional Risk Factors in Celiac Disease," *Journal of Pediatric Gastroenterology and Nutrition* 7 (1988): 395–99.

20. American Urological Association, "Urinary Tract Infections in Children," http://www.urologyhealth.org/print/index.cfm?topic=146 (accessed August 30, 2006).

21. Alfredo Pisacone and others, "Breastfeeding and Urinary Tract Infection," *The Journal of Pediatrics* 120 (1992): 87–88.

22. Micheline Beaudry, Renee Dufour, and Sylvie Marcoux, "Relation Between Infant Feeding and Infections During the First Six Months of Life," *The Journal of Pediatrics* 126 (1995): 191–97.

23. Aimin Chen and Walter J. Rogan and others, "Breastfeeding and the Risk of Postneonatal Death in the United States," *Pediatrics* 113 (2004): 435–39; Anne L. Wright and others, "Breastfeeding and Lower Respiratory Tract Illness in the First Year of Life," *British Medical Journal* 299 (1989): 946–49; and Anne L. Wright and others, "Relationship of Infant Feeding to Recurrent Wheezing at Age 6 Years," *Archives of Pediatrics and Adolescent Medicine* 149 (1995): 758–63.

24. CDC Division of Bacterial and Mycotic Diseases, "*Haemophilus Influenzae* Serotype B (Hib) Disease" (2005), http://www.cdc.gov/ncidod/dbmd/diseaseinfo/haeminfluserob_t.htm (accessed August 30, 2006).

25. Beaudry and others, "Relation Between;" Stephen L. Cochi and others, "Primary Invasive *Haemophilus Influenzae* Type B Disease: A Population-Based Assessment of Risk Factors," *The Journal of Pediatrics* 108 (1985): 887–96; Gregory R. Istre and others, "Risk Factors for Primary Invasive Haemophilius Influenzae Disease: Increased Risk from Day Care Attendance and School-Aged Household Members," *The Journal of Pediatrics* 106 (1985): 190–95; and Arthur L. Frank and others, "Breastfeeding and Respiratory Virus Infection," *Pediatrics* 70 (1982): 239–45.

26. Kathryn Dewey and Laurie A. Nommsen-Rivers, "Differences in Morbidity Between Breast-fed and Formula-Fed Infants," *The Journal of Pediatrics* 126 (1995): 696–702; G. B. Aniansson and others, "A Prospective Cohort Study on Breast-feeding and Otitis Media in Swedish Infants," *Pediatric Infectious Diseases Journal* 13 (1993): 183–88; Burris Duncan and others, "Exclusive Breast-Feeding for at Least 4 Months Protects Against Otitis Media," *Pediatrics* 91 (1993): 867–72; and Jack L. Paradise, Barbara A. Elsterl, and Lingshi Tan, "Evidence in Infants with Cleft Palate That Breast Milk Protects Against Otitis Media," *Pediatrics* 94 (1994): 853–60.

27. CDC, "Sudden Infant Death Syndrome: Home" (2006), http://www.cdc.gov/SIDS/index.htm (accessed September 21, 2006); and CDC NCHS, "Infant Mortality Statistics from the 2003 Period Linked Birth/Infant Death Data Set," *National Vital Statistics Reports* 54 (2006).

28. R.P.K. Ford and others, "Breastfeeding and the Risk of Infant Death Syndrome," *International Journal of Epidemiology* 22 (1993): 885–90; and E. A. Mitchell and others, "Four Modifiable and Other Major Risk Factors for Cot Death: The New Zealand Study," *Journal of Paediatric and Child Health* 28 (1992): S3–8.

29. NIH, NIDDKD, "Prevalence of Diagnosed Diabetes in People Aged 20 Years and Younger, United States, 2005," http://diabetes.niddk.gov.dm/pubs/statistics/index.htm (accessed August 30, 2006).

30. AAP, "Breastfeeding and the Use of Human Milk," *Pediatrics* 115 (2005): 496–506; "Hertzel Gertstein, "Cow's Milk Exposure and Type I Diabetes Mellitus: A Critical Overview of the Clinical Literature," *Diabetes Care* 17 (1994): 13–19; Elizabeth J. Mayer and others, "Reduced Risk of IDDM Among Breastfed Children," *Diabetes* 37 (1988): 1625–32; and Suvi M. Virtanen and others, "Infant Feeding in Finnish Children <7 Yr Age with Newly Diagnosed IDDM," *Diabetes Care* 14 (1991): 415–17.

31. American Cancer Society, *Cancer Facts & Figures, 2006.* http://www.cancer.org/down loads/STT/CAFF2006PWSecured.pdf (accessed August 30, 2006); Chen and Rogan, "Breastfeeding and the Risk of Postneonatal Death in the United States;" Margaret K. Davis, David A. Savitz, and Barry I. Graubard, "Infant Feeding and Childhood Cancer," *The Lancet* 2 (1988): 365–68; and Xiao-Ou Shu and others, "Infant Breastfeeding and the Risk of Childhood Lymphoma and Leukaemia," *International Journal of Epidemiology* 24 (1995): 27–32.

32. American Academy of Allergy, Asthma and Immunology, "Media Resources Kit: Allergy Statistics," http://www.aaaai.org/media/resources/media_kit/allergy_statistics.stm (accessed September 8, 2006); and NIH, National Institute of Arthritis, Musuloskeletal and Skin Diseases (NIAMSD), *Handout on Health: Atopic Dematitis* (n.d.), http://www.niams.nih.gov/hi/topics/dermatitis/index.html (accessed November 14, 2006).

33. Ulla M. Saarinen and Merja Kajosaari, "Breastfeeding as Prophilaxis Against Atopic Disease: Prospective Follow-Up Study until 17 Years Old," *The Lancet* 346 (1995): 1065–69.

34. Ya Sun Wang and Shi Yi Wu, "The Effect of Exclusive Breastfeeding on Development and Incidence of Infection in Infants," *Journal of Human Lactation* 12 (1996): 27–30.

35. Mary Morrow-Tlucak, Richard H. Haude, and Claire B. Ernhart, "Breastfeeding and Cognitive Development in the First Two Years of Life," *Social Science and Medicine* 26 (1988): 635–39.

36. Erik Lyle Mortensen and others, "The Association between Duration of Breastfeeding and Adult Intelligence," *JAMA: The Journal of the American Medical Association* 287 (2002): 2365–72.

37. Chen and Rogan, "Breastfeeding and the Risk of Postneonatal Death in the United States."

38. S. Chua and others, "Influence of Breastfeeding and Nipple Stimulation on Postpartum Uterine Activity," *British Journal of Obstetrics and Gynaecology* 101 (1994): 804–5

39. Kathryn G. Dewey, M. Jane Henig, and Laurie A. Nommsen, "Maternal Weight-Loss Patterns During Prolonged Lactation," *American Journal of Clinical Nutrition* 58 (1993): 162–66.

40. Ronald H. Gray and others, "Risk of Ovulation During Lactation," *The Lancet* 335 (1990): 25–29.

41. National Osteoporosis Foundation, "Fast Facts," http://www.nof.org/osteoporosis/disease facts.htm (accessed November 14, 2006).

42. J. Melton III, and others, "Influence of Breastfeeding and Other Reproductive Factors on Bone Mass Later in Life," *Osteoporosis International* 3 (1993): 76–83.

43. Robert G. Cumming, and Robin J. Klineberg, "Breastfeeding and Other Reproductive Factors and the Risk of Hip Fractures in Elderly Women," *International Journal of Epidemiology* 22 (1993): 684–91.

44. American Cancer Society, *Breast Cancer Facts & Figures: 2005–2006*, http://www.cancer. org (accessed November 14, 2006).

45. Polly A. Newcomb and others, "Lactation and Reduced Risk of Premenopausal Breast Cancer," *The New England Journal of Medicine* 330 (1994): 81–87.

46. American Cancer Society, *Cancer Facts & Figures, 2006*.

47. Karin A. Rosenblatt, David B. Thomas, and the WHO Collaborative Study of Neoplasia and Steroid Contraceptives, "Lactation and the Risk of Epithelial Ovarian Cancer," *International Journal Epidemiology* 22 (1993): 192–97.

48. AAP, "Breastfeeding and the Use of Human Milk," 2005.

49. AAP, "Breastfeeding and the Use of Human Milk," 2005; AAP, "Human Milk, Breastfeeding and Transmission of Human Immunodeficiency Virus in the United States," *Pediatrics* 95 (1995): 977–79; and Elizabeth Cohen and Mirian Falco, "CDC Probes West Nile in Breast Milk," http://www.CNN.com/2002/HEALTH/conditions/09/27/west.nile.nursing/index.html (accessed October 4, 2002).

50. Kathryn Harrison, "Too Close to Home: Dioxin Contamination of Breast Milk and the Political Agenda," *Policy Sciences* 34 (2001): 35–62.

51. United States Department of Health and Human Services, "Breastfeeding, Newborn Screening and Service Systems," Goal 16–19, *Healthy People 2010*, http://www.health.gov/healthypeople/document/html (accessed June 6, 2002).

52. CDC, "CDC's National Immunization Data: Socioeconomic: 2003," http://www.cdc.gov/breastfeeding/data/NIS_data/2003/socio-demographic.htm (accessed August 29, 2006).

53. CDC, "CDC's National Immunization Data: Socioeconomic: 2003." These factors—highly educated mothers, and parents in a stable relationship who can afford wholesome foods during pregnancy and stimulating toys during infancy—may also explain why breastfed babies are more intelligent, on average, than formula-fed babies.

54. CDC, "CDC's National Immunization Data: Socioeconomic: 2003."

55. U.S. Department of Labor Bureau of Labor Statistics, *Women in the Labor Force: A Databook*, Report 973 (2004), http://www.bls.gov/cps/wlf-databook.htm (accessed August 29, 2006).

56. Barbara Downs, "Fertility of American Women: June 2002," U.S. Census Bureau, Current Population Survey, http://www.census.gov/prod/2003pubs/p20-548.pdf (accessed November 28, 2006).

57. Downs, "Fertility of American Women."

58. Anne Schneider and Helen Ingram, "Social Construction of Target Populations: Implications for Politics and Policy," *American Political Science Review* 87 (1993): 334–47.

CHAPTER 2

1. Patricia Stuart-Macadam, "Biocultural Perspectives on Breastfeeding," in *Breastfeeding: Biocultural Perspectives*, ed. Patricia Stuart-Macadam and Katherine A. Dettwyler (New York: Aldine De Gruyter, 1995), 7.

2. Valerie Fildes, "The Culture and Biology of Breastfeeding: An Historical Review of Western Europe," in *Breastfeeding: Biocultural Perspectives*, 101–2.

3. Fildes, "The Culture and Biology," 102.

4. Fildes, "The Culture and Biology," 102.

5. Fildes, "The Culture and Biology," 104.

6. Fildes, "The Culture and Biology," 104.

7. Paula A. Treckel, "Breastfeeding and Maternal Sexuality in Colonial America," *Journal of Interdisciplinary History* 20 (1989): 25–51.

8. Treckel, "Breastfeeding," 32–33.

9. Treckel, "Breastfeeding," 27.

10. Nancy Schrom Dye and Daniel Blake Smith, "Mother Love and Infant Death, 1750–1920," *The Journal of American History* 73 (1986): 329–53.

11. Dye and Smith, "Mother Love," 343.

12. Londa Schiebinger, *Nature's Body: Gender in the Making of Modern Science* (Boston: Beacon Press, 1993), 53.

13. Katherine A. Dettwyler, "Beauty and the Breast: The Cultural Context of Breastfeeding in the United States," in *Breastfeeding: Biocultural Perspectives*, 181.

14. Dettwyler, "Beauty and the Breast," 171.

15. Marilyn Yalom, *A History of the Breast* (New York: Ballantine Books, 1997).

16. Yalom, *A History*, 147–58.

17. Carolyn Latteier, *Breasts: The Women's Perspective on an American Obsession* (Binghamton, NY: The Haworth Press, 1998), 61–73.

18. As cited in Rebecca Kukla, "Ethics and Ideology in Breastfeeding Advocacy Campaigns," *Hypatia* 21 (2006): 166–67.

19. Kukla, "Ethics and Ideology," 167. See also Yalom, *A History*, 254–55, and Latteier, *Breasts*, 75.

20. Kukla, "Ethics and Ideology."

21. Lauri Umansky, "Breastfeeding in the 1990s: The Karen Carter Case and the Politics of Maternal Sexuality," in *Bad Mothers: The Politics of Blame in Twentieth Century America*, ed. Molly Ladd-Taylor and Lauri Umansky (New York: New York University Press, 1998). 299–309.

22. Rima Apple, *Mothers and Medicine: A Social History of Infant Feeding, 1890–1950* (Madison: The University of Wisconsin Press, 1987), 5.

23. Linda Blum, *At the Breast, Ideologies of Breastfeeding and Motherhood in the Contemporary United States* (Boston: Beacon Press, 1999), 21.

24. Blum, *At the Breast*, 21.

25. Blum, *At the Breast*, 21–22.

26. Blum, *At the Breast*, 22.

27. Blum, in fact, hypothesizes that lower rates of breastfeeding by contemporary black women reflects the indirect effect of this history in which they did not have ownership of their own bodies. This does not, in her view, mean that these women find themselves "deficient." Rather, she found that "some used humor or irony to criticize the moralism of the 'natural' and few used the term positively. After such a long history of oppression justified by their closeness to nature, their primitive, subhuman being, it makes sense that they would wary of such ideologies." Blum, *At the Breast*, 13–14.

28. Apple, *Mothers and Medicine*, 5–6.

29. Apple, *Mothers and Medicine*, 7.

30. Jacqueline H. Wolfe, "What Feminists Can Do for Breastfeeding and What Breastfeeding Can Do for Feminists," *Signs: Journal of Women in Culture and Society* 31 (2006): 397–424.

31. Wolfe, "What Feminists," 404–5.

32. Wolfe, "What Feminists, 404.

33. For a detailed discussion of the emergent women's movement during this period, see Barbara Ryan, *Feminism and the Women's Movement: Dynamics of Change in Social Movement Ideology and Activism* (New York: Routledge, 1992), 21–38.

34. Ryan, *Feminism and the Women's Movement*, 337.

35. Ryan, *Feminism and the Women's Movement*, 347.

36. For a discussion see Naomi Baumslag and Dia L. Michels, *Milk, Money and Madness: The Culture and Politics of Breastfeeding* (Westport, CT: Bergin and Garvey, 1995).

37. Blum, *At the Breast*, 28.

38. Jacqueline Wolfe, "Low Breastfeeding Rates and Public Health in the United States," *American Journal of Public Health* 93 (2003): 2,000–2,010.

39. Gerry E. Hendershoot, "Trends in Breast-Feeding," *Pediatrics* 74 (Suppl., 1984): 591–602.

40. Penny Van Esterik, *Beyond the Breast—Bottle Controversy* (New Brunswick, NJ: Rutgers University Press, 1989), 112.

41. Wolfe, "Low Breastfeeding Rates."

42. As quoted in Wolfe, "Low Breastfeeding Rates," 2,000.

43. Dye and Smith, "Mother Love and Infant Death," 353.

44. John P. Swann, "A History of the FDA," http://www.fda.gov/oc/history/historoffda/full text.html (accessed June 16, 2007).

45. Barbara Downs, "Fertility of American Women: June 2002," United States Census Bureau, Current Population Survey, http://www.census.gov/prod/2003pubs/p20–548.pdf (accessed November 28, 2006).

46. Wolfe, "What Feminists," 407.

47. Bernice L. Hausman, *Mother's Milk: Breastfeeding Controversies in American Culture* (New York: Routledge, 2003).

48. The notion of the disembodied mother is taken from Blum, *At the Breast,* 53.

49. Lynn Y. Weiner, "Reconstructing Motherhood: The La Leche League in Postwar America," *The Journal of American History* 80 (1994): 1357–81.

50. Wiener, "Reconstructing Motherhood." See also Christina G. Bobel, "Bounded Liberation: A Focused Study of La Leche League International," *Gender and Society* 15 (2001): 130–50.

51. Bobel, "Bounded Liberation," 131.

52. Bobel, "Bounded Liberation," 131.

53. La Leche League International, "Our Philosophy," http://www.lalecheleague.org/ (accessed June 16, 2007). These statements are taken verbatim from LLLI's Web page.

54. Blum, *At the Breast,* 72.

55. Blum, *At the Breast,* 72.

56. Julie DeJager Ward, *La Leche League: At the Crossroads of Medicine, Feminism, and Religion* (Chapel Hill: The University of North Carolina Press, 2000).

57. Ward, *La Leche League,* 3.

58. Ward, *La Leche League,* 3.

59. Ward, *La Leche League,* 4.

60. See Robert Karen, *Becoming Attached: Unfolding the Mystery of the Infant-Mother Bond and Its Impact on Later Life* (New York: Warner Books, 1994).

61. Chris Bobel, *The Paradox of Natural Mothering* (Philadelphia: Temple University Press, 2002), 48–72.

62. Bobel, *The Paradox,* 49.

63. Bobel, *The Paradox,* 67.

64. Bobel, *The Paradox,* 61–62.

65. Ward, *La Leche League,* 3.

66. American Academy of Pediatrics Work Group on Breastfeeding, "Breastfeeding and the Use of Human Milk," *Pediatrics* 100, no. 6 (December 1997): 1035.

67. American Dietetic Association, "Promoting and Supporting Breastfeeding," http://www.eatright.org/cps/rde/xchag/ada/hs.xsl/advocacy_1728_ENU_HTML.htm (accessed June 5, 2006), 1

68. Katherine R. Shealy and others, *The CDC Guide to Breastfeeding Interventions* (Atlanta, GA: Centers for Disease Control and Prevention, 2005); American Medical Association, "H-245.982 AMA Support for Breastfeeding," http://www.ana-assn.org/apps/pf_new/pf_online? (accessed June 5, 2006); U.S. Breastfeeding Committee, *Breastfeeding in the United States, A National Agenda* (Atlanta: U.S. Department of Health and Human Services Centers for Disease Control, 2001); Elizabeth Toledo and Jan Erickson, "NOW Demands Greater Acceptance and Access for Breastfeeding Mothers," http://www.now.org/nnt/05–98/breastfd.html (accessed June 5, 2006); and March of Dimes, "Breastfeeding," http://www.marchofdimes.com/pnhec/298_1061.asp (accessed June 5, 2006).

69. For a classic statement of the environmental justice ethos, see Robert Bullard, *Dumping in Dixie: Race, Class, and Environmental Quality* (Boulder: Westview Press, 2000).

70. For a discussion of this tension, see Maia Boswell-Penc, *Tainted Milk: Breastmilk, Feminisms, and the Politics of Environmental Degradation* (Albany: State University Press of New York, 2006), 6–7.

71. Edith White, *Breastfeeding and HIV/AIDS: The Research, the Politics, the Women's Responses* (Jefferson, NC: McFarland and Company, 1999).

72. Marian Thompson, Speech to the South Carolina La Leche League, April 29, 2006, Sullivan's Island, SC.

73. Hausman, *Mother's Milk*, 14.

74. Bobel, "Bounded Liberation."

75. Blum, *At the Breast*, 138–39.

76. See Kukla, "Ethics and Ideology."

CHAPTER 3

Earlier versions of this chapter were presented at the 2004 American Political Science Association meeting, the 2005 South Carolina Political Science Association meeting, and the 2006 Western Political Science Association meeting. We gratefully acknowledge the research assistance of Renee Capstraw and Emily Heckl. We are also indebted to the Winthrop University Research Council, which funded this research, and to the Winthrop University Social and Behavioral Research Laboratory which conducted the public opinion survey.

1. Associated Press, "Burger King Apologizes to Breast-feeding Mom," November 12, 2003, http://www.CNN.com (accessed November 12, 2003).

2. Associated Press, "Woman Kicked Off Plane for Breast-feeding: Files Complaint Saying She Was Being Discreet, Airline Disagrees," November 11, 2006, http://www.msnbc.com (accessed November 16, 2006).

3. Associated Press, "Lactivists: Where Is It OK to Breastfeed? *Babytalk* Magazine Generates Controversy with Nursing Cover," July 28, 2006, http://www.cnn.com.

4. "Man Assaulted in Breast-feeding on the Beach Brouhaha," *The (Myrtle Beach, SC) Sun News*, May 8, 2006, (accessed through Lexis Nexis database, December 5, 2006).

5. Holly Auer, "SC Laws Don't Protect Mothers Nursing in Public AH: Some Moms Struggle to Find Places to Breast-feed," *The (Charleston, SC) Post and Courier*, June 26, 2005, A1 (accessed through Custom Newspapers database, December 5, 2006); Christopher Evans, "Victoria's Secret Welcomes Breast-feeding Protesters," *The (Cleveland, OH) Plain Dealer*, July 2, 2006, B1 (accessed through Custom Newspapers database, December 5, 2006); and Jessica Heslam, "Moms Reveal Bust-Up Over Breast-feeding," *The Boston Herald*, June 24, 2006, 3 (accessed through Custom Newspapers database, December 5, 2006).

6. "Stars Who Are Normal or . . . Not Normal," *Star*, September 6, 2004, 36–37.

7. Samir Arora and others, "Major Factors Influencing Breastfeeding Rates: Mother's Perception of Father's Attitude and Milk Supply," *Pediatrics* 106 (2000): 67–71.

8. Arora and others, "Major Factors;" Heidi Littman, Sharon VanderBrug Medendorp, and Johanna Goldfarb, "The Decision to Breastfeed," *Clinical Pediatrics* 33 (2004): 214–19.

9. Gary L. Freed, J. Kennard Fraley, and Richard J. Schanler. "Attitudes of Expectant Fathers Regarding Breastfeeding," *Pediatrics* 90 (1992): 224–27.

10. "The 1995 Parenting Poll," *Parenting* (November 1995): 146–49.

11. Christine E. Peterson and Julie DeVanzo, "Why Are Teenagers in the United States Less Likely to Breast-Feed than Older Women?" *Demography* 29 (1992): 431–50.

12. Karen S. Corbett, "Explaining Infant Feeding Style of Low Income Black Women," *Journal of Pediatric Nursing* 15 (2000): 73–81; see also Arora and others, "Major Factors."

13. Arora and others, "Major Factors."

14. Nurit Guttman and Deena R. Zimmerman, "Low-income Mothers' Views on Breastfeeding," *Social Science and Medicine* 50 (2000): 1457–73.

15. Peterson and DeVanzo, "Why Are Teenagers?"

16. A third survey found in this database is a study of parents of children under age three. This study asked parents whether they had received any information about breastfeeding or bottle feeding from the hospital or birthing center. A large majority (81%) reported they had received such information. The entire survey is available at http://www.kaisernetwork.org.

17. This survey included a question to assess public knowledge of breast cancer. The survey was a 1979 study conducted by the National Cancer Institute. The survey found that only five percent of respondents were aware of the protective effect of breastfeeding. The entire survey is available at http://www.kaisernetwork.org.

18. The study included a question about news coverage of the 1998 World AIDS conference, where transmission of HIV through breast milk was discussed. Two-thirds of the survey respondents reported that they did not hear or see any coverage of this story. The entire survey is available at http://www.kaisernetwork.org.

19. Tawnya D. O'Keefe, Susan J. Henly, and Cindy M. Anderson, "Breastfeeding on Campus: Personal Experiences, Beliefs, and Attitudes of the University Community," *Journal of American College Health* (November 1998): 129.

20. Cordon B. Forbes and others, "Perceptions of the Woman Who Breastfeeds: The Role of Erotophobia, Sexism and Attitudinal Variables," *Sex Roles: A Journal of Research* 49 (2003): 379–88.

21. Ruowei li, Fred Fridinger, and Laurence Grummer-Strawn, "Public Perceptions of Breastfeeding Constraints," *Journal of Human Lactation* 18(2002): 227–35 and Rouwei Li and others, "Public Beliefs about Breastfeeding Politics in Various Settings, " *Journal of American Dietetic Association* 104 (2004): 1162–68.

22. Li, Fridinger, and Grummer-Strawn, "Public Perceptions" and Li and others, "Public Beliefs."

23. Abeda Hannan and others, "Regional Variation in Public Opinion about Breastfeeding in the United States," *Journal of Human Lactation* 21 (2005): 284.

24. Li and others, "Public Beliefs."

25. Margin of error of +/– 4.4%. The sample included telephone numbers within the Rock Hill exchange, but some respondents live outside the city limits of Rock Hill.

26. South Carolina is approximately 67 percent white, 29 percent African American, and 2.4 percent Latino; and the United States is 75 percent white, 12 percent African American, and 12.5 percent Latino. U.S. Census Bureau, "Quick Facts," http://www.census.gov (accessed March 7, 2006).

27. Seventy-six percent of adults in South Carolina hold a high school diploma and 20 percent have a Bachelor's degree or higher; median family income in South Carolina is $37,000. In the United States, 80 percent of the adult population holds a high school diploma, and 24 percent hold a Bachelor's degree or higher; median family income is $41,000. U.S. Census Bureau, "Quick Facts."

28. *USA Today*, "Presidential Vote by County—South Carolina," http://www.usatoday.com/news/politicselections/vote2004/PresidentialByCounty (accessed August 29, 2006).

29. Daniel J. Elazar, *American Federalism: A View from the States,* 3rd ed. (New York: Harper and Row, 1984).

30. Institute for Women's Policy Research, "The Status of Women in the States 2004: An Overview," Report # R265 (2004), http://www.iwpr.org (accessed March 7, 2006).

31. Centers for Disease Control and Prevention, "CDC's National Immunization Data: Socioeconomic: 2003," http://www.cdc.gov/breastfeeding/data/NIS_data/2003/socio-demographic.htm (accessed August 29, 2006).

32. Chi-square = 36.50; p < 0.000.

33. Li and others, "Public Beliefs."

34. Chi-square = 47.38, p < 0.001.

35. Chi-square = 18.51, p < 0.047.

36. Sonya Charles and Tricha Shivas, "Mothers in the Media: Blamed and Celebrated—An Examination of Drug Abuse and Multiple Births," *Pediatric Nursing* 28 (2002): 142–46; Dierdre D. Johnston and Debra H. Swanson, "Invisible Mothers: A Content Analysis of Motherhood Ideologies and Myths in Magazines," *Sex Roles: A Journal of Research* 21(2003): 13–33; Bronwyn Naylor, "The 'Bad' Mother in Media and Legal Texts," *Social Semiotics* 11 (2001): 155–76; Fiona E. Raitt and M. Suzanne Zeedyk, "Mothers on Trial: Discourses of Cot Death and Munchausen's Syndrome by Proxy," *Feminist Legal Studies* 12 (2004): 257–78; and Angela Wall, "Monstrous Mothers: Media Representations of Post-Menopausal Pregnancy," *Afterimage* 25 (1997): 14–16.

37. r = 0.187 for extra break time; r = 0.142 for a clean, private place; and r = 0.230 for a refrigerator; *p* < 0.05 in each case.

38. Chi-square = 6.33, p < 0.042.

39. Chi-square = 18.14, p < 0.001.

40. Chi-square = 16.65, p < 0.002.

41. Chi-square = 28.17, p < 0.000.

42. Chi-square = 10.03, p < 0.018.

43. Chi-square = 12.31, p < 0.002.

44. See for instance Thomas C. Wilson, "Trends in Tolerance toward Rightist and Leftist Groups," *Public Opinion Quarterly* 58 (1994): 539–56.

45. For a longer discussion about the rights of incarcerated women, please see Chapters 4 and 5. We also note that this survey did frame the issue of rights purely within the context of the mother; the study did not attempt to assess whether the public perceives that a child has a right to be breastfed.

46. J. David Johnson, "Factors Distinguishing Regular Readers of Breast Cancer Information in Magazines," *Women & Health* 26, no. 1 (1997): 7–27.

47. Ann M. Henderson, "Mixed Messages About the Meanings of Breast-feeding Representations in the Australian Press and Popular Magazines," *Midwifery* 15 (1999): 24–31.

48. Lesley Henderson, Jenny Kitzinger, and Josephine Green, "Representing Infant Feeding: Content Analysis of British Media Portrayals of Bottle Feeding and Breast Feeding," *British Medical Journal* 321 (2000): 1196–98.

49. Judith Manniën and others, "Breastfeeding Articles in the Australian Press: 1996–1999," *Breastfeeding Review* 10 (2002): 5–10.

50. James K. Friel and others, "The Effect of a Promotion Campaign on Attitudes of Adolescent Females Toward Breastfeeding," *Canadian Journal of Public Health* 80 (1989): 195–99.

51. Beth Potter, Judy Sheeshka, and Ruta Valaitis, "Content Analysis of Infant Feeding Messages in a Canadian Women's Magazine, 1945–1995," *Journal of Nutrition Education* 32

(2000): 196–203; and Kathryn T. Young, "American Conceptions of Infant Development from 1955 to 1984: What Experts Are Telling Parents," *Child Development* 61 (1990): 17–28.

52. Julie L. Andsager and Angela Powers, "Social or Economic Concerns: How News and Women's Magazines Framed Breast Cancer in the 1990s," *Journalism and Mass Communication Quarterly* 76 (1999): 531–50.

53. Wylie Burke and others, "Misleading Presentation of Breast Cancer in Popular Magazines." *Effective Clinical Practice* 4 (2001): 58–64; and Karen M. Kedrowski and Marilyn Stine Sarow, *Cancer Activism: Gender, Media and Public Policy* (Champaign: University of Illinois Press, 2007).

54. Renee Marinez, Ingrid Johnson-Robledo, Heather M. Ulsh, and Joan C. Chrisler, "Singing 'The Baby Blues': A Content Analysis of Popular Press Articles about Postpartum Affective Disturbances," *Women & Health* 31 (2000): 37–56.

55. Joseph E. Scott and Jack L. Franklin, "The Changing Nature of Sex References in Mass Circulation Magazines," *The Public Opinion Quarterly* 36 (1972): 80–86; and Gaye Tuchman, "Women's Depiction by the Mass Media," *Signs: The Journal of Women in Culture and Society* 4 (1979): 528–42.

56. Josephine Ballenger, "Uncovering Abortion: Sisterhood is Cautious," *Columbia Journalism Review* 30 (1992): 16; Myra Marx Ferree, "Resonance and Radicalism: Feminist Framing in the Abortion Debates of the United States and Germany," *The American Journal of Sociology* 109 (2003): 304–46; and Frederick Fico and Michael Drager, "News Stories about Conflict Generally Balanced," *Newspaper Research Journal* 22 (2001): 2.

57. Johnston and Swanson, "Invisible Mothers."

58. Anna M. Smith, "Mass-Market Magazine Portrayals of Working Mothers and Related Issues, 1987 and 1997," *Journal of Children and Poverty* 7 (2001): 101–19.

59. Charles and Shivas, "Mothers in the Media"; Johnston and Swanson, "Invisible Mothers"; Naylor, "The 'Bad' Mother in Media and Legal Texts"; Raitt and Zeedyk, "Mothers on Trial"; and Wall, "Monstrous Mothers."

60. Charles and Shivas, "Mothers in the Media."

61. All are among the women's magazines with the highest circulation rates in each category, according to the EP Magazine Database. These same publications also were used by Laurie Hoffman-Goetz and colleagues in their study of tobacco advertising targeted to African American women. Laurie Hoffman-Goetz and others, "Cancer Coverage and Tobacco Advertising in African-American Women's Popular Magazines," *Journal of Community Health* 22 (1997): 261–70.

62. Newspaper, television, and women's magazine.

63. Hard news stories are those with time-sensitive information and are considered information of general importance, such as events, discoveries, or conflicts. Soft news stories are defined as those with an emphasis on human interest, novelty, or have less immediacy than hard news. These definitions are adapted from Carole Rich, *Writing and Reporting News*, 3rd ed. (Belmont, CA: Wadsworth, 1998). See also Lesley Henderson and Jenny Kitzinger, "The Human Drama of Genetics: 'Hard' and 'Soft' Media Representations of Inherited Breast Cancer," *Sociology of Health and Illness* 21 (1999): 560–78.

64. A categorical level variable coded as 1 = positive; 2 = negative (breastfeeding is dangerous); 3 = negative (breastfeeding is difficult); 4 = negative (other); 5 = mixed; 0 = neutral.

These codes were derived from the findings of Ann Henderson in her study of mass media depictions of breastfeeding in Australia. Henderson, "Mixed Messages."

65. Judith Galtry, "Extending the 'Bright Line': Feminism, Breastfeeding, and the Workplace in the United States," *Gender & Society* 14, no. 2 (2000): 295–317.

66. Kim Painter, "A Little Breastmilk May Not Go a Long Way," *USA Today,* December 31, 1998, 6D.

67. Tabatha Walrond is a New York mother whose baby died of malnutrition even though she was breastfeeding him. In all likelihood, Walrond did not produce sufficient breast milk because she had undergone breast reduction surgery, and she had not been warned that this surgery might interfere with her ability to produce milk. Bernice L. Hausman, *Mother's Milk: Breastfeeding Controversies in American Culture* (New York: Routledge, 2003), 33–34.

68. Henderson, "Mixed Messages."

69. In addition, 64 stories, including all television news stories, were coded as neutral; the tone in another eight stories could not be determined (Chi-square 79.9, $p < .000$).

70. Judges and police were included as separate sources because of the cases such as Tabitha Walrond, and the experiences of women who were arrested on public indecency charges while breastfeeding in public. Judges are also important in child custody decisions and employment discrimination cases. This figure combines the coding categories of government official, judge, and police.

71. The American Academy of Pediatrics (AAP) could be classified as either medical/scientific professionals or a breastfeeding advocate. The AAP was a source in 5.8 percent of stories (see Table 3.7).

72. Elizabeth Olson, "U.S. Urged to Educate Women about Foods Linked to Dioxin," *New York Times,* July 2, 2003, A22.

73. Liz Galst, "Prevention: Babies Aren't the Only Beneficiaries of Breastfeeding," *New York Times,* June 22, 2003, Women's Health, p. 4.

74. Pass along readers are those who do not purchase the magazine themselves, but may read the stories at a doctor's office or library, or because the magazine was given to them by a friend or relative. Chi-square = 60.7; $p < 0.000$.

75. Chi-square = 12.5 $p < 0.002$.

76. Chi-square = 7.8; $p < 0.02$.

77. Chi-square = 12.5; $p < 0.002$.

78. Chi-square = 5.6; $p < 0.06$.

79. Chi-square = 6.8; $p < 0.033$.

80. Chi-square = 10.1; $p < 0.006$.

81. Chi-squire = 13.1; $p < 0.001$.

82. Chi-square = 15.3 and $p < 0.000$ in the case of mothers; Chi-square = 18.5 and $p < 0.000$ in the case of La Leche League; and Chi-square = 7.7 and $p < 0.021$ in the case of other advocates.

83. Julia DeJager Ward, *La Leche League: At the Crossroads of Medicine, Feminism and Religion* (Raleigh: University of North Carolina Press, 2000).

84. Linda Blum, *At the Breast: Ideologies of Breastfeeding and Motherhood in the Contemporary United States* (Boston: Beacon Press, 1999).

85. Laura Woliver, *The Political Geographies of Pregnancy* (Champaign-Urbana: University of Illinois Press, 2002).

86. Chi-square = 9.6; $p < 0.002$.

87. Chi-square = 13.8; $p < 0.000$.

88. Chi-square = 7.9; $p < 0.005$.

89. Chi-square = 4.7; $p < 0.032$ for positive stories and chi-square = 5.2; $p < 0.037$ for negative stories.

90. Chi-square = 5.2; $p < 0.037$.

91. Chi-square = 14.5; $p < 0.000$.

92. Chi-square = 7.3; $p < 0.011$.

93. Chi-square = 6.2; $p < 0.013$.

94. Blum, *At the Breast*; Ward, *La Leche League*.

95. Nancy Fraser, *Justice Interruptus: Critical Reflections on the "Postsocialist" Condition* (New York: Routledge, 1997).

CHAPTER 4

1. S. Prakash Sethi, *Multinational Corporations and the Impact of Public Advocacy on Corporate Strategy: Nestle and the Infant Formula Controversy* (Boston: Kluwer Academic Publishers, 1994).

2. United States Department of Health and Human Services (DHHS) Office on Women's Health, *HHS Blueprint for Action on Breastfeeding* (Washington, D.C.: DHHS, 2000).

3. David Satcher, "Healthy People 2000 Progress Review: Maternal and Infant Health," May 5, 1999, http://odphp.osophs.dhhs.gov/pubs/HP2000/PDF/prog_rvw/matinf99.pdf (accessed June 16, 2007). See also National Center for Health Statistics, *Healthy People 2000 Review, 1992* (Hyattsville, MD: Public Health Service, 1993).

4. DHHS Office of Disease Prevention and Health Promotion, *Healthy People 2010 Mid-Course Review*, December 19, 2006, http://www.healthypeople.gov/data/midcourse/ (accessed March 7, 2007).

5. DHHS Office on Women's Health, *HHS Blueprint*.

6. DHHS and the Ad Council, "Public Service Campaign to Promote Breastfeeding Awareness Launched," News Release, June 4, 2004; Suzanne G. Haynes, "National Breastfeeding Awareness Campaign Results: Babies were Born to Be Breastfed!" Presentation on Breastfeeding Campaign with Campaign Research Findings, August 1, 2005, http://www.4woman.gov/breastfeeding/campaign_results.pdf/ (accessed March 7, 2007).

7. Donna V. Porter, "Breastfeeding: Impact on Health, Employment and Society," CRS Report for Congress, RL 32002, July 18, 2003; and Douglas Reid Weimar, "Breastfeeding: Federal Legislation," CRS Report for Congress, RL 32908, October 12, 2006.

8. U.S. Department of Agriculture, "Legislative History of Breastfeeding Promotion Requirements in WIC" (2004), http:www.fns.usda.gov/wic/Breastfeeding/bfleghistory.htm (accessed February 14, 2004).

9. Food Research and Action Center, "Summary of Women, Infants and Children (WIC) Provisions of the 2004 Child Nutrition Reauthorization Act, Fact Sheet," http://www.frac.org/html/federal_food_programs/cnreauthor/WIC_Summary.html (accessed March 6, 2007).

10. U.S. Government Accountability Office (GAO), "Breastfeeding: Some Strategies Used to Market Infant Formula May Discourage Breastfeeding; State Contracts Should Better Protect Against Misuse of WIC Name," Report No. GAO-06–282, December 14, 2005; U.S.

Department of Agriculture, Food and Nutrition Service, "How to Apply: WIC Income Eligibility Guidelines 2006–2007," http://www.fns.usda.gov/wic/howtoapply/incomeguidelines.htm (accessed March 8, 2007).

11. Sara B. Fein and Brian Roe, "The Effect of Work Status on Initiation and Duration of Breast-Feeding," *American Journal of Public Health* 88 (1998): 1042–46; Judith Galtry, "Lactation and the Labor Market: Breastfeeding, Labor Market Changes and Public Policy in the United States," *Health Care for Women International* 18 (1997): 467–80; Porter, "Breastfeeding."

12. U.S. Department of Labor (DOL), Employment Standards Administration, "Fact Sheet #28: The Family and Medical Leave Act of 1993," http://dol.gov/esa/regs/compliance/whd/printpage.asp?REF+whdfs28.htm (accessed February 14, 2004).

13. Henry Wyatt Christup, "Litigating a Breastfeeding and Employment Case in the New Millenium," *Yale Journal of Law and Feminism* 12 (2000): 263–86; Isabelle Schallreuter Olson, "Out of the Mouth of Babes: No Mother's Milk for U.S. Children: The Law and Breastfeeding," *Hamline Law Review* 19 (1995): 269–311.

14. M. Margaret Conway, David W. Ahern, and Gertrude A. Steuernagel, *Women and Public Policy: A Revolution in Progress*, 3rd ed. (Washington, D.C.: Congressional Quarterly Press, 2005).

15. Transportation Safety Administration, "Traveling with Children," http://www.tsa.gove/travelers/airtravel/children/formula.shtm (accessed May 29, 2007).

16. La Leche League International, "Employed Breastfeeding Mothers Face New Obstacle," News release, September 12, 2006, http://www.lalecheleague.org/Release/employedobs.html (accessed May 29, 2007).

17. National Breastfeeding Campaign, "Log Rolling Spot" PSA text, November 2005, http://www.4woman.gov/breastfeeding/index.cfm?page=logroll (accessed March 7, 2007); Jacqueline Wolf, "What Feminists Can Do for Breastfeeding and What Breastfeeding Can Do for Feminists," *Signs: A Journal of Women in Culture and Society* 31 (2006): 397–424.

18. Rebecca Kukla, "Ethics and Ideology in Breastfeeding Advocacy Campaigns," *Hypatia* 21, no. 1 (2006): 157–80.

19. J. Chen and R. Li, "Racial and Socioeconomic Disparities in Breastfeeding—United States, 2004," *Morbidity and Mortality Weekly Report* 55 (2006): 335–39.

20. U.S. GAO, "Breastfeeding: Some Strategies."

21. Nazlie Baydar and others, "WIC Infant Feeding Practices Study: Summary of Findings," United States Department of Agriculture Food and Nutrition Service Office of Evaluation and Analysis, Contract No. 54–1398–003, November 1997; Srimathi Kannan, Betty Ruth Carruth, and Jean Skinner, "Cultural Influences on Infant Feeding Beliefs of Mothers," *Journal of American Dietetic Association* 99 (1999): 88–92.

22. Chen and Li, "Racial and Socioeconomic Disparities."

23. U.S. GAO, "Food Assistance: Information on WIC Sole-Source Rebates and Infant Formula Prices," Report no. GAO/RCED-98–146, May 1998.

24. DOL, "News Release: U.S. Department of Labor Takes Action to Protect Integrity of Unemployment Insurance Trust Funds," December 3, 2002, http://www.dol.gov/opa/media/press/opa/OPA2002672.htm (accessed December 4, 2002); DOL, "Commentary," UIPL 26–00 Attachment II, http://www.ows.doleta.gov/dmstree/uipl2k/uipl_2600a2.htm (accessed December 4, 2002).

25. DHHS Administration for Children and Families, Office of Public Affairs, "Welfare Reform Reauthorized," News Release, February 8, 2006, http://www.acf.hhs.gov/opa/spotlight/welfarereauthorized.htm (accessed March 6, 2007); DHHS Administration for Children and Families, "Office of Family Assistance Fact Sheet," October, 2006, http://www.acf.hhs.gov/opa/spotlight/welfarereauthorized.htm (accessed March 6, 2007); Deficit Reduction Act of 2005.

26. Linda Blum, *At the Breast: Ideologies of Breastfeeding and Motherhood in the Contemporary United States* (Boston: Beacon Press, 1991); Judith Galtry, "Maternal Employment and Breastfeeding: Policies and Practices in the United States and Sweden," BLCC Working paper #01–12 (Ithaca: Cornell Employment and Family Careers Institute, September, 2001); Galtry, "Lactation and Labor Market."

27. See Harry D. Krause and David D. Mayer, *Family Law in a Nutshell,* 4th ed. (St. Paul: Thomson West, 2003).

28. *Dike v. The School Board of Orange County, Florida,* 650 F. 2d. 783 (1981 U.S. App.).

29. As quoted in *Jacobson v. Regent Assisted Living* (1999 U.S. Dist.).

30. *Martinez v. NBC Inc. and MSNBC Inc.,* 49 F. Supp. 2d. 305 (1999 U.S. Dist.); and Maureen E. Eldredge, "The Quest for a Lactating Male: Biology, Gender and Discrimination," *Chicago-Kent Law Review* 80 (2005): 875–901.

31. *Bond v. Sterling, Inc.,* 77 F. Supp. 2d. 300 (1999 U.S. Dist.).

32. *Bond v. Sterling* (1999).

33. *Martinez v. MSNBC Inc.* (1999). All direct quotations are taken from this decision.

34. *Tozzi v. Advanced Medical Equipment, Inc. et al.* (2001 U.S. Dist.).

35. *Toyota v. Williams,* 534 U.S. 184; 122 S. Ct. 651 (2002).

36. DOL, Office of Disability Employment Policy, "Frequently Asked Questions," http://www.dol.gov/odep/faqs/federal.htm (accessed May 23, 2007).

37. *Bond v. Sterling* (1999).

38. *Gallegos v. Department of Interior,* 6 Fed. Appx. 865 (2001 U.S. App.).

39. See relevant portions of *Fejes v. Gilpin Ventures,* 960 F. Supp. 1487 (1997 U.S. Dist.) and *Jacobson v. Regent Assisted Living* (1999 U.S. Dist.).

40. *Wallace v. Pyro Mining Company,* 789 F. Supp. 867 (1990 U.S. Dist.).

41. *McNill v. New York City Department of Corrections,* 950 F. Supp. 564 (1996 U.S. Dist.).

42. Candace Saari Kovacic-Fleischer, "Litigating Against Employment Penalties for Pregnancy, Breastfeeding and Child Care," *Villanova Law Review* 44 (1999): 355–93; and Christup, "Litigating a Breastfeeding and Employment Case."

43. *Barrash v. Bowen,* 846 F. 2d. 927 (1988 U.S. App.).

44. *Fortier and Fortier v. US Steel Group* (2002 U.S. Dist.).

45. *Ruffino v. State Street Bank and Trust Company et al.,* 908 F. Supp. 1019 (1995 U.S. Dist.).

46. *Bremiller v. Cleveland Psychiatric Institute et al.,* 195 F. R. D. 1 (2000 U.S. Dist.).

47. *Donaldson et al. v. American Banco Corporation, Inc.,* 945 F. Supp. 1456 (1996 U.S. Dist.).

48. *Southerland v. Thigpen,* 784 F. 2d. 713 (1986 U.S. App.).

49. All quotations are from *Southerland v. Thigpen* (1986).

50. *U.S. v. Dyce,* 320 U.S. App. D.C. 1 91 F. 3d. 1462 (1996 U.S. App.).

51. *Berrios-Berrios v. Thornburg*, 716 F Supp. 987 (1989 U.S. Dist.).

52. Monique Anikwue, "Breast Is Still Best: An Argument in Favor of One HIV Positive Mother's Right to Breastfeed," *William and Mary Journal of Women and Law* 9 (2003): 479–454.

53. *Ploski v. Feder et al.*, 1999 U.S. Dist.

54. *Giguere v. Massanari*, 74 Soc. Sec. Rep. Service 55 (2001 U.S. Dist.).

55. *Walls v. Barnhart*, 79 Soc. Sec. Rep. Service 183 (2002 U.S. Dist.).

56. At least one scholar argues that the *Martinez* decision is flawed because the court failed to distinguish between pregnancy and lactation, considering the two as one event. Rather, when the two are separated, lactation does meet the definition of "disability" under the ADA because lactation does affect multiple bodily systems and limits women's capacity to work because of the need to eat and express milk or nurse frequently. See Hillary Von Rohr, "Lactation Litigation and the ADA Solution: A Response to *Martinez v. NBC*," *Washington University Journal of law and Policy* 4 (2000): 341–59.

57. *McNill v. New York City Department of Correction* (1996).

58. *Gilbert v. General Electric*, 429 U.S. 125 (1976).

59. See specifically *Wallace v. Pyro Mining* (1990), also Christup, "Litigating Breastfeeding"; Eldredge, "The Quest for a Lactating Male."

60. *Gallegos v. Deprtment of Interior* (2001).

61. *Southerland v. Thigpen* (1986).

62. Anne Schneider and Helen Ingram, "Social Construction of Target Populations: Implications for Politics and Policy," *American Political Science Review* 87 (1993): 334–47.

63. Helen Ingram and Anne Schneider, "The Choice of Target Populations," *Administration and Society* 23 (1991): 333–57.

64. Mark C. Donovan, *Taking Aim: Target Populations and the Wars on AIDS and Drugs* (Washington, D.C.: Georgetown University Press, 2001); Nancy Lynn Hoga, "The Social Construction of Target Populations and the Transformation of Prison-based AIDS Policy: A Descriptive Case Study," *Journal of Homosexuality* 32 (1997): 77–114; Jean Reith Schroedel and Daniel R. Jordan, "Senate Voting and Social Construction of Target Populations: A Study of AIDS Policy making, 1987–1992," *The Journal of Health Politics, Policy and Law* 23 (1998): 107–32.

65. One major drawback to using social construction theory, of course, is that it reduces women to one dimension: their lactation function. Certainly women are far more complex.

66. *Berrios-Berrios v. Thornburg* (1989).

67. *Southernland v. Thigpen* (1986) and *Berrios-Berrios v. Thornburg* (1989).

68. *Dike v. School Board of Orange County* (1981) and *Wallace v. Pyro Mining* (1990).

69. *Southerland v. Thigpen* (1986) and *Berrios-Berrios v. Thornburg* (1989).

70. Blum, *At the Breast*.

71. GAO, "Breastfeeding: Some Strategies."

72. HR 2236, 110th Congress, Breastfeeding Promotion Act of 2007.

73. HR 1369, 110th Congress, Family and Medical Leave Expansion Act.

74. S. 1074, 109th Congress, "HeLP America Act," "Harkin Pushes Comprehensive Wellness Initiative to Fight Chronic Disease, Obesity and Reduce Health Care Costs," News Release, May 18, 2005; Douglas R. Weimer, "Breastfeeding: Federal Legislation," CRS Report for Congress RL 32908, October 12, 2006.

75. Kukla, however, makes the point that the images typically proffered in breastfeeding campaigns—usually white, comfortably clothed, secluded in a private space—alienate some

women, particularly lower-class women and women of color, who do not have these types of bodies, or access to these kinds of spaces. Kukla, "Ethics and Ideology."

CHAPTER 5

1. The Supremacy Clause found in Article VI of the U.S. Constitution stipulates that all federal laws are supreme over all states and that federal laws preempt contradictory state laws.

2. Elizabeth N. Baldwin and Kenneth A. Friedman, "A Current Summary of Breastfeeding Legislation in the U.S." (2002), http://www.lalecheleague.org/Law?Bills8a.html (accessed May 28, 2002).

3. National Conference of State Legislatures (NCSL), "50 State Summary of Breastfeeding Laws," (February 2007), http://www.ncsl.org/programs/health/breast50.htm (accessed February 28, 2007).

4. NCSL, "50 State Summary."

5. NCSL, "50 State Summary."

6. 2003 Florida Statutes, Title XLVI, Chapter 847; Kentucky SB 106, http://www.lrc.ky.gov/record/06rs/sb106.htm (accessed May 22, 2007); NCSL, "50 State Laws."

7. These states are Connecticut, Georgia, Hawaii, Illinois, Minnesota, Tennessee, Oklahoma, and Rhode Island. NCSL, "50 State Summary."

8. The states that require employers to provide space are California, Connecticut, Georgia, Illinois, Minnesota, Rhode Island, and Tennessee. NCSL "50 State Summary."

9. These states are Texas, Virginia, Washington, and Wyoming. NCSL, "50 State Summary."

10. NCSL, "50 State Summary."

11. NCSL, "50 State Summary"; Mississippi Senate Bill 2419, 2006.

12. NCSL, "50 State Summary." This document also reports that Minnesota allows nursing mothers to be excused from jury service if they are not employed. We were not able to find this provision in our own search of the Minnesota state code, legislative Web site, and the state courts site. Therefore, we omitted it from Table 5.1.

13. Alaska code section 09.20.030.

14. New Jersey state code 2B:20-10.

15. South Carolina state code 14-7-860.

16. Tennessee state code, 22-1-104.

17. Texas state code, Art. 19.25. This law refers specifically to "grand jury service."

18. Michigan state code, 722.27a.

19. Maine state code, Title 19-A, section 1653.

20. S.B. 33, "Child Visitation Guidelines," 1997 General Session.

21. NCSL, "50 State Summary."

22. NCSL, "50 State Summary"; Michigan Vehicle Code, 257.710d; Douglas Reid Weimer, "Summary of State Breastfeeding Laws," CRS Report for Congress RL 31633, July 23, 2003.

23. Dumeriss Cruver-Smith, "Protecting Breast-feeding in Theory But Not in Practice," *Women's Rights Law Reporter* 19 (1998): 167–80; and Elizabeth N. Baldwin, "A Summary of Breastfeeding Legislation as of 2001," http://www.lalecheleague.org (accessed May 28, 2002).

24. Isabelle Schallreuter Olson, "Out of the Mouth of Babes: No Mother's Milk for U.S. Children. The Law and Breastfeeding," *Hamline Law Review* 19, no. 2 (Winter 1995): 269–311.

25. Cruver-Smith, "Protecting Breast-feeding."

26. Cruver-Smith, "Protecting Breast-feeding," 170.

27. Cruver-Smith, "Protecting Breast-feeding," 168.

28. Representative Chip Limehouse, Testimony before the Subcommittee on Special Laws, Judiciary Committee, South Carolina State Assembly, February 2006; Karen M. Kedrowski, Testimony before the Subcommittee on Special Laws, Judiciary Committee, South Carolina State Assembly, February 2006.

29. Carl Manning, "Bill Protects Breast-Feeding but Discreet a Wording Problem," *Associated Press*, March 11, 2005; and Carl Manning, "Breast-Feeding Bill Gets Renewed Life in Senate," *Associated Press*, February 16, 2006.

30. Emily F. Suski, "In One Place But Not the Other: When the Law Encourages Breastfeeding in Public While Simultaneously Discouraging It at Work," *UCLA Women's Law Journal* 12 (2001). 109–48.

31. Ohio Legislative Service Commission, "S.B. 41" Bill Summary and Comment, http://www.legislature.state.oh.us/analysis.cfm (accessed June 4, 2006).

32. *Derungs et al. v. Wal-MartStores Inc.*, 374 F.3d. 428; 2004 U.S. App. (6th Cir.).

33. For descriptions of these differing state laws see Laura Woliver, *Political Geographies of Pregnancy* (Champaign: University of Illinois Press, 2002); Melody Rose, *Safe, Legal and Unavailable? Abortion Politics in the United States* (Washington, D.C.: Congressional Quarterly Press, 2007); and Jean Reith Schroedel, *Is the Fetus a Person? A Comparison of Policies Across the 50 States* (Ithaca, NY: Cornell University Press, 2000).

34. Daniel J. Elazar, *American Federalism: A View from the States*, 3rd ed. (New York: Harper and Row, 1984); Cindy Simon Rosenthal, *When Women Lead: Integrative Leadership in State Legislatures* (New York: Oxford University Press, 1998); and Sue Thomas, *How Women Legislate* (New York: Oxford University Press, 1994).

35. The statistical tests we use are independent samples, t-tests, and correlations, as appropriate. We also report those findings that are statistically significant at the $p < 0.05$ level or approach significance at $0.05 < p < 0.10$ level.

36. Thomas, *How Women Legislate*; Rosenthal, *When Women Lead*; Ruth Mandel and Debra L. Dodson, "Do Women Office Holders Make a Difference?" in *The American Woman 1992–1993: A Status Report*, ed. Paula Reis and Anne J. Stone (New York: W.W. Norton, 1992), 149–77. For a conflicting view see Caroline J. Tolbert and Gertrude A. Steuernagel, "Women Lawmakers, State Mandates and Women's Health," *Women & Politics* 22 (2001): 1–39.

37. Center for American Women and Politics (CAWP), "Fact Sheet: Women in State Legislative Office," http://www.rci.rutgers.edu/~cawp/Facts.html#leg/ (accessed March 31, 2007).

38. Jocelyn Elise Crowley, "When Tokens Matter," *Legislative Studies Quarterly* 29 (2004): 109–36.

39. We chose to use this typology of state politics because it has been found to be strongly predictive in related policy areas, particularly family law. It also has some predictive power in the economic policy domain. Given the role of employers in the breastfeeding rights debate, this typology appeared all the more germane.

40. Elazar, *American Federalism*.

41. See Elazar, *American Federalism*, and Shirley Zimmerman, *Family Policies and Family Well-Being: The Role of Political Culture* (Newbury Park, CA: Sage Publications, 1992).

42. $p = 0.079$.

43. Coded as a "1" when the Democrats controlled both houses in the state legislature, and a "0" when there was Republican or shared control of the legislature. Nebraska was omitted from this analysis because its legislature is nonpartisan.

44. *p* < 0.037.

45. CAWP, "Fact Sheet."

46. Manning, "Bill Protects" and Manning, "Breast-feeding bill."

47. Harry D. Krause and David D. Meyer, *Family Law in a Nutshell*, 4th ed. (St. Paul: Thomson/Wadsworth, 2003).

48. *Stephon v. Malmed*, 30 PS. D. & C. 4th 510. 1996.

49. *Lalama v. Lalama*, 94 C.A. 1996 Ohio App.

50. *In Re: Marriage of Norton*, 640 P.2d. 254.

51. Mark Momjian, "Winning the Weaning War: Breastfeeding as a Factor in Child Custody Litigation," *American Journal of Family Law* 8 (1994): 135–39.

52. Kristen D. Hofheimer, "Breastfeeding as a Factor in Child Custody and Visitation Decisions," *Virginia Journal of Social Policy and Law* 5 (1998): 433.

53. Hofheimer, "Breastfeeding as a Factor."

54. *VCE v. JBE*, File No. CNo1–09752, Family Court of Delaware, 2003.

55. *Stelluto v. Stelluto*, Supreme Court of Louisiana, 914 So. 2d. 34, 2005.

56. *Stelluto v. Stelluto*.

57. *In Re. Austin L. and Brandon L.*, 2003 Cal. App.

58. *In Re: James et al.*, 1998 Ohio.

59. Monique Anikwue, "Breast Is Still Best: An Argument in Favor of One HIV Positive Mother's Right to Breastfeed," *William and Mary Journal of Women and Law* 9 (2003): 479–74.

60. *Juliette S. v. The Superior Court of Alameda County*, 2005 Cal. App.

61. *Commonwealth v. Michaud*, 14 Mass. App. Ct. 471; 440 N.E. 2d. 768, 1982 Mass., *The People v. Pointer*, 151 Cal. App. 3d. 1128 199 Cal. 1984.

62. *In the Matter of Justin Smith*, 2005 Ohio App. 149; *Laura T. v. Texas Department of Protective and Regulatory Services*, 1999 Tex. App.; *Snyder and Smith v. Scheerer and Scheerer*, 190 W. Va. 64; 436 S.E. 2d. 299 1993.

63. *In the Matter of Jeffrey S.*, 1998 Ohio App.

64. *In the Interest of Jane Doe*, 95 Haw. 183 20 P 3d. 616 2001.

65. Lauri Umansky, "Breastfeeding in the 1990s: The Karen Carter Case and the Politics of Maternal Sexuality," in *Bad Mothers: The Politics of Blame in Twentieth Century America*, ed. Molly Ladd-Taylor and Lauri Umansky (New York: New York University Press, 1998), 299–309.

66. *Kallir v. Friendly Ice Cream*, 93 A.D. 2d. 246 463 N.Y.S. 2d. 56 1983 N.Y. App. Div.

67. *American Red Cross v. Workers' Compensation Appeal Board*, 741 A. 2d. 244; 1999 Pa. Commw.

68. *Board of School Directors v. Rossetti*, 488 Pa. 125; 411 A. 2d. 486 1979.

69. *Perdrix-Wang v. Director, Employment Security Department* 42 Ark. App. 218; 856 S.W. 2d. 636 1993.

70. *Slivka v. Camden-Clark Memorial Hospital*, 215 W. Va. 109 S.E. 2d. 616, 2004 W. Va.

71. *Champagne v. Mid-Maine Medical Center*, 1998 ME 87; 711 a.2d. 842.

72. *Casey v. Southern Baptist Hospital*, 526 So. 2d. 1332; 1988 La. App.

73. *Finley et al. v. Culligan et al.*, 201 Wis. 2d. 611; 548 N.W. 2d. 854; 1996 Wisc. App.

74. *Bailey v. Lombard*, 101 Misc. 2d. 56; 420 N.Y.S. 2d. 650, 1979 NY Misc; *Pendergrass v. Toombs*, 24 Ore. App. 719; 546 P. 2d. 1103; 1976 Ore. App.

75. *Picco et al. v. Marmor et al.*, 203 Cal. App.

76. *Murillo v. Rite Stuff Foods*, 65 Cal. Ap. 4th 833; 77 Cal. Rpt. 2d. 12 1998 Cal. App.; *Trecost v. Trecost*, 202 W. Va. 129; 502 S.E. 2d. 445. 1998 W. Va.

77. *Hughes v. Moore*, 214 Va. 27; 197 S.E. 2d. 214; 1973 Va.

78. Martha Fineman, *The Neutered Mother: The Sexual Family and Other 20th Century Tragedies* (Oxford, UK: Routledge, 1995).

79. Lara M Gardner, "A Step Toward True Equality in the Workplace: Requiring Employer Accommodation for Breastfeeding Women," *Wisconsin Women's Law Journal* 7 (2002): 259–90.

80. Karen M. Kedrowski, correspondence to members of South Carolina Assembly Judiciary Committee members, February 3, 2006.

81. Krause and Meyer, *Family Law*, 179.

82. Gerar H. Seijts, "Milking the Organization? The Effect of Breastfeeding Accommodation on Perceived Fairness and Organizational Attractiveness," *Journal of Business Ethics* 40 (2002): 1–13.

CHAPTER 6

1. For a discussion of the negative connotations of "feminism," see Susan Faludi, *Backlash: The Undeclared War Against American Women* (New York: Doubleday, 1991), particularly the introductory chapter, "Blame It on Feminism."

2. For more detailed discussions of breastfeeding practices among African American women, see Kathi Barber, *The Black Women's Guide to Breastfeeding: The Definitive Guide to Nursing for African American Mothers* (Naperville, IL: Sourcebooks, Inc., 2005).

3. *Dike v. The School Board of Orange County, Florida* 650 F. 2d. 783. (1981 U.S. App.).

4. As summarized on La Leche League International's Web page: "Breastfeeding is enhanced and the nursing couple sustained by the loving support, help, and companionship of the baby's father. A father's unique relationship with his baby is an important element in the child's development from early infancy." La Leche League International, "La Leche League Philosophy," http://www.lalecheleague.org/philosophy.html?m=1,0,1 (accessed March 30, 2007).

5. See Julia DeJager Ward, *La Leche League: At the Crossroads of Medicine, Feminism and Religion* (Raleigh: University of North Carolina Press, 2000).

6. Workoptions.com, "Flexible Work for New Mothers," http://www.workoptions.com/bf_FWA.htm (accessed June 17, 2007).

7. Patricia Williams, *The Alchemy of Race and Rights: Diary of a Law Professor* (Cambridge, MA: Harvard University Press, 1991).

8. Jürgen Habermas, *The Inclusion of the Other: Studies in Political Theory*, ed. Ciaran Cronin and Pablo De Greiff (Cambridge, MA: The MIT Press, 1998), xxx–xxxvi.

9. Wendy Brown, *States of Injury: Power and Freedom in Late Modernity* (Princeton: Princeton University Press, 1995), 98.

10. Nancy Fraser and Linda Gordon, "A Genealogy of Dependency: Tracing a Keyword of the U.S. Welfare State," in *Justice Interruptus: Critical Reflections on the "Postsocialist" Condition*, ed. Nancy Fraser (New York: Routledge, 1997).

11. Brown, *States of Injury*, 8.

12. A similar dilemma faces breastfeeding advocates when confronting the devastation of the HIV/AIDS virus. Though some advocates would minimize the risk of transmitting the disease through breast milk, most of the medical community accepts findings that breastfeeding while infected with the virus doubles a child's risk of contracting the virus. More importantly may be the need for advocates to join their work in coalition with the fight against this disease. See Edith White, *Breastfeeding and HIV/AIDS: The Research, the Politics, the Women's Responses* (Jefferson, NC: McFarland and Company, 1999).

13. See Maia Boswell-Penc, *Tainted Milk: Breastmilk, Feminisms, and the Politics of Environmental Degradation* (Albany: State University Press of New York, 2006).

Bibliography

American Academy of Allergy, Asthma and Immunology. "Media Resources Kit: Allergy Statistics." Available: http://www.aaaai.org/media/resources/media_kit/allergy_statistics.stm. (Accessed September 8, 2006.)

American Academy of Pediatrics. "Human Milk, Breastfeeding and Transmission of Human Immunodeficiency Virus in the United States." *Pediatrics* 95, no. 5 (1995): 997–79.

———. "Breastfeeding and the Use of Human Milk." *Pediatrics* 100, no. 6 (1997): 1035–39.

———. "Breastfeeding and the Use of Human Milk." *Pediatrics* 115, no. 2 (2005): 496–506.

American Cancer Society. *Cancer Facts & Figures, 2006.* Available: http://www.cancer.org/downloads/STT/CAFF2006PWSecured.pdf. (Accessed August 30, 2006.)

———. *Breast Cancer Facts & Figures: 2005–2006.* Available: http://www.cancer.org. (Accessed November 14, 2006.)

American Dietetic Association. "Promoting and Supporting Breastfeeding." Available: http://www.eatright.org/cps/rde/xchag/ada/hs.xsl/advocacy_1728_ENU_HTML.htm. (Accessed June 5, 2006.)

American Liver Foundation. "Alpha-1 Antitrypsin Deficiency." Available: http://www.liverfoundation.org/cgi-bin/dbs/articles.cgi?db=articles&uid=default&ID=1044&view_records=1. (Accessed September 7, 2006.)

American Medical Association. "H-245.982 AMA Support for Breastfeeding." Available: http://www.ama-assn.org/apps/pf_new/pf_online? (Accessed June 5, 2006.)

American Urological Association. "Urinary Tract Infections in Children." Available: http://www.urologyhealth.org/print/index.cfm?topic=146. (Accessed August 30, 2006.)

Aniansson, G., B. Alm, B. Andersson, A. Hakansson, P. Larsson, O. Nylen, H. Peterson, P. Rigner, M. Svanborg, H. Sabharwal, and C. Svanborg. "A Prospective Cohort Study on Breast-feeding and Otitis Media in Swedish Infants." *Pediatric Infectious Diseases Journal* 13 (1993): 183–88.

Anikwue, Monique. "Breast Is Still Best: An Argument in Favor of One HIV Positive Mother's Right to Breastfeed." *William and Mary Journal of Women and Law* 9 (2003): 479–94.

Apple, Rima. *Mothers and Medicine: A Social History of Infant Feeding, 1890–1950.* Madison: The University of Wisconsin Press, 1987.

Arora, Samir, Cheryl McJunkin, Julie Wehrer, and Phyllis Kuhn. "Major Factors Influencing Breastfeeding Rates: Mother's Perception of Father's Attitude and Milk Supply." *Pediatrics* 106, no. 5 (2000): 67–71.

Associated Press. "Burger King Apologizes to Breast-feeding Mom." November 12, 2003. Available: http://www.CNN.com. (Accessed November 12, 2003.)

———. "Woman Kicked Off Plane for Breast-feeding: Files Complaint Saying She Was Being Discreet, Airline Disagrees." November 11, 2006. Available: http://www.msnbc.com. (Accessed November 16, 2006.)

———. "Lactivists: Where Is It OK to Breastfeed? *Babytalk* Magazine Generates Controversy with Nursing Cover." July 27, 2006. Available: http://www.cnn.com. (Accessed July 28, 2006.)

Auer, Holly. "SC Laws Don't Protect Mothers Nursing in Public AH: Some Moms Struggle to Find Places to Breast-feed." *The (Charleston, SC) Post and Courier,* June 26, 2005, p. A1. (Accessed through Custom Newspapers database, December 5, 2006.)

Baldwin, Elizabeth N. "A Summary of Breastfeeding Legislation as of 2001." Available: http://www.lalecheleague.org. (Accessed May 28, 2002.)

———, and Kenneth A. Friedman. "A Current Summary of Breastfeeding Legislation in the U.S." Available: http://www.lalecheleague.org/Law?Bills8a.html. (Accessed May 28, 2002.)

Barber, Kathi. *The Black Woman's guide to Breastfeeding: The Definitive Guide to Nursing for African American Mothers.* Naperville, IL: Sourcebooks, Inc., 2005.

Baumslag, Naomi, and Dia L. Michels. *Milk, Money and Madness: The Culture and Politics of Breastfeeding.* Westport, CT: Bergin and Garvey, 1995.

Baydar, Nazli, Margaret McCann, Rick Williams, Eric Vesper, and Patricia McKinney. "WIC Infant Feeding Practices Study: Summary of Findings." U.S. Department of

Agriculture Food and Nutrition Service Office of Evaluation and Analysis. Contract No. 54–1398–003, November 1997.

Beaudry, Micheline, Renee Dufour, and Sylvie Marcoux. "Relation Between Infant Feeding and Infections During the First Six Months of Life." *The Journal of Pediatrics* 126, no. 2 (1995): 191–97.

Blum, Linda. *At the Breast: Ideologies of Breastfeeding and Motherhood in the Contemporary United States*. Boston: Beacon Press, 1991.

Bobel, Christina. "Bounded Liberation: A Focused Study of La Leche League International." *Gender and Society* 15, no. 1 (2001): 130–50.

———. *The Paradox of Natural Mothering*. Philadelphia: Temple University Press, 2002.

Boswell-Penc, Maia. *Tainted Milk: Breastmilk, Feminisms, and the Politics of Environmental Degradaton*. Albany: State University of New York Press, 2006.

Brown, Wendy. *States of Injury: Power and Freedom in Late Modernity*. Princeton, NJ: Princeton University Press, 1995.

Bullard, Robert. *Dumping in Dixie: Race, Class, and Environmental Quality*. Boulder, CO: Westview Press, 2000.

Center for American Women and Politics. "Fact Sheet: Women in State Legislative Office." Available: http://www.rci.rutgers.edu/~cawp/Facts.html#leg/. (Accessed March 31, 2007.)

Centers for Disease Control and Prevention. "CDC's National Immunization Data: Socioeconomic: 2003." http://www.cdc.gov/breastfeeding/data/NIS_data/2003/socio-demographic.htm. (Accessed August 29, 2006.)

———. "Sudden Infant Death Syndrome: Home." http://www.cdc.gov/SIDS/index.htm. (Accessed September 21, 2006.)

———. Division of Bacterial and Mycotic Diseases. "*Haemophilus Influenzae* Serotype B (Hib) Disease." http://www.cdc.gov/ncidod/dbmd/diseaseinfo/haeminfluserob_t.htm. (Accessed August 30, 2006.)

———. National Center for Health Statistics. "Births/Natality (2004)." http://www.cdc.gov/nchs/faststas/births.htm. (Accessed September 7, 2006.)

———. "Infant Mortality Statistics from the 2003 Period Linked Birth/Infant Death Data Set." *National Vital Statistics Reports*, 54, no. 16 (2006).

Charles, Sonya, and Tricha Shivas. "Mothers in the Media: Blamed and Celebrated—An Examination of Drug Abuse and Multiple Births." *Pediatric Nursing* 28, no. 2 (2002): 142–46.

Chen, Aimin, and Walter J. Rogan. "Breastfeeding and the Risk of Postneonatal Death in the United States." *Pediatrics* 113, no. 5 (2004): 435–39.

Chen, J., and R. Li. "Racial and Socioeconomic Disparities in Breastfeeding—United States, 2004." *Morbidity and Mortality Weekly Report* 55, no. 12 (2006): 335–39.

Chen, Yue. "Synergistic Effect of Passive Smoking and Artificial Feeding on Hospitalization for Respiratory Illness in Early Childhood." *Ches*, 95, no. 5 (1989): 1004–7.

Christup, Henry Wyatt. "Litigating a Breastfeeding and Employment Case in the New Millenium." *Yale Journal of Law and Feminism* 12, no. 2 (winter): 263–86.

Chua, S., S. Arulkumaran, I. Lim, N. Selamat, and S. S. Ratnam. "Influence of Breastfeeding and Nipple Stimulation on Postpartum Uterine Activity." *British Journal of Obstetrics and Gynaecology* 101 (1994): 804–5.

Cochi, Stephen L., David W. Fleming, Allen W. Hightower, Khanchit Limpakarn-janarat, Richard R. Facklam, J. David Smith, R. Keith Sikes, and Claire V. Broome. "Primary Invasive *Haemophilus Influenzae* Type B Disease: A Population-Based Assessment of Risk Factors." *The Journal of Pediatrics* 108, no. 6 (1985): 887–96.

Cohen, Elizabeth, and Mirian Falco. "CDC Probes West Nile in Breast Milk." http://www.CNN.com/2002/HEALTH/conditions/09/27/west.nile.nursing/index.html. (Accessed October 4, 2002.)

Collins, Patricia Hill. *Black Sexual Politics: African Americans, Gender, and the New Racism.* New York: Routledge, 2005.

Conway, M. Margaret, David W. Ahern, and Gertrude A. Steuernagel. *Women and Public Policy: A Revolution in Progress,* 3rd ed. Washington, D.C.: Congressional Quarterly Press, 2005.

Conway, M. Margaret, Gertrude Steuernagel, and David W. Ahern. *Women and Political Participation,* 2nd ed. Washington, D.C.: Congressional Quarterly Press, 2005.

Corbett, Karen S. "Explaining Infant Feeding Style of Low Income Black Women." *Journal of Pediatric Nursing* 15, no. 2 (2000): 73–81.

Costello, Cynthia, and Anne J. Stone, eds. *The American Woman 1994–1995: Where We Stand, Women and Health.* New York: W.W. Norton, 1994.

"Crohn's Disease in Children." http://digestive-disorders.health-cares.net/crohns-disease-children.php. (Accessed August 30, 2006.)

Crowley, Jocelyn Elise. "When Tokens Matter." *Legislative Studies Quarterly* 29, no. 1 (2004): 109–36.

Cruver-Smith, Dumeriss. "Protecting Breast-Feeding in Theory But Not in Practice." *Women's Rights Law Reporter* 19, no. 2 (1998): 167–80.

Cumming, Robert G., and Robin J. Klineberg. "Breastfeeding and Other Reproductive Factors and the Risk of Hip Fractures in Elderly Women." *International Journal of Epidemiology* 22, no. 4 (1993): 684–91.

Davis, Margarett K., David A. Savitz, and Barry I. Graubard. "Infant Feeding and Childhood Cancer." *The Lancet* 2, no. 8607 (1988): 365–68.

De Plaen, Isabelle, and Michael Caplan. "Necrotizing Entercolitis." Available: http://www.pediatrie.be/NECROT_%20ENTEROCOL.htm. (Accessed August 30, 2006.)

Dewey, Kathryn G., M. Jane Henig, and Laurie A. Nommsen. "Maternal Weight-Loss Patterns During Prolonged Lactation." *American Journal of Clinical Nutrition* 58 (1993): 162–66.

Dewey, Kathryn G., M. Jane Henig, and Laurie A. Nommsen-Rivers. "Differences in Morbidity Between Breast-fed and Formula-Fed Infants." *The Journal of Pediatrics* 126, no. 5 (1995): 696–702.

Donovan, Mark C. *Taking Aim: Target Populations and the Wars on AIDS and Drugs.* Washington, D.C.: Georgetown University Press, 2001.

Downs, Barbara. "Fertility of American Women: June 2002." U.S. Census Bureau, Current Population Survey. Available: http://www.census.gov/prod/2003pubs/ p20–548.pdf. (Accessed November 28, 2006.)

Duncan, Burris, John Ey, Catharine J. Holberg, Anne L. Wright, Fernando D. Martinez, and Lynn M. Taussig. "Exclusive Breast-Feeding for at Least 4 Months Protects Against Otitis Media." *Pediatrics* 91, no. 5 (1993): 867–72.

Dye, Nancy Schrom, and Daniel Blake Smith. "Mother Love and Infant Death, 1750–1920." *The Journal of American History* 73, no. 2 (1986): 329–53.

Ehrenreich, Barbara, and Deirdre English. *For Her Own Good: Two Centuries of Experts' Advice to Women*, rev. ed. New York: Anchor Books, 2005.

Elazar, Daniel J. *American Federalism: A View from the States*, 3rd ed. New York: Harper and Row, 1984.

Eldredge, Maureen E. "The Quest for a Lactating Male: Biology, Gender and Discrimination." *Chicago-Kent Law Review* 80 (2005): 875–901.

Evans, Christopher. "Victoria's Secret Welcomes Breast-feeding Protesters." *The (Cleveland, OH) Plain Dealer,* July 2, 2006, p. B1. (Accessed through Custom Newspapers database, December 5, 2006.)

Faludi, Susan. *Backlash: The Undeclared War Against American Feminism.* New York: Doubleday, 1991.

Fein, Sara B., and Brian Roe. "The Effect of Work Status on Initiation and Duration of Breast-Feeding." *American Journal of Public Health* 88, no. 7 (1998): 1042–46.

Fineman, Martha. *The Neutered Mother: The Sexual Family and Other 20th Century Tragedies.* Oxford, UK: Routledge, 1995.

Food Research and Action Center. "Summary of Women, Infants and Children (WIC) Provisions of the 2004 Child Nutrition Reauthorization Act. Fact Sheet. Available: http://www.frac.org/html/federal_food_programs/cnreauthor/WIC_ Summary.html. (Accessed March 6, 2007.)

Forbes, Gordon B., Leah E. Adams-Curtis, Nicole R. Hamm, and Kay B. White. "Perceptions of the Woman Who Breastfeeds: The Role of Erotophobia, Sexism and Attitudinal Variables." *Sex Roles: A Journal of Research* 49, no. 7–8 (2003): 379–88.

Ford, R.P.K., B. J. Taylor, E. A. Mitchell, S. A. Enright, A. W. Stewart, D. M. O. Becroft, R. Scragg, I. B. Hassall, D.M.J. Barry, E. M. Allen, and A. P. Roberts. "Breastfeeding and the Risk of Infant Death Syndrome." *International Journal of Epidemiology* 22, no. 5 (1993): 885–90.

Ford, Richard T. *Racial Culture: A Critique.* Princeton, NJ: Princeton University Press, 2006.

Frank, Arthur L., Larry H. Taber, W. P. Glezen, Gary L. Kasel, Christine R. Wells, and Abel Paredes. "Breastfeeding and Respiratory Virus Infection." *Pediatrics* 70, no. 2 (1982): 239–45.

Fraser, Nancy. *Justice Interruptus: Critical Reflections on the "Postsocialist" Condition.* New York: Routledge, 1997.

Freed, Gary L., J. Kennard Fraley, and Richard J. Schanler. "Attitudes of Expectant Fathers Regarding Breastfeeding." *Pediatrics* 90, no. 2 (1992): 224–27.

Friedan, Betty. *The Feminine Mystique.* New York: W. W. Norton, 1997. First published 1963 by Dell.

Friel, James K., Nancy I. Hudson, Suzan Banoub, and Abraham Ross. "The Effect of a Promotion Campaign on Attitudes of Adolescent Females Toward Breastfeeding." *Canadian Journal of Public Health* 80, no. 3 (1989): 195–99.

Galst, Liz. "Prevention: Babies Aren't the Only Beneficiaries of Breastfeeding." *New York Times* June 22, 2003, Women's Health, p. 4.

Galtry, Judith. "Lactation and the Labor Market: Breastfeeding, Labor Market Changes and Public Policy in the United States." *Health Care for Women International* 18 (1997): 467–80.

———. "Extending the 'Bright Line': Feminism, Breastfeeding, and the Workplace in the United States." *Gender & Society* 14, no. 2 (2000): 295–317.

———. "Maternal Employment and Breastfeeding: Policies and Practices in the United States and Sweden." BLCC Working paper #01–12. September. Ithaca: Cornell Employment and Family Careers Institute, September, 2001.

Gardner, Lara M. "A Step Toward True Equality in the Workplace: Requiring Employer Accommodation for Breastfeeding Women." *Wisconsin Women's Law Journal* 7 (2002): 259–90.

Gerstein, Hertzel. "Cow's Milk Exposure and Type I Diabetes Mellitus: A Critical Overview of the Clinical Literature." *Diabetes Care* 17, no. 1 (1994): 13–19.

Gray, Ronald H., Oona M. Campbell, Ruben Apelo, Susan S. Eslami, Howard Zacur, Rebecca M. Ramos, Judith C. Gehret, and Miriam H. Labbock. "Risk of Ovulation During Lactation." *The Lancet* 335, no. 8680 (1990): 25–29.

Greco, L., S. Auricchio, M. Mayer, and M. Grimaldi. "Case Control Study on Nutritional Risk Factors in Celiac Disease." *Journal of Pediatric Gastroenterology and Nutrition* 7 (1998): 395–99.

Guttman, Nurit, and Deena R. Zimmerman. "Low-income Mothers' Views on Breastfeeding." *Social Science and Medicine* 50 (2000): 1457–73.

Habermas, Jürgen. *The Inclusion of the Other: Studies in Political Theory.* Ed. Ciaran Cronin and Pablo De Greiff. Cambridge, MA: The MIT Press, 1998.

Hannan, Abeda, Ruowei Li, Sandra Benton-Davis, and Laurence Gummer- Strawn. "Regional Variation in Public Opinion About Breastfeeding in the United States." *Journal of Human Lactation* 21, no. 3 (2005): 284.

"Harkin Pushes Comprehensive Wellness Initiative to Fight Chronic Disease, Obesity and Reduce Health Care Costs." News Release, Senator Tom Harkin. May 18, 2005.

Harrison, Kathryn. "Too Close to Home: Dioxin Contamination of Breast Milk and the Political Agenda." *Policy Sciences* 34 (2001): 35–62.

Hausman, Bernice L. *Mother's Milk: Breastfeeding Controversies in American Culture*. New York: Routledge, 2003.

Haynes, Suzanne G. "National Breastfeeding Awareness Campaign Results: Babies were Born to Be Breastfed!" Presentation on Breastfeeding Campaign with Campaign Research Findings, August 1, 2005. Available: http://www.4woman.gov/ breastfeeding/campaign_results.pdf/. (Accessed March 7, 2007.)

Heath-Cares.net. "Crohn's Disease in Children." Available: http://disgestive-disorders.health-cares.net/. (Accessed August 30, 2006.)

Hendershoot, Gerry E. "Trends in Breast-Feeding." *Pediatrics* 74 (Suppl, 1984): 591–602.

Henderson, Ann M. "Mixed Messages About the Meanings of Breast-feeding Representations in the Australian Press and Popular Magazines." *Midwifery* 15 (1999): 24–31.

Henderson, Lesley, and Jenny Kitzinger. "The Human Drama of Genetics: 'Hard' and 'Soft' Media Representations of Inherited Breast Cancer." *Sociology of Health and Illness* 21 (1999): 560–78.

Henderson, Lesley, Jenny Kitzingerand Josephine Green, "Representing Infant Feeding: Content Analysis of British Media Portrayals of Bottle Feeding and Breast Feeding." *British Medical Journal* 321: (2000) 1196–98.

Heslam, Jessica. "Moms Reveal Bust-Up Over Breast-feeding." *The Boston Herald*. June 24, 2006, p. 3. (Accessed through Custom Newspapers database, December 5, 2006.)

Hofheimer, Kristen D. "Breastfeeding as a Factor in Child Custody and Visitation Decisions." *Virginia Journal of Social Policy and the Law* 5 (1998): 433.

Hoga, Nancy Lynn. "The Social Construction of Target Populations and the Transformation of Prison-based AIDS Policy: A Descriptive Case Study." *Journal of Homosexuality* 32, no. 3–4 (1997): 77–114.

Ingram, Helen, and Anne Schneider. "The Choice of Target Populations." *Administration and Society* 23, no. 3 (1991): 333–57.

Institute for Women's Policy Research. "The Status of Women in the States 2004: An Overview." Report # R265. Available: http://www.iwpr.org. (Accessed March 7, 2006.)

Istre, Gregory R., Judy S. Conner, Claire V. Broome, Allen Hightower, and Richard S. Hopkins. "Risk Factors for Primary Invasive Haemophilius Influenzae Disease: Increased Risk from Day Care Attendance and School-Aged Household Members." *The Journal of Pediatrics* 106 no. 2 (1985): 190–95.

Johnston, Dierdre D., and Debra H. Swanson. 2003. "Invisible Mothers: A Content Analysis of Motherhood Ideologies and Myths in Magazines." *Sex Roles: A Journal of Research* 21 (2003): 13–33.

Kannan, Sirmathi, Betty Ruth Carruth, and Jean Skinner. "Cultural Influences on Infant Feeding Beliefs of Mothers." *Journal of American Dietetic Association* 99, no. 1 (1999): 88–92.

Karen, Robert. *Becoming Attached: Unfolding the Mystery of the Infant-Mother Bond and Its Impact on Later Life*. New York: Warner Books, 1994.

Kedrowski, Karen M. "Testimony Before Special Laws Subcommittee." February 1, 2006.

———. Memo to Members of the State Judiciary Committee. February 3, 2006.

Kedrowski, Karen M., and Marilyn Stine Sarow. *Cancer Activism: Gender, Media and Public Policy*. Champaign: University of Illinois Press, 2007.

Koletzko, S., P. Sherman, M. Corey, A. Griffiths, and C. Smith. "Role of Infant Feeding Practices in Development of Crohn's Disease in Childhood." *British Medical Journal* 298 (1989): 1617–18.

Kovacic-Fleischer, Candace Saari. "Litigating Against Employment Penalties for Pregnancy, Breastfeeding and Childcare." *Villanova Law Review* 44, no. 3 (1999): 355–93.

Kovar, Mary Grace, Mary K. Serdula, James S. Marks, and David W. Fraser. "Review of the Epidemiologic Evidence for an Association between Infant feeding and Infant Health." *Pediatrics* 74, Suppl. (184): 615–38.

Krause, Harry D., and David D. Meyer. *Family Law in a Nutshell*, 4th ed. St. Paul: Thomson/Wadsworth, 2003.

Kukla, Rebecca. "Ethics and Ideology in Breastfeeding Advocacy Campaigns." *Hypatia* 21, no. 1 (2006): 157–80.

La Leche League International. "La Leche League Philosophy." Available: http://www.lalecheleague.org/philosophy.html?m=1,0,1. (Accessed March 30, 2007.)

———. "Employed Breastfeeding Mothers Face New Obstacle." News Release, September 12, 2006. Available: http://www.llli.org/Release/employedobs.html. (Accessed May 29, 2007.)

Latteier, Carolyn. *Breasts: The Women's Perspective on an American Obsession*. New York: The Haworth Press, 1998.

Li, Rouwei, Fred Fridinger, and Laurence Grummer-Strawn. "Public Perceptions of Breastfeeding Constraints." *Journal of Human Lactation* 18, no. 3 (2002): 227–35.

Li, Rouwei, Jason Hsia, Fred Fridinger, Abeda Hussain, Sandra Benton-Davis, and Laurence Grummer-Strawn. "Public Beliefs about Breastfeeding Politics in Various Settings." *Journal of American Dietetic Association* 104, no. 7 (2004): 1162–68.

Littman, Heidi, Sharon VanderBrug Medendorp, and Johanna Goldfarb. "The Decision to Breastfeed." *Clinical Pediatrics* 33, no. 4 (2004): 214–19.

"Man Assaulted in Breast-feeding on the Beach Brouhaha." *The (Myrtle Beach, SC) Sun News*, May 8, 2006. (Accessed through Lexis Nexis database, December 5, 2006.)

Mandel, Ruth, and Debra L. Dodson. "Do Women Office Holders Make a Difference?" In *The American Woman 1992–1993: A Status Report*, ed. Paula Reis and Anne J. Stone. New York: W. W. Norton, 1992, pp. 149–77.

Manniën, Judith, Winette E. van den Brandhof, Ellen McIntyre, and Janet E. Hiller. "Breastfeeding Articles in the Australian Press: 1996–1999." *Breastfeeding Review* 10, no. 1 (2002): 5–10.

Manning, Carl. "Bill Protects Breast-feeding but Discreet Wording a Problem." Associated Press State and Local Wire. March 11, 2005. (Accessed through Lexis-Nexis database, March 31, 2007.)

———. "Breast-feeding Bill Gets Renewed Life In Senate." Associated Press State and Local Wire. February 16, 2006. (Accessed through Lexis-Nexis database, June 2006.)

March of Dimes. "Breastfeeding." Available: http://www.marchofdimes.com/pnhec/298_1061.asp. (Accessed June 5, 2006.)

Mayer, Elizabeth J., Richard F. Hamman, Elizabeth C. Gay, Dennis C. Lezotte, David A. Savitz, and Georgeanna J. Klingensmith. "Reduced Risk of IDDM Among Breastfed Children." *Diabetes* 37 (1988): 1625–32.

Melton, L. J. III, S. C. Bryant, H. W. Wahner, W. M. O'Fallon, G. D. Malkasian, H. L. Judd, and B. L. Riggs. "Influence of Breastfeeding and Other Reproductive Factors on Bone Mass Later in Life." *Osteoporosis International* 3 (1993): 76–83.

Mitchell, E. A., B. J. Taylor, R.P.K. Ford, A. W. Stewart, D.M.O. Becroft, J.M.D. Thompson, R. Scragg, I. B. Hassall, D.M.J. Barry, E. M. Allen, and A. P. Roberts. "Four Modifiable and Other Major Risk Factors for Cot Death: The New Zealand Study." *Journal of Paediatric and Child Health* 28, Suppl. 1 (1992): S3–8.

Momjian, Mark. "Winning the Weaning War: Breastfeeding as a Factor in Child Custody Litigation." *American Journal of Family Law* 8 (1994): 135–39.

Morrow-Tlucak, Mary, Richard H. Haude, and Claire B. Ernhart. "Breastfeeding and Cognitive Development in the First Two Years of Life." *Social Science and Medicine* 26, no. 6 (1988): 635–39.

Mortensen, Erik Lyle, Kim Fleisher Michelsen, Stephanie A. Sanders, and June Machover Reinisch. "The Association Between Duration of Breastfeeding and Adult Intelligence." *JAMA: The Journal of the American Medical Association* 287, no. 18 (2002): 2365–72.

National Breastfeeding Campaign. "Log Rolling Spot" PSA text. November, 2005. Available: http://www.4woman.gov/breastfeeding/index.cfm?page=logroll. (Accessed March 7, 2007.)

National Center for Health Statistics. *Healthy People 2000 Review, 1992.* Hyattsville, MD: Public Health Service, 1993.

National Conference of State Legislatures. "50 State Summary of Breastfeeding Laws." February 2007. Available: http://www.ncsl.org/programs/health/breast50.htm. (Accessed February 28, 2007.)

National Institutes of Health, National Institute of Arthritis, Musuloskeletal and Skin Diseases (NIAMSD). *Handout on Health: Atopic Dematitis.* http://www.niams.nih.gov/hi/topics/dermatitis/index.html. (Accessed November 14, 2006.)

National Institutes of Health, National Institute of Diabetes, and Digestive and Kidney Diseases (NIDDKD). "Prevalence of Diagnosed Diabetes in People Aged 20 Years and Younger, United States, 2005." Available: http://diabetes.niddk.gov.dm/pubs/statistics/index.htm. (Accessed August 30, 2006.)

National Institutes of Health, National Institute of Diabetes, and Digestive and Kidney Diseases (NIDDKD), National Digestive Diseases Information Clearinghouse. "What Is Celiac Disease?" Available: http://digestive.niddk.nih.gov/ddiseases/pubs/celiac/#1. (Accessed December 19, 2006.)

National Osteoporosis Foundation. "Fast Facts." Available: http://www.nof.org/osteoporosis/diseasefacts.htm. (Accessed November 14, 2006.)

Naylor, Bronwyn. "The 'Bad' Mother in Media and Legal Texts." *Social Semiotics* 11, no. 2 (2001): 155–76.

Newcomb, Polly A., Barry E. Storer, Matthew P. Longnecker, Robert Mittendorf, E. Robert Greenberg, Richard W. Clapp, Kenneth Burke, Walter C. Willett, and Brian MacMahon. "Lactation and Reduced Risk of Premenopausal Breast Cancer." *The New England Journal of Medicine* 330, no. 2 (1994): 81–87.

O'Keefe, Tawnya D., Susan J. Henly, and Cindy M. Anderson. "Breastfeeding on Campus: Personal Experiences, Beliefs, and Attitudes of the University Community." *Journal of American College Health* (November 1998): 129–34.

Olson, Elizabeth. "U.S. Urged to Educate Women about Foods Linked to Dioxin." *New York Times*, July 2, 2003, p. A22.

Olson, Isabelle Schallreuter. "Out of the Mouth of Babes: No Mother's Milk for U.S. Children. The Law and Breastfeeding." *Hamline Law Review* 19, no. 2 (Winter 1995): 269–311.

Paradise, Jack L., Barbara A. Elsterl, and Lingshi Tan. "Evidence in Infants with Cleft Palate That Breast Milk Protects Against Otitis Media." *Pediatrics* 94, no. 6 (1994): 853–60.

Peterson, Christine E., and Julie DeVanzo. "Why Are Teenagers in the United States Less Likely to Breast-feed than Older Women?" *Demography* 29, no. 3 (1992): 431–50.

Pisacone, Alfredo, Liberatore Graziano, Gianfranco Mazzarella, Benedetto Scarpellino, and Gregorio Zona. "Breastfeeding and Urinary Tract Infection." *The Journal of Pediatrics* 120, no. 1 (1992): 87–88.

Porter, Donna V. "Breastfeeding: Impact on Health, Employment and Society." CRS Report for Congress, RL 32002. July 18, 2003.

Potter, Beth, Judy Sheeshka, and Ruth Valaitis. "Content Analysis of Infant Feeding Messages in a Canadian Women's Magazine, 1945 to 1995." *Journal of Nutrition Education* 32, no. 4 (2000): 196–203.

Raitt, Fiona E., and M. Suzanne Zeedyk. "Mothers on Trial: Discourses of Cot Death and Munchausen's Syndrome by Proxy." *Feminist Legal Studies* 12 (2004): 257–78.

Rich, Carole. *Writing and Reporting News*, 3rd ed. Belmont, CA: Wadsworth, 1998.

Rose, Melody. *Safe, Legal and Unavailable? Abortion Politics in the United States.* Washington, D.C.: Congressional Quarterly Press, 2007.

Rosenblatt, Karin A., David B. Thomas, and the WHO Collaborative Study of Neoplasia and Steroid Contraceptives. "Lactation and the Risk of Epithelial Ovarian Cancer." *International Journal Epidemiology* 22, no. 2 (1993): 192–97.

Rosenthal, Cindy Simon. *When Women Lead: Integrative Leadership in State Legislatures.* New York: Oxford University Press, 1998.

Ruzek, Sheryl Burt. *The Women's Health movement: Feminist Alternatives to Medical Control.* New York: Praeger, 1978.

Ryan, Barbara. *Feminism and the Women's Movement: Dynamics of Change in Social Movement Ideology and Activism.* New York: Routledge, 1992.

Saarinen, Ulla M., and Merja Kajosaari. "Breastfeeding as Prophilaxis Against Atopic Disease: Prospective Follow-Up Study until 17 Years Old." *The Lancet* 346, no. 8982 (1995): 1065–69.

Satcher, David. "Healthy People 2000 Progress Review: Maternal and Infant Health." May 5, 1999. Available: http://odphp.osophs.dhhs.gov/pubs/HP2000/PDF/prog_rvw/matinf99.pdf. (Accessed June 16, 2007.)

Schiebinger, Londa. *Nature's Body: Gender in the Making of Modern Science.* Boston: Beacon Press, 1993.

Schneider, Anne, and Helen Ingram. "Social Construction of Target Populations: Implications for Politics and Policy." *American Political Science Review* 87, no. 2 (1993): 334–47.

Schroedel, Jean Reith. *Is the Fetus a Person? A Comparison of Policies Across the 50 States.* Ithaca, NY: Cornell University Press, 2000.

Schroedel, Jean Reith, and Daniel R. Jordan. "Senate Voting and Social Construction of Target Populations: A Study of AIDS Policy Making, 1987–1992." *The Journal of Health Politics, Policy and Law* 23, no. 1 (1998): 107–32.

Seijts, Gerard H. "Milking the Organization? The Effect of Breastfeeding Accommodation on Perceived Fairness and Organizational Attractiveness." *Journal of Business Ethics* 40 (2002): 1–13.

Sethi, S. Prakash. *Multinational Corporations and the Impact of Public Advocacy on Corporate Strategy: Nestle and the Infant Formula Controversy.* Boston: Kluwer Academic Publishers, 1994.

Shealy, Katherine R., Ruowei Li, Sandra Benton-Davis, and Laurence M. Grummer-Strawn. *The CDC Guide to Breastfeeding Interventions.* Atlanta: U.S. Department of Health and Human Services and Centers for Disease Control and Prevention, 2005.

Shu, Xiao-Ou, John Clemens, Wei Zheng, Da Ming Ying, Bu Tian Ji, and Fan Jin. "Infant Breastfeeding and the Risk of Childhood Lymphoma and Leukaemia." *International Journal of Epidemiology* 24, no. 1 (1995): 27–32.

"Stars Who Are Normal or…Not Normal." *Star,* September 6, 2004: 36–37.

Stuart-Macadam, Patricia, and Katherine A. Dettwyler, eds. *Breastfeeding: Biocultural Perspectives*. New York: Aldine De Gruyer, 1995.

Suski, Emily F. "In One Place But Not Another: When the Law Encourages Breastfeeding in Public While Simultaneously Discouraging it at Work." *UCLA Women's Law Journal* 12, no. 19 (2001): 109–148.

Swann, John P. "History of the FDA." Available: http://www.fda.gov/oc/history/historyoffda/fulltext.html. (Accessed June 16, 2007.)

"The 1995 Parenting Poll." *Parenting*, November 1995: 146–49.

Thomas, Sue. *How Women Legislate*. New York: Oxford University Press, 1994.

Thompson, Marian. Speech to the South Carolina La Leche League. Sullivan's Island, SC. April 29, 2006.

Tolbert, Caroline J., and Gertrude A. Steuernagel. "Women Lawmakers, State Mandates and Women's Health." *Women & Politics* 22, no. 1 (2001): 1–39.

Toledo, Elizabeth, and Jan Erikson. "NOW Demands Greater Acceptance and Access for Breastfeeding Mothers." Available: http://www.now.org/nnt/05–98/breastfd.html. (Accessed June 5, 2006.)

Transportation Safety Administration. "Traveling with Children." Available: http://www.tsa.gov/travelers/airtravel/children/index.shtm#4. (Accessed May 29, 2007).

Treckel, Paula A. "Breastfeeding and Maternal Sexuality in Colonial America." *Journal of Interdisciplinary History* 20, no. 1 (989): 25–51.

Udall, John N., Marvin Dixon, Anna Newman, James Wright, Brent James, and Kurt J. Bloch. "Liver Disease in alpha-1 Antitrypsin Deficiency: A Retrospective Analysis of the Influence of Early Breast- vs. Bottle-feeding." *JAMA: Journal of the American Medical Association* 253, no. 18 (1985): 2679–82.

Umanksy, Lauri. "Breastfeeding in the 1990s: The Karen Carter Case and the Politics of Maternal Sexuality." In *Bad Mothers: The Politics of Blame in Twentieth Century America*, ed. Molly Ladd-Taylor and Lauri Umansky. New York: New York University Press, 1998, 299–309.

United States Breastfeeding Committee. *Breastfeeding in the United States: A National Agenda*. Rockville, MD: U.S. Department of Health and Human Services, Health Resources and Services Administration, Maternal and Child Health Bureau, 2001.

United States Census Bureau. "Quick Facts." Available: http://www.census.gov. (Accessed March 7, 2006.)

United States Department of Agriculture. "Legislative History of Breastfeeding Promotion Requirements in WIC." Available: http:www.fns.usda.gov/wic/Breastfeeding/bfleghistory.htm. (Accessed February 14, 2004.)

United States Department of Agriculture, Food and Nutrition Service. "How to Apply: WIC Income Eligibility Guidelines 2006–2007." Available: http://www.fns.usda.gov/wic/howtoapply/incomeguidelines.htm. (Accessed March 8, 2007.)

United States Department of Health and Human Services. "Breastfeeding, Newborn Screening and Service Systems." Goal 16–19. *Healthy People 2010*. Available: http://www.health.gov/healthypeople/document/html. (Accessed June 6, 2002.)

United States Department of Health and Human Services and the Ad Council. "Public Service Campaign to Promote Breastfeeding Awareness Launched." News Release, June 4, 2004.

United States Department of Health and Human Services, Administration for Children and Families, Office of Public Affairs. "Welfare Reform Reauthorized." News Release, February 8, 2006. Available: http://www.acf.hhs.gov/opa/spotlight/welfare reauthorized.htm. (Accessed March 6, 2007.)

United States Department of Health and Human Services, Administration for Children and Families, Office of Public Affairs. "Office of Family Assistance Fact Sheet." October, 2006. Available: http://www.acf.hhs.gov/opa/spotlight/welfarere authorized.htm. (Accessed March 6, 2007.)

United States Department of Health and Human Services, Office of Disease Prevention and Health Promotion. *Healthy People 2010 Mid-Course Review*. December 19, 2006. Available: http://www.healthypeople.gov/data/midcourse/. (Accessed March 7, 2007.)

United States Department of Labor. "News Release: U.S. Department of Labor Takes Action to Protect Integrity of Unemployment Insurance Trust Funds." December 3, 2002. Available: http://www.dol.gov/opa/media/press/opa/OPA2002672. htm. (Accessed December 4, 2002.)

———. "Commentary." UIPL 26–00 Attachment II. N.d. Available: http://www. ows.doleta.gov/dmstree/uipl2k/uipl_2600a2.htm. (Accessed December 4, 2002.)

United States Department of Labor, Bureau of Labor Statistics. *Women in the Labor Force: A Databook*. Report 973. (2004). Available: http://www.bls.gov/cps/ wlf-databook.htm. (Accessed August 29, 2006.)

United States Department of Labor, Employment Standards Administration. "Fact Sheet #28: The Family and Medical Leave Act of 1993." Available: http://dol. gov/esa/regs/compliance/whd/printpage.asp?REF+whdfs28.htm. (Accessed February 14, 2004.)

United States Department of Labor, Office of Disability Employment Policy. "Frequently Asked Questions." Available: http://www.dol.gov/odep/faqs/federal.htm. (Accessed May 23, 2007.)

United States Government Accountability Office. "Food Assistance: Information on WIC Sole-Source Rebates and Infant Formula Prices." Report No. GAO/ RCED-98–146. May, 1998.

———. "Breastfeeding: Some Strategies Used to Market Infant Formula May Discourage Breastfeeding; State Contracts Should Better Protect against Misuse of WIC Name." Report No. GAO-06–282, December 4, 2005.

USA Today. "Presidential Vote by County—South Carolina." Available: http://www. usatoday.com/news/politicselections/vote2004/PresidentialByCounty. (Accessed August 29, 2006.)

Van Esterik, Penny. *Beyond the Breast-Bottle Controversy*. New Brunswick, NJ: Rutgers University Press, 1989.

Virtanen, Suvi M., Leena Rasanen, Antti Aro, Jaana Lindstrom, Henna Sippola, Raisa Lounamaa, Liisa Toivanen, Jaakko Tuomilehto, Hans K. Akerblom, and Childhood Diabetes in Finland Study Group. "Infant Feeding in Finnish Children <7 Yr Age with Newly Diagnosed IDDM." *Diabetes Care* 14, no. 5 (1991): 415–17.

Von Rohr, Hillary. "Lactation Litigation and the ADA Solution: A Response to *Martinez v. NBC.*" *Washington University Journal of law and Policy* 4, no. 341 (2000): 341–59.

Wall, Angela. "Monstrous Mothers: Media Representations of Post-Menopausal Pregnancy." *Afterimage* 25, no. 2 (1997): 14–16.

Wang, Ya Sun, and Shi Yi Wu. "The Effect of Exclusive Breastfeeding on Development and Incidence of Infection in Infants." *Journal of Human Lactation* 12, no. 1 (1996): 27–30.

Ward, Julia DeJager. *La Leche League: At the Crossroads of Medicine, Feminism and Religion.* Raleigh: University of North Carolina Press, 2000.

Weimar, Jon. *The Economic Benefits of Breastfeeding: A Review and Analysis.* U.S. Department of Agriculture, Food and Assistance and Nutrition Research Report No. 13, 2001.

———. "Summary of State Breastfeeding Laws." CRS Report for Congress RL 31633. July 23, 2003.

Weimer, Douglas Reid. 2006. "Breastfeeding: Federal Legislation." CRS Report for Congress RL 32908, October 12, 2006.

Weiner, Lynn Y. "Reconstructing Motherhood: The La Leche League in Postwar America." *The Journal of American History* 80, no. 4 (1994): 1357–81.

White, Edith. *Breastfeeding and HIV/AIDS: The Research, the Politics, the Women's Responses.* Jefferson, NC: McFarland and Company, 1999.

Williams, Patricia. *The Alchemy of Race and Rights: Diary of a Law Professor.* Cambridge, MA: Harvard University Press, 1991.

Wilson, Thomas C. "Trends in Tolerance toward Rightist and Leftist Groups." *Public Opinion Quarterly* 58 (1994): 539–56.

Wolfe, Jacqueline H. "What Feminists Can Do for Breastfeeding and What Breastfeeding Can Do for Feminists." *Signs: Journal of Women in Culture and Society* 31, no. 2 (2006): 397—424.

———. "Low Breastfeeding Rates and Public Health in the United States." *American Journal of Public Health* 93, no. 12 (2003): 200–210.

Woliver, Laura. *The Political Geographies of Pregnancy.* Champaign: University of Illinois Press, 2002.

World Health Organization. *The World Health Report 2002: Reducing Risks, Promoting Healthy Life.* Available: http://www.who.int/whr/2002/en/. (Accessed November 14, 2006).

Workoptions.com. "Flexible Work for New Mothers." Available: http://www.workoptions.com/BF_FWA.htm. (Accessed June 17, 2007).

Wright, Anne L., Catharine J. Holberg, Fernando D. Martinez, Wayne J. Morgan, and Lynn M. Taussig. "Breastfeeding and Lower Respiratory Tract Illness in the First Year of Life." *British Medical Journal* 299 (1989): 946–49.

Wright, Anne L., Catharine J. Holberg, Lynn M. Taussig, and Fernando D. Martinez. "Relationship of Infant Feeding to Recurrant Wheezing at Age 6 Years." *Archives of Pediatrics and Adolescent Medicine* 149, no. 7 (1995): 758–63.

Yalom, Marilyn. *A History of the Breast*. New York: The Ballantine Publishing Group, 1997.

Young, Kathryn T. "American Conceptions of Infant Development from 1955 to 1984: What the Experts Are Telling Parents." *Child Development* 61, no. 1 (1990): 17–28.

Zimmerman, Shirley. *Family Policies and Family Well-Being: The Role of Political Culture*. Newbury Park, CA: Sage Publications, 1992.

COURT CASES

American Red Cross v. Workers' Compensation Appeal Board, 741 A. 2d. 244; 1999 Pa. Commw.

Bailey v. Lombard, 101 Misc. 2d. 56; 420 N.Y.S. 2d 650, 1979 NY Misc.

Barrash v. Bowen, 846 F. 2d. 927 (1988 U.S. App.).

Berrios-Berrios v. Thornburg, 716 F Supp. 987 (1989 U.S. Dist.).

Board of School Directors v. Rossetti, 488 Pa. 125; 411 A. 2d. 486 1979.

Bond v. Sterling, Inc., 77 F. Supp. 2d. 306. (1998 U.S. Dist.) and 77F. Supp. 2d. (1999 U.S. Dist.).

Bremiller v. Cleveland Psychiatric Institute et al., 195 F.R.D. 1 (2000 U.S. Dist.).

Casey v. Southern Baptist Hospital, 526 So. 2d. 1332; 1988 La. App.

Champagne v. Mid-Maine Medical Center, 1998 ME 87; 711 a.2d. 842.

Commonwealth v. Michaud, 14 Mass. App. Ct. 471; 440 N.E. 2d. 768, 1982 Mass.

Derungs v. Wal-Mart Stores Inc., 374 F. 3d. 428 (2004 U.S. App)

Dike v. The School Board of Orange County, Florida., 650 F. 2d. 783. (1981 U.S. App.).

Donaldson et al. v. American Banco Corporation, Inc. et al., 945 F. Supp. 1456 (1996 U.S. Dist.).

Fejes v. Gilpin Industries (1999 U.S. Dist.).

Finley et al. v. Culligan et al., 201 Wis. 2d. 611; 548 N.W. 2d. 854; 1996 Wisc. App.

Fortier and Fortier v. US Steel Group (2002 US Dist.).

Gallegos v. Department of Interior, 6 Fed. Appx. 865 (2001).

Giguere v. Massanari, 74 Soc. Sec. Rep. Service 55 (2001 U.S. Dist.).

Griswold v. Connecticut, 85 S. Ct. 1678; 1965.

Hughes v. Moore, 214 Va. 27; 197 S.E. 2d. 214; 1973 Va.

In the Interest of Jane Doe, 95 Haw. 183 20 P 3d. 616 2001.

In the Matter of Jeffrey S., 1998 Ohio App.

In the Matter of Justin Smith, 2005 Ohio App. 149.

In Re. Austin L. and Brandon L., 2003 Cal. App.

In Re: James et al., C.A. no. 18936, 1998 Ohio.

In Re: Marriage of Norton, 640 P.2d. 254.

Jacobson v. Regent Assisted Living (1999 U.S. Dist.).

Juliette S. v. The Superior Court of Alameda County, 2005 Cal. App.

Kallir v. Friendly Ice Cream, 93 A.D. 2d. 246 463 N.Y.S. 2d. 56 1983 N.Y. App. Div.

Lalama v. Lalama, 94 C.A. 1996 Ohio App.

Laura T. v. Texas Department of Protective and Regulatory Services, 1999 Tex. App.

Lawrence v. Texas, 539 U.S. 558; 123 S. Ct. 2472; 2003.

Martinez v. NBC Inc. and MSNBC Inc., 49F Supp. 2d. 205. (1999 U.S. Dist.).

McNill v. New York City Department of Correction (1996. 95 F. Supp. 564).

Meyer v. Nebraska, 43 S. Ct. 625; 1923.

Murillo v. Rite Stuff Foods, 65 Cal. Ap.. 4th 833; 77 Cal. Rpt. 2d. 12 1998 Cal. App.

Pendergrass v. Toombs, 24 Ore. App. 719; 546 P. 2d. 1103; 1976 Ore. App.

The People v. Pointer, 151 Cal. App. 3d. 1128 199 Cal. 1984.

Perdrix-Wang v. Director, Employment Security Department, 42 Ark. App. 218; 856 S.W. 2d. 636 1993.

Picco et al. v. Marmor et al., 203 Cal. App.

Pierce v. Society of Sisters, 45 S. Ct. 571; 1925.

Ploski v. Feder et al., 1999 U.S. Dist.

Roe v. Wade, 93 S. Ct. 1409 1973.

Ruffino v. State Street Bank and Trust Company, 908 F. Supp. 1019 (1995 U.S. Dist.).

Slivka v. Camden-Clark Memorial Hospital, 215 W. Va. 109 S.E. 2d. 616, 2004 W. Va.

Snyder and Smith v. Scheerer and Scheerer, 190 W. Va. 64; 436 S.E. 2d. 299 1993.

Southerland v. Thigpen, 784 F.2d. 713 (1986 U.S. App.).

Stelluto v. Stelluto Supreme Court of Louisiana, 914 So. 2d. 34, 2005.

Stephon v. Malmad, 30 Pa.D. &C. 4th 510 1996.

Toyota v. Williams, 534 U.S. 184; 122 S. Ct. 651 (2002).

Tozzi v. Advanced Medical Equipment, Inc. et al. (2001 U.S. Dist.).

Trecost v. Trecost, 202 W. Va. 129; 502 S.E. 2d. 445. 1998 W. Va.

U.S. v. Dyce, 320 U.S. App. D.C. 1 91 F. 3d. 1462 (1996 U.S. App.).

VCE v. JBE, File No. CNo1–09752, Family Court of Delaware. 2003.

Wallace v. Pyro Mining Company., 789 F. Supp. 867 (1990 U.S. Dist.).

Walls v. Barnhart, 79 Soc. Sec. Rep. Service 183 (2002 U.S. Dist.).

Index

About the Authors

KAREN M. KEDROWSKI is Professor and Chair of the Department of Political Science at Winthrop University. Her research and teaching areas include media and politics, women and politics, American politics, and public policy. She is author of *Media Entrepreneurs and the Media Enterprise in the U.S. Congress* (1996) and coauthor of *Cancer Activism: Gender, Media and Public Policy* (2007). She has also published articles that have appeared in *Armed Forces and Society, Journal of Political Science, Perspectives on Politics, Political Communication, PS,* and *Teachers College Record.*

MICHAEL E. LIPSCOMB is Associate Professor of Political Science at Winthrop University, where he teaches political theory and American politics. Dr. Lipscomb has written on the areas of critical theory, postmodern political theory, and environmental politics. He is currently working on a book on the relationship between the constructed tempos of modern life and the experiential sensibilities that underwrite various commitments to environmental politics. His work has appeared in *New German Critique* and *Administrative Theory and Praxis.*

**CARDS MUST REMAIN IN THIS
POCKET AT ALL TIMES**
a charge will be made for
lost or damaged cards